Tristram and Coote's Probate Practice

Tristram and Coote's Probate Practice

Second Supplement to Thirty-first edition (Cumulative)

R D'Costa
Formerly District Probate Registrar, Oxford

P Teverson
Master of the Senior Courts, Chancery Division

T Synak
Formerly HMRC Inheritance Tax

LexisNexis® | 200

Members of the LexisNexis Group worldwide

United Kingdom	RELX (UK) Limited, trading as LexisNexis, 1-3 Strand, London WC2N 5JR
Australia	Reed International Books Australia Pty Ltd trading as LexisNexis, Chatswood, New South Wales
Austria	LexisNexis Verlag ARD Orac GmbH & Co KG, Vienna
Benelux	LexisNexis Benelux, Amsterdam
Canada	LexisNexis Canada, Markham, Ontario
China	LexisNexis China, Beijing and Shanghai
France	LexisNexis SA, Paris
Germany	LexisNexis GmbH, Dusseldorf
Hong Kong	LexisNexis Hong Kong, Hong Kong
India	LexisNexis India, New Delhi
Italy	Giuffrè Editore, Milan
Japan	LexisNexis Japan, Tokyo
Malaysia	Malayan Law Journal Sdn Bhd, Kuala Lumpur
New Zealand	LexisNexis New Zealand Ltd, Wellington
Singapore	LexisNexis Singapore, Singapore
South Africa	LexisNexis, Durban
USA	LexisNexis, Dayton, Ohio

Published by LexisNexis

A CIP Catalogue record for this book is available from the British Library.

ISBN for this volume: 9781474310383

Printed and bound in Great Britain by Hobbs the Printers Ltd, Totton, Hampshire

Visit LexisNexis at www.lexisnexis.co.uk

Preface

When the first supplement to the main work was published, the Non-Contentious Probate Rules had just been amended (SI 2016/972). The amended rules allow a personal applicant for a grant at any probate registry to make the application online if invited to do so by the registry. This online process was introduced on a pilot basis and the Non-Contentious Probate (Amendment) Rules 2017 (SI 2017/1034) extend the pilot further to include applications submitted by solicitors or probate practitioners.

For the time being the Probate Service has concentrated its efforts in setting up and implementing the pilot on dealing with personal applications, and at the time of publication of this update the indications are that the practice will extend to solicitor and probate practitioner applications later in 2018. This supplement deals with the rule changes.

The anticipated modernisation of the complete Non-Contentious Probate Rules appears to have been sidelined for the moment in favour of the pilot process.

In *Payne v Payne* [2018] EWCA Civ 985 the Court of Appeal provided clarity in construing the term 'sign' used in the Wills Act 1837, s 9 (as amended and in respect of deaths on or after 1 January 1983). The term is to be given the same meaning as the term 'subscribe' originally enacted and applying to deaths before 1 January 1983. The amended term is merely the modern English equivalent of the previous archaic one.

The Business and Property Courts ('B&PCs') were launched in July 2017 and became operational on 2 October 2017. The work in the B&PCs is divided between specialist courts and lists. The relevant list for contentious probate claims is the Property, Trusts and Probate List (ChD). In the High Court in London, the claim will be issued in the Rolls Building. Outside London, Business and Property Courts have been or will shortly be established in Birmingham, Bristol, Leeds, Liverpool, Manchester, Newcastle and Cardiff. These are known as the B&PCs District Registries. A claimant wishing to issue a claim in the Business and Property Courts must determine whether to issue the claim in London or in one of the B&PCs District Registries. Outside London, the claimant must issue a probate claim in a Chancery District Registry. All the B&PCs District Registries are at locations which are also Chancery District Registries. Preston, Mold and Caernarfon are the only Chancery District Registries not designated as one of the B&PCs District Registries.

In the County Court, the appropriate venues for contentious probate claims, where jurisdiction exists or is conferred by transfer from the High Court, are the County Court at Central London, Birmingham, Bristol, Cardiff, Manchester, Newcastle, Leeds, Liverpool and Preston.

The Practice Direction giving effect to the B&PCs came into force on 21 November 2017.

On 13 July 2017 the Law Commission published Consultation Paper 231 'Making a Will'. The paper includes a proposal that the scope of undue influence be broadened to increase protection for vulnerable testators.

It is also provisionally proposed that a dispensing power be introduced in England and Wales 'to soften the rough edges of the formality rules'.

So far as the Inheritance Tax aspects are concerned, as indicated in the first supplement to the 31st edition, revisions to the IHT 400 series of forms have been made to take into account the provision for a portion of the main family home to be exempted if passing to direct descendants. Additionally, legislation has now been effected to reduce the qualifying period for 'deemed domicile' from 17 years down to 15 years out of the last 20 years.

RD'C

PT

TS

June 2018

Contents

List of abbreviations

AC (preceded by date)	Law Reports, Appeal Cases, House of Lords and Privy Council
Add	Addams' Ecclesiastical Reports
A & E, Ad & El	Adolphus and Ellis, QB reports
Adam	Adam's Justiciary Reports
All ER (preceded by date)	All England Law Reports
All ER Rep (preceded by date)	All England Law Reports Reprint
App Cas	Law Reports, Appeal Cases
B & Ad	Barnewall and Adolphus
B & PCs	Business and Property Courts
Beav	Beavan's Rolls Court
Bos & Pu	Bosanquet and Puller
Bro CC	Brown's Chancery Reports
CA	Court of Appeal
CB	Common Bench Reports
Ch	Law Reports, Chancery Division (1890 onwards)
Ch D	Law Reports, Chancery Division (1875–1890)
Cox	Cox's Chancery Reports
CPD	Law Reports, Common Pleas Division
CPR	Civil Procedure Rules 1998

Curt	Curteis's Ecclesiastical Reports
Deane Ecc R	Deane's Ecclesiastical Reports
Dea & Sw	Dean and Swabey's Ecclesiastical Reports
De GM & G	De Gex, MacNaughten and Gordon's Reports
Dick	Dickens's Reports
Dir Ag	Directions to Agents
E & B	Ellis and Blackburn's Reports
Eq Cas	Equity Cases
Fam	Family Division, Series of Law Reports
F & F	Foster and Finlayson's Reports
Gow	NP Gow's Nisi Prius Cases
Hag Cons	Haggard's Consistory Court Cases
Hag Ecc	Haggard's Ecclesiastical Reports
Hare	Hare's Chancery Reports
HL	House of Lords
Ir Eq Rep	Irish Equity Reports
ITELR	International Trusts & Estates Law Reports
JP	Justice of the Peace Reports
JP Jo	Justice of the Peace and Local Government Review
Johns & H	Johnson and Hemming's Reports
Jur	Jurist Reports
KB (preceded by date)	Law Reports, King's Bench Division
Knapp	Knapp's Privy Council Cases
LGR	Local Government Reports
LJR	Law Journal Reports
LR Ir	Law Reports (Ireland)
LRP & D	Law Reports, Probate and Divorce
LT	Law Times Reports
LTJo	Law Times Newspaper
Lee	Lee's Ecclesiastical Reports
Lev	Levinz, KB
M & W	Meeson and Welsby's Reports
Moo	Moore's Privy Council Reports

NC	Notes of Cases
NC	Non-Contentious
NCPR	Non-Contentious Probate Rules 1987
NLJ	New Law Journal
P (preceded by date)	Law Reports, Probate, etc, Division
PC	Privy Council Cases
PCC	Prerogative Court of Chancery
PD	Law Reports, Probate Division
P & D	Law Reports, Probate and Matrimonial
P & M	Law Reports, Probate and Matrimonial
Phill	Phillimore's Ecclesiastical Reports
Phill Ch R	Phillip's Chancery Reports
Plowd	Plowden, KB
Prec C	Precedents in Chancery
P Wms	Peere Williams' Chancery Reports
QB	Queen's Bench Reports
QBD	Law Reports, Queen's Bench Division
R	The Reports
RR	Revised Reports
Rob	Robertson's Ecclesiastical Reports
RSC	Rules of the Supreme Court
Russ Ch Rep	Russell's Chancery Reports
SCF	Supreme Courts Fees
Sim	Simon's Chancery Reports
Sol Jo	Solicitor's Journal
Spinks	Spinks' Ecclesiastical and Admiralty Reports
S & T	Swabey and Tristram's Reports
Sw & Tr	Swabey and Tristram's Reports
Sugd Pow	Sugden on Powers
TLR	Times Law Reports
Vern	Vernon's Chancery Reports
Ves	Vesey's Chancery Reports
Ves Sen	Vesey's Chancery Reports

WLR	Weekly Law Reports
WN (preceded by date)	Law Reports, Weekly Notes
WR	Weekly Reporter
WTLR	Wills & Trusts Law Reports
WW & D	Willmore, Woolaston and Davisson, KB or QB
Y & CCC	Young and Collier's Chancery Reports

Table of Statutes

Paragraph references printed in **bold** type indicate where an Act is set out in part or in full.

Other Jurisdictions

New Zealand

Table of Statutory Instruments

Paragraph references printed in **bold** type indicate where an Act is set out in part or in full.

Table of Cases

D

E

F

G

L

M

N

O

P

R

S

T

W

Y

Part I

THE COMMON FORM PROBATE PRACTICE

of the Family Division of the High Court of Justice

Chapter 1

THE PROBATE JURISDICTION OF THE FAMILY DIVISION

COMMON FORM BUSINESS

1.30 Grants of representation may be applied for either through a probate practitioner or in person at the Principal Registry of the Family Division or at any of the district probate registries.

1.36A The Legal Services Act 2007 (Designation as a Licensing Authority) Order 2017 (SI 2017/27) came into force on 17 February 2017. It designates the General Council of the Bar as a licensing authority in relation to:

(a) the exercise of a right of audience;
(b) the conduct of litigation;
(c) reserved instrument activities;
(d) probate activities, and
(e) the administration of oaths.

1.36B The General Council to the Bar is already an approved regulator of reserved activities and the Order allows it to license alternative business structures to provide legal services to the public. Alternative businesses may be wholly or partly owned or controlled by non-lawyers.

1.41 For the time being, approved regulators responsible under the Legal Services Act 2007 (as amended) for authorising their members to carry on probate activities are:

– The Law Society (through the Solicitors Regulation Authority);
– The General Council of the Bar (through the Bar Standards Board);
– The Master of Faculties (Notaries);
– The Council of Licenced Conveyancers;
– The Association of Chartered Accountants;
– The Institute of Chartered Accountants in England and Wales;
– The Chartered Institute of Legal Executives.

Rules

1.49 The current rules are the Non-Contentious Probate Rules 1987 (SI 1987/2024) (see **1.52** below), as amended by the Non-Contentious Probate (Amendment) Rules 1991, 1998, 1999, 2003, 2004, 2016 and 2017. The Rules were further amended with effect from 1 October 2007 by the Mental

Capacity Act (Transitional and Consequential Provisions) Order 2007 (SI 2007/1898). The most recent are the Non-Contentious Probate (Amendment) Rules 2009 (SI 2009/1893) (effective from 1 September 2009) which reflect amendments to the Children Act 1989 consequential upon the Human Fertilisation and Embryology Act 2008. These rules govern the practice in the case of death on or after 1 January 1926. Where the deceased died before 1 January 1926 the right to a grant is, subject to the provisions of any enactment, to be determined by the principles and rules under which the court would have acted at the date of the death (see r 23 of the 1987 Rules).

1.50 In 2009 Sir Mark Potter, then President of the Family Division, invited the then Lord Justice Mumby (now President of the Family Division) to chair a working group to undertake the revision of the Non-Contentious Probate Rules 1987 and produce a set of draft rules and supporting practice directions, which set out fair and efficient procedures which are both simple and simply addressed. The working party produced a consultation paper following which draft rules were prepared. The working party has since reported to the President and the implementation of these revised rules is now awaited. In anticipation of these rules, this work includes references to some of the new practice changes which will emerge.

PROPERTY FOR WHICH GRANT REQUIRED

Vesting of property prior to issue of grant

1.70 When an estate has so vested and it is necessary to serve on the Public Trustee a notice to quit the notice should be served direct on the Public Trustee at the Office of the Official Solicitor and Public Trustee, Victory House, 30–34 Kingsway, London WC2B 6EX *or* DX 0012 Chancery Lane. Tel: 020 3681 2759. Fax: 020 3681 2762. Email: enquiries@offsol.gov.gsi.uk.

SMALL SUMS: PAYMENT WITHOUT GRANT

Production of unproved wills to National Savings and Investments

1.93 In dealing with applications for payment under the provisions set out in the preceding paragraphs without the production of a grant of representation National Savings and Investments (NS&I) will normally accept, in lieu of the original will, a clear photocopy or other facsimile of the will, certified personally by a solicitor to be a true copy of the original. Typewritten copies are not accepted[1].

1 Notice by Department for National Savings: *Law Society's Gazette*, 6 October 1976.

Chapter 2

GENERAL PROCEDURE IN REGISTRY

Note: In anticipation of the revision of the Non-Contentious Probate Rules the expression 'witness statement' where it is used in this work refers to the form of application or evidence required with reference to any rule in force at the time of the application.

AT THE PRINCIPAL REGISTRY

Situation of offices

2.01 Section 105 of the Senior Courts Act 1981[1] provides that application for a grant of probate or administration may be made at the Principal Registry of the Family Division. The Principal Registry is situated at First Avenue House, 7th Floor, 42–49 High Holborn, London WC1V 6NP or DX160011 Kingsway 7. The Principal Registry's Probate Department's Public Enquiries telephone number is 0207 421 8509. Email enquiries are to: londonprobate@hmcts.gsi.gov.uk

1 See para **A1.324**.

2.03 The Principal Registry is a member of the British Document Exchange and its box number is DX 160011 Kingsway 7.

Administration pending determination of a probate claim

2.05 Previously, a grant of administration pending determination of a probate claim (formerly administration pending suit) could only be made at the Principal Registry[1]. It may now be made to any district probate registry. As to application for an order for such a grant, see paras **38.01** ff.

1 Direction, 1935; NCPR SI 1987/2024 r 7(1).

AT DISTRICT PROBATE REGISTRIES AND SUB-REGISTRIES

Situation of registries

2.08 The function of sub-registries is to receive applications for grants and transmit them to their parent registries for the issue of the grants. Although the District Probate Registries Order 1982 (SI 1982/379) remains in force, the sub-registries are not open to the public, and callers (except by arrangement) and post from probate practitioners is directed to the parent registries. The sub-registries do not accept applications from probate practitioners. It is advisable to contact the parent district registry before making a personal call to a sub-registry. To avoid delay, it is therefore desirable that all applications and enquiries be submitted to a district probate registry. The following table lists the sub-registries for information only.

Further and current details may be obtained at: https://courttribunalfinder.serv ice.gov.uk/search/

2.09 The court and tribunal finder webpage lists district probate registries and sub-registries as situated at the following places[1]. However, in practice many of the offices are not open save by prior arrangement:

Registries	**Sub-registries**	**Addresses, telephone numbers, fax number and document exchange number**
Birmingham		The Priory Courts, 33 Bull Street, Birmingham B4 6DU Tel: 0121 681 3400/3401 DX 701990 Birmingham 7 Email: birminghamdprsolicitorsenquiries@hmcts.gsi.gov.uk
	Nottingham	
	Stoke on Trent	
Brighton		William Street, Brighton BN2 0RF Tel: 01273 573510 Fax: 01273 625845 DX 98073 Brighton 3 Email: brightondprsolicitorsenquiries@hmcts.gsi.gov.uk
	Maidstone	
Bristol	*address correspondence to:*	The Probate Registry of Wales, 3rd Floor, Cardiff Magistrates' Court, Fitzalan Place, Cardiff CF24 0RZ Tel 1: 02920 474373 DX 743940 Cardiff 38 Email: cardiffdprsolicitorsenquiries@hmcts.gsi.gov.uk
Probate Registry of Wales [*Cardiff*]		3rd Floor, Cardiff Magistrates Court, Fitzalan Place, Cardiff CF24 0RZ Tel: 029 2047 4373 Email: cardiffdprsolicitorsenquiries@hmcts.gsi.gov.uk DX 743940 Cardiff 38
	Bodmin	

Registries	Sub-registries	Addresses, telephone numbers, fax number and document exchange number
	Caernarfon [*Bangor*]	
	Carmarthen	
	Exeter	
Ipswich		Ground Floor, 8 Arcade Street, Ipswich IP1 1EJ Tel: 01473 284260 Fax: 01473 231 951 Email: ipswichdprsolicitorsenquiries@hmcts.gsi.gov.uk DX 97733 Ipswich 3
	Norwich	
	Peterborough	
Leeds		York House, York Place, Leeds LS1 2BA Tel: 0113 3896 133 Email: leedsdprsolicitorsenquiries@hmcts.gsi.gov.uk DX 26451 Leeds Park Square
	Lincoln	
	Sheffield	
	York	
Liverpool		Queen Elizabeth II Law Courts, Derby Square, Liverpool L2 1XA Tel: 0151 236 8264 Email: liverpooldprsolicitorsenquiries@hmcts.gsi.gov.uk DX 14246 Liverpool 1
	Chester	
	Lancaster	
Manchester		Ground Floor, Manchester Civil Justice Centre, 1 Bridge Street West, PO Box 4240, Manchester M60 9DJ Tel: 0161 240 5701/2 Email: manchesterdprsolicitorsenquiries@hmcts.gsi.gov.uk

Registries	Sub-registries	Addresses, telephone numbers, fax number and document exchange number
		DX 724784 Manchester 44
	Nottingham	[*Details as for Birmingham*]
Newcastle upon Tyne		1 Waterloo Square, Newcastle upon Tyne NE1 4AL Tel: 0191 211 2170 Email: newcastledprsolicitorenquiries@hmcts.gsi.gov.uk DX 61081 Newcastle upon Tyne 14
	Carlisle	
	Middlesbrough	
	York	
Oxford		Combined Court Building, St Aldates, Oxford OX1 1TL Tel 1: 01865 793050 Tel 2: 01865 793055 Fax: 01865 793090 Email: OxfordDPRsolicitorsenquiries@hmcts.gsi.gov.uk DX 96454 Oxford 4
	Gloucester	
	Leicester	
Winchester		1st Floor, Southside Offices, The Law Courts Winchester SO23 9EL Tel: 01962 814100 Email: winchesterdprsolicitorsenquiries@hmcts.gsi.gov.uk DX 96900 Winchester 2

The opening hours of district registries and those sub-registries which are open to the public are 9.30am until 4.00pm, Monday to Friday.

1 The District Probate Registries Order 1982 (SI 1982/379) as amended (see paras **A2.30** ff).

Administration pending determination of a probate claim

2.16 A grant of administration pending determination of a probate claim (formerly administration pending suit) can be made only at the Principal Registry[1]. As to application for an order for such a grant, see paras **38.01** ff.

1 Direction, 1935; NCPR SI 1987/2024 r 7(1). As to practice, see paras **11.364** ff.

Powers of district probate registrars

2.19 No grant may, however, be made by a district probate registrar in any case where there is contention until the contention is disposed of, or in any case where it appears to the district registrar that a grant ought not to be made without the directions of a High Court judge or a district judge of the Principal Registry[1]. Formerly, it was for this reason that an application for a grant pending determination of a probate claim could only be made to the Principal Registry. It is assumed that under delegated power the district probate registrar may now issue a grant in such an application. In any case where the district probate registrar seeks directions under the aforesaid provision, he is required to send a statement of the matter in question to the Principal Registry for directions[2]. Where directions are sought, a district judge of the Principal Registry may either confirm that the matter be referred to a High Court judge and give directions accordingly or he may direct the district probate registrar to proceed with the matter in accordance with such instructions as are deemed necessary, or direct him to take no further action in relation to the matter[3]. In practice this procedure is rarely used.

1 Direction, 1935; NCPR SI 1987/2024 r 7(1).
2 NCPR SI 1987/2024 r 7(2).
3 NCPR SI 1987/2024 r 7(3).

Settling documents to lead grant

2.28 While it is not the practice to settle affidavits (*witness statements, when the Non-Contentious Probate Rules are revised*) of facts (eg affidavits to lead an order of the district judge, or affidavits as to due execution of wills) the probate manager or registrar may at his or her discretion peruse and comment on these complex draft affidavits.

Application for grant at district registry

2.30 A probate practitioner makes an application for a grant at a district probate registry by lodging at, or sending by post or document exchange to, the registry (see para **2.09**) the papers to lead the grant, namely, the will and codicils (if any) together with two plain copies of each testamentary paper on A4 size paper, the oath, the HMRC account summary Form IHT 241 (unless such an account is not required, see Chapter 8) or return of estate in Form IHT205 as appropriate (see Chapter 8) and any affidavits etc, which the particular circumstances of the case may render necessary A personal applicant may apply for a grant at any district probate registry.

Procedure in district registry

2.43 Sub-registries have no power to issue grants.

Form of grant

2.57 The wording at the foot of the form of grant is now as follows:

'It is hereby certified that it appears from information supplied on the application for this grant that the gross value of the said estate in the United Kingdom amounts to £ and that the net value of such estate amounts to £ .'

PERSONAL APPLICATIONS

Personal application for grant

2.81 A personal application for a grant of probate or letters of administration (with will) or letters of administration may be made by the person entitled to the grant[1]. There is no financial limit on the value of the estate.

1 NCPR SI 1987/2024 r 5(1).

Where made

2.88 A personal application may be made at the Principal Registry or any district probate registry. There are no territorial limits on jurisdiction.

2.89 In addition to the probate registries and sub-registries there are a few probate offices throughout England and Wales at which a personal applicant may be interviewed and swear the oath. These offices are open occasionally and attendance is by appointment only.

Procedure

2.90A With effect from 1 November 2016, the Non-Contentious Probate Rules have been amended to allow a personal applicant to apply to any probate registry to make an application for a grant online if invited to do so by that registry[1]. Under Rule 5A the personal applicant completes and sends the application online in accordance with instructions given by the registry. The new rule provides that the applicant shall produce original documents and information required in instructions given by the registry. In place of swearing an oath, the applicant verifies his application by a statement of truth in the online application. Any will is marked by the applicant's signature only. If the application is for probate, the applicant also confirms in the online form in accordance with instructions given by the registry that notice has been given to any executor to whom power is reserved in accordance with r 27(1). Where original documents are required in accordance with the registry's instructions, they must be sent separately to the registry. *This practice is in its infancy and may be subject to revision.*

1 NCP(A)R SI 2016/973 r 5A. The revised rules are incorporated in Appendix II of this supplement; see para **A2.39**.

2.91 Save as stated in the preceding paragraph on receipt of the completed forms, notice of an appointment to attend at the chosen registry or office will be sent to the applicant. A second visit is sometimes necessary, and this will be arranged at the time of the first attendance or subsequently.

2.94 The revised probate rule 5A requires only that a personal application be completed in the form of a questionnaire in which the applicant verifies the answers in a statement of truth, as may be required by any instruction given by the registry. Unless otherwise directed, no attendance will be necessary.

Chapter 3

WILLS AND CODICILS

Note: In anticipation of the revision of the Non-Contentious Probate Rules the expression 'witness statement' where it is used in this work refers to the form of application or evidence required with reference to any rule in force at the time of the application.

REVOCATION OF WILLS

Revocation by subsequent marriage

Will made on or after 1 January 1983

3.40A With effect from 29 March 2014 marriage includes a reference to the marriage of a same sex couple[1].

1 See Marriage (Same Sex Couples) Act 2013, Sch 3, Pt 1.

Revocation by subsequent formation of Civil Partnership

3.43 The effect of this Act is that it places a civil partnership on similar footing to a marriage. Section 71 and Sch 4 of this Act amend the Wills Act 1837 and other enactments so that they apply in relationship to a civil partnership as they apply to marriage. In *Wilkinson v Kitzinger* [2006] EWHC 2022 (Fam), [2007] 1 FCR 183, [2007] 1 FLR 295 the English court declined on grounds of public policy to recognise a form of marriage between two persons of the same sex which is valid and lawful in the jurisdiction in which it took place. Such relationship would qualify in the United Kingdom as a formation of a civil partnership. Schedule 4 amends the Wills Act 1837 to provide in s 18B:

'(1) Subject to subsections (2) to (6), a will is revoked by the formation of a civil partnership between the testator and another person.

(2) A disposition in a will in exercise of a power of appointment takes effect despite the formation of a subsequent civil partnership between the testator and another person unless the property so appointed would in default of the appointment pass to the testator's personal representatives.

(3) If it appears from a will –

(a) that at the time it was made the testator was expecting to form a civil partnership with a particular person, and

(b) that he intended that the will should not be revoked by the formation of the civil partnership,

the will is not revoked by its formation.

(4) Subsections (5) and (6) apply if it appears from a will–

(a) that at the time it was made the testator was expecting to form a civil partnership with a particular person, and

(b) that he intended that a disposition in the will should not be revoked by the formation of the civil partnership.

(5) The disposition takes effect despite the formation of the civil partnership.

(6) Any other disposition in the will also takes effect, unless it appears from the will that the testator intended the disposition to be revoked by the formation of the civil partnership.'

3.43A A form of marriage between two persons of the same sex which is lawful and valid in a jurisdiction in which it took place outside the United Kingdom before the Civil Partnership Act 2004 and the Marriage (Same Sex Couples) Act 2013 came into force is not recognised. However, where such a marriage was subsequently treated as a civil partnership in England and Wales, it is now recognised as a marriage.

EXECUTION OF WILLS—INTERNAL LAW OF ENGLAND AND WALES

By mark

3.75 Where a testator had his hand guided in making his mark, it was held to be a sufficient signature within the Statute of Frauds[1]. The object of guiding the testator's hand is to steady it rather than lead it.

1 *Wilson v Beddard* (1841) 12 Sim 28.

Re-execution by acknowledgment

3.95 Practitioners who are instructed to draft a will but do not supervise its execution are under a duty to check that it is properly executed when it is returned to them for safekeeping[1].

1 *Humblestone v Martin Tolhurst Partnership (a Firm)* [2004] EWHC 151 (Ch), (2004) Times, 27 February (it was found on examination after the death of the deceased that the will was not signed by him). See also *Marley v Rawlings* [2014] UKSC 2, [2015] AC 129, [2014] 1 All ER 807.

Presence of witnesses

3.102 The witnesses must have seen, or have had the opportunity of seeing, the testator's signature[1], even though they were unaware of the nature of the document they were asked to sign[2], and they must both subscribe their names (or sign or acknowledge their signatures *where the testator's death occurred on or after 1 January 1983*) after this has occurred in their joint presence[3]. The will is not duly executed if the testator acknowledges his signature in the presence of one witness who thereupon signs the will, and subsequently the testator acknowledges his signature in the joint presence of the two witnesses, after which the second witness signs[4] but see para **3.103**.

1 *Re Gunstan's Goods, Blake v Blake* (1882) 7 PD 102; *Re Groffman, Groffman and Block v Groffman* [1969] 2 All ER 108, [1969] 1 WLR 733.

2 *Daintree v Butcher and Fasulo* (1888) 13 PD 67; on appeal (1888) 13 PD 102, CA.

3 *Hindmarsh v Charlton* (1861) 8 HL Cas 160.

4 *Wyatt v Berry* [1893] P 5, following *Hindmarsh v Charlton* (1861) 8 HL Cas 160; *Re Colling, Lawson v von Winckler* [1972] 3 All ER 729, [1972] 1 WLR 1440.

Attestation

3.107 *'Attests and signs the will in the presence of the testator'*. The witnesses must sign the will in the presence of the testator after he has signed it, or acknowledged his previously made signature, when all of them were present together; but under English law it is not essential that the witnesses should sign in the presence of each other.

3.108 No form of attestation is necessary; but to make a valid signature or subscription and attestation, either the name or initials of each witness, or some mark or name intended to represent his name, must be written or made by him in the presence of the testator[1].

1 *Re Sperling's Goods* (1863) 3 Sw & Tr 272; see also *Hindmarsh v Charlton* (1861) 8 HL Cas 160; *Charlton v Hindmarsh* (1859) 1 Sw & Tr 433.

3.108A The Court of Appeal held that the term 'sign' used in s 9 of the Wills Act 1837 as amended with effect from 1 January 1983 by the Administration of Justice Act 1982 should be construed as meaning the same as the original requirement to 'subscribe'[1]. The change of term was a modernisation and not intended to be of any substance. A signature in the sense of an identifiable and personal mark as when signing a cheque or other formal document was not required. The court further held that a witness merely had to write his name with the intention that the act of writing it should operate as an attestation.

1 *Payne v Payne* [2018] EWCA Civ 985.

Position of witnesses' signatures

3.113 A testatrix wrote her will, consisting of the date, dispositive words and her signature, on a small single sheet of paper. There was no attestation clause. On the reverse side, upside down, were written in different handwritings the names of two persons whom it had proved impossible to trace. It was held, applying *Re Peverett's Goods* [1902] P 205, and the maxim *omnia praesumuntur rite esse acta* (all things are presumed to have been done rightly), that the document was a duly executed will, there being no practical reason why the names should be on the reverse of the document unless for the purpose of attesting the will[1].

1 *Re Denning, Harnett v Elliott* [1958] 2 All ER 1, [1958] 1 WLR 462.

Refusal of probate

Fiat against a will. Probate refused

3.140 The procedure for obtaining the district judge's or registrar's marking 'Probate refused' on a testamentary document is as follows:

(a) *Prior to an application for a grant.* An application by a solicitor or probate practitioner to a district judge or registrar for a document to be marked 'Probate refused' must be made through the probate department in the Principal Registry or to a probate registry or a sub-registry. If and when so marked, the refused document together with the affidavits (*witness statements*) leading to the district judge's or registrar's fiat is retained and it will not be handed out without the leave of a district judge or registrar. Upon the issue of a grant in respect of the estate of the deceased the refused document and its accompanying affidavits will be filed with the oath to lead the grant.

(b) *Simultaneously with the application for a grant.* Where the application for refusal of probate and for a grant are simultaneous, the purported will and the affidavits (*witness statements*) by the witnesses should be lodged with the remainder of the papers at the probate department, probate registry or sub-registry.

Two or more wills

Conditional will

3.206 If the later will is wholly conditional, eg on an event which never occurred, the earlier one will be proved. A revocation clause in a conditional will is effective only if the condition is fulfilled and so makes the whole will operative[1]. See also paras **3.224** ff.

1 *Re Hugo's Goods* (1877) 36 LT 518.

Joint and mutual wills

3.211 The term 'mutual will' is commonly used to denote one of two testamentary instruments made respectively by two persons whereby each gives the other corresponding rights in his property although the doctrine of mutual wills can also apply to cases where the two testators leave their property to particular beneficiaries rather than each other[1]. As to enforceability of an agreement between testators who made mutual wills in reliance on the agreement, see *Legg v Burton*[2].

1 See *Re Dale, Proctor v Dale* [1994] Ch 31, [1993] 4 All ER 129.
2 [2017] EWHC 2088 (Ch), [2017] 4 WLR 186.

Revocation of joint and mutual wills

3.222 If after the death of one testator, the survivor revokes his will, the revocation is recognised in the probate registry as operative, but his personal representative may be directed[1] to hold the estate on trust to carry out the terms of the contract, or implied contract (if any), originally made[2]. It does not necessarily follow, because joint or mutual wills are made, that there was a contract: and this is a question to be decided in the Chancery Division[3], the probate registry being concerned only with the formal validity of the dispositions.

1 By the Chancery Division.
2 *Dufour v Pereira* (1769) 1 Dick 419; *Stone v Hoskins* [1905] P 194; *Re Oldham, Hadwen v Myles* [1925] Ch 75 (the probability of a contract is greater if the mutual gifts are for life only); *Re Green, Lindner v Green* [1951] Ch 148, [1950] 2 All ER 913 (the wills themselves may contain a clear indication of a contract); *Re Cleaver, Cleaver v Insley* [1981] 2 All ER 1018,

[1981] 1 WLR 939 (the whole evidence must be looked at to determine whether there was a definite agreement between the testators: the mere fact that the wills were to the same effect, though a relevant circumstance, was not in itself sufficient).

3 *Re Heys' Estate, Walker v Gaskill* [1914] P 192 at 200; *Re Goodchild* [1997] 3 All ER 63, [1997] 1 WLR 1216 (the court confirmed that for the doctrine of mutual wills to apply there had to be a contract at law between two testators that both wills would be irrevocable and remain unaltered. It was not sufficient that both testators merely had a mutual desire that the wills should remain unaltered); *Legg v Burton* [2017] EWHC 2088 (Ch), [2017] 4 WLR 186.

Incorporation of papers by reference

Production of document

3.301 Whenever a will or codicil refers to any list, memorandum, or other document in such a manner as to suggest that such document was in existence at the time the will or codicil referring to it was executed, such document must be produced with a view to ascertaining if it is entitled to probate (NCPR SI 1987/2024 r 14(3)) (save that where a will incorporates by reference standard will forms or clauses as contained in a published document, production of that document will not be required in any individual case, unless otherwise directed, if the published document containing the standard forms or clauses (together with as many copies as may be required) has been previously lodged with the Senior District Judge and accepted by him as sufficient lodgement for the purposes—*District Judge's Direction*, 10 April 1995).

WILLS ACT 1963

Requirements of foreign law to be treated as formal

3.417 Where a law in force outside the United Kingdom applies in relation to a will, any requirement of that law whereby special formalities are to be observed by testators answering a particular description, or witnesses to the execution of a will are to possess certain qualifications is notwithstanding any rule of that law to the contrary, to be treated as a formal requirement only (s 3).

Chapter 4

PROBATES

Note: In anticipation of the revision of the Non-Contentious Probate Rules the expression 'witness statement' where it is used in this work refers to the form of application or evidence required with reference to any rule in force at the time of the application.

EXECUTORS

Executor according to the tenor

4.21A The term 'personal representative' may be accepted as meaning executor subject to the direction of the registrar being sought as to the sufficiency.

Corporation not a trust corporation

4.39 Where a corporation (not being a trust corporation) and an individual are appointed executors the individual's right to probate has priority under NCPR SI 1987/2024 r 20, and probate may be granted to the individual only, it being recited in the oath that the corporation is not a trust corporation as defined by NCPR SI 1987/2024 r 2(1). Alternatively, application for the grant of probate may be made by the individual alone, with power being reserved to the non-trust corporation: so the status of the corporation to extract a grant of double probate will be tested at the time when application is made for the subsequent grant[1].

1 Registrar's Direction (1977) 6 December.

Alternative business structures

4.49 Nowadays the situation may arise where the appointment of an executor applies to a firm which is a corporate body comprised of share owner lawyers or probate practitioners (authorised persons) as well as other share owners or persons (non-authorised persons) who exercise control or have an interest in the body but are not lawyers or probate practitioners. Such a firm may provide a mixture of legal and other professional services (alternative business structure). It is licensable by the Solicitors Regulation Authority, an approved regulator under the Legal Services Act 2007. Unless the will expresses a contrary intention, the appointment of the firm as executor would appear to apply to all the shareholders. The question may arise as to who would constitute the executors where the appointment applies to a successor firm and the instituted executors were all share-owning probate practitioners or other legal practitioners.

TRANSMISSION OF EXECUTORSHIP

4.86 However, if the proving executor leaves an executor who proves his will there is a chain of representation which is liable to be broken, as the chain ceases to apply if an executor to whom power was reserved afterwards exercises his power to take double probate: see Administration of Estates Act 1925, s 7(1). The non-proving executor may be cited to accept or refuse double probate with a view to the extinction of his rights: see paras **24.16** ff and **24.89** ff.

HOW SOON A WILL CAN BE PROVED

Expedition of grant

4.90 For good reason, the issue of a grant may be expedited at the discretion of the district judge, registrar or probate manager.

REQUIREMENTS ON PROVING A WILL

The executor's oath (witness statement of application)

4.92A The current programme for modernisation of the courts has led to the Non-Contentious Probate (Amendment) Rules 2016 and 2017 (SI 2016/972 and SI 2017/1034 respectively). These amend the Non-Contentious Probate Rules 1987 to provide new rules 4A and 5A. A personal applicant (SI 2016/972 with effect from 1 November 2016) or a solicitor or probate practitioner (together referred to as a probate practitioner in this work) (SI 2017/1034 with effect from 20 November 2017) may apply for a grant of probate or administration online at any registry if invited to do so by that registry. The amendment rules for the new alternative online process are introduced on a pilot basis. The Non-Contentious Probate Rules 1987 as amended are set out in Appendix II.

4.92B At the time of publication the pilot has begun and is being trialled for personal applicants in the District Probate Registry at Oxford. The procedure for making online applications will extend and be trialled for applications from solicitors and probate practitioners at the District Probate Registry at Birmingham during 2018 and migrate to other registries in due course. At present the criteria for personal applications are as follows:

- applications for probate by up to four executors;
- the original will and codicils are in existence; and
- the deceased died domiciled in England and Wales.

The criteria in applications for probate by practitioners should be broadly similar. When invited to do so, a probate practitioner makes the application by completing and sending an online application form in accordance with instructions given by the registry. The applicant must verify the application by a statement of truth in the online application form. As well as completing the online form, the original will and any codicils (with two copies), inheritance tax forms and any supporting documents such as renunciations must be posted to the registry. At the present time the online project is in its infancy and the amendment rules have not been supplemented by any explanatory practice direction. It would seem that in individual cases the registry gives directions about the provision of evidence to support the application in matters such as evidence of identity or in support of execution of a will or codicil. In due course this online process will begin in the probate registries for other types of applications for grants (letters of administration with and without will) as the pilot scheme works out difficulties and improves the online process.

4.93 The following paragraphs set out the requirements in an order corresponding to the usual form of oath for executors. Similar care should be taken when completing an online application form together with any modifications required by the registry. In this work references to executor's witness statement include a statement of truth contained in an online application form.

Name of deponent

4.96 Care should be taken to ascertain, and include in the oath or online application form, the true full name of the deponent, whether or not this is correctly stated in the will.

Description of documents to be proved

4.119 Where the original will is not available and the court has ordered a copy of the document to be proved in its stead, this document is referred to in the oath (*executor's witness statement*) as the will 'as contained in a copy (*or* draft) thereof', or 'as contained in the exhibit to the affidavit (*witness statement*) of sworn on the —— day of —— 19—', as the case may be, in accordance with the order of the court.

Marking testamentary documents

4.124 The executor, and the person before whom the oath is sworn, must 'mark' the will and codicils or other testamentary papers by signing their names upon these documents (NCPR SI 1987/2024 r 10). In an online application r 10 applies as if, instead of signatures of the applicant and person before whom the oath is sworn, the will is marked by the signature of the applicant or the solicitor or probate practitioner through whom the application is made. Each document should be marked, but when two documents are written on the same sheet of paper, one marking is sufficient. It is not necessary that the exhibit clause, required on all other occasions when a document (including a will) is exhibited to an affidavit, should be endorsed.

Name of testator. Alias

4.130 A grant should always issue in the true name of the deceased. The inclusion of one or more alternative names (known as alias names) may be necessary because the deceased held assets in a name other than the true full name, or for some other sufficient reason.

> 'Where it is sought to describe the deceased in a grant by some name in addition to his true name, the applicant shall depose to or state in an online application the true name of the deceased and shall specify some part of the estate which was held in the other name, or give any other reason for the inclusion of the other name in the grant.' (r 9).

Change of name

4.131 In the absence of evidence of a change of name, or of any discrepancy in the papers lodged, it is assumed that the name of the deceased given in the sworn documents or online application is the true name. A surname may, however, be abandoned, and another adopted or assumed, in various ways; eg by succession or elevation to a title of nobility, by change of name by Royal Licence, or simply by constant use and repute. Subject to any statutory restriction, the law of this country allows any person to assume and use any name, provided that its use is not calculated to deceive and inflict pecuniary loss[1].

1 *Fendall v Goldsmid* (1877) 2 PD 263; *Cowley (Earl) v Countess of Cowley* [1901] AC 450, 70 LJP 83, HL.

Alias name required in grant

4.139 In cases, whether of testacy or intestacy, where the deceased held property standing in a name other than his true full name, an alias may be included in the grant to facilitate the administration. The oath (*executor's witness statement*) should depose specifically or state to the true name and any alias name. It should identify the estate that the deceased held in the alternative name or names: at least one item of property in each alternative name must be specified. If the inclusion of an alias is desired for some other reason, this must be deposed to.

Certificates under Merchant Shipping Acts 1970 and 1995

4.160 The address of the Registry of Shipping and Seamen is Anchor Court, Keen Road, Ocean Way, Cardiff CF24 5JW (tel: 02920 448813). Evidence of death is provided by the Registrar General of Shipping and Seamen and death certificates are issued in the following instances:

(a) known deaths or losses in United Kingdom ships;
(b) known deaths or losses of citizens of the United Kingdom and Colonies in other ships which call at United Kingdom ports;
(c) known deaths abroad of seamen employed in United Kingdom ships.

Clearing off executors

4.200 If power is to be reserved to one or more executors, a statement to that effect should be made in the oath (*witness statement*). The oath or witness statement must state that notice of the application for probate has been given to the executor or executors to whom power is to be reserved, unless the district judge or registrar directs otherwise or dispenses with the giving of such notice or the appointment is of partners in a firm and one (or more) of the other partners is applying (see paras **4.55** and **4.57**).

4.202 Where one executor is a minor the oath (witness statement) should show that power is reserved to him on attaining the age of 18 (see also para **4.32**). As to grant where the sole executor is a minor, see paras **4.30–4.31** and **11.142** and **11.143**.

Notice to Treasury Solicitor

4.229 In any case in which it appears that the Crown is or may be beneficially interested in the estate of a deceased person, notice of the intended application for a grant must be given by the applicant to the Treasury Solicitor. The district judge or registrar may direct that no grant shall issue within 28 days after such notice has been given[1]. The notice should be sent to: The Treasury Solicitor (BVD), PO Box 70165, London WC1A 9HG *or* DX 123240 Kingsway (tel 020 7210 4700. Email: bvestates@governmentlegal.gov.uk).

1 NCPR SI 1987/2024 r 38.

FEES

Fees on the grant

4.259A In 2016 the government issued a consultation paper setting out proposals for reforming fees payable on an application for a grant. The main proposals were to move from the current flat fee approach and introduce a banded structure where the fee increases in line with the value of the estate and to remove probate fees from the fees remission scheme. The senior judiciary, legal practitioners and representative groups, charities and members of the public responded to the consultation. At the time of publication of this supplement, the government announced it would proceed with all the proposals set out in the consultation. When the necessary statutory instrument takes effect, the threshold below which an application would not attract a fee will rise from £5,000 to £50,000 and above that increase according to the value of the estate up to a maximum of £20,000. See para **4.209A** and Appendix III, 'Fees' for further details of the fees increase.

Remission of probate fees

4.264A See para **4.259A.** The remission of fees scheme for probate applications will be removed when the proposed fee changes come into force.

Estate on which fees are assessed

4.267 The fees payable for the issue of a grant of probate or administration (or resealing of a grant, as to which, see Chapter 18) are assessed on the 'assessed value' being the value of the net real and personal estate (excluding settled land if any) before payment of inheritance tax passing under the grant as shown either in the HMRC Inheritance Tax account or Capital taxes affidavit, or, where an IHT 205 is delivered, in the oath (witness statement) to lead the grant[1]. This provision is not applicable in the case of those applications specified in Fee No 3 of the Non-Contentious Probate Fees Order 2004 (SI 2004/3120) as amended by the Non-Contentious Probate Fees (Amendment) Order 2011 (SI 2011/588), for which a fixed fee of £20 is provided.

1 NC Probate Fees (Amendment) Order 2014 (SI 2014/876), Fee 1, as interpreted by para 2(b).

Chapter 5

LETTERS OF ADMINISTRATION WITH THE WILL ANNEXED

Note.—This chapter deals only with grants of administration (with will) in cases where the deceased died **domiciled** in England and Wales. For the practice in cases where the deceased died domiciled elsewhere, see Chapter 12. For interpretation of wills (including codicils), see Chapter 3.

Note: In anticipation of the revision of the Non-Contentious Probate Rules the expression 'witness statement' where it is used in this work refers to the form of application or evidence required with reference to any rule in force at the time of the application.

ORDER OF PRIORITY

5.05A As to the effect of a disclaimer by a beneficiary under the will, see para 5.99.

PERSONS INTERESTED IN THE RESIDUARY ESTATE

Gift to charities

5.86 Under the Charities Act 2011, the trustees of any charity for religious, educational, literary, scientific or public charitable purposes may apply to the Charity Commissioners for a certificate of registration as a corporate body. If the certificate is granted, the trustees become a corporate body able to hold and acquire property, and thereafter all gifts of property to the charity or the trustees or otherwise for the purposes thereof take effect as if made to the incorporated body for the like purposes. The Charities Act 2011 came into force on 14 March 2012; it is a consolidating Act and replaces previous Charities Acts (including the Charitable Trustees Incorporation Act 1872, which governed this matter formerly).

5.87 Where a gift of residue is made to charity generally, or for charitable purposes or objects without specifying particular institutions, the Attorney General, by royal prerogative, has the sole right to represent the beneficial interest of charity. The Treasury Solicitor acts on his behalf in charity matters. On application to him the Attorney General will make a direction nominating a particular charity or charities so that a residuary beneficiary may be constituted to take a grant of letters (with will annexed). Enquiry or application to the Attorney General should be addressed to: The Government Legal Department, One Kemble Street, London WC2B 4TS or DX 123242. Tel. 020 7210 4700. Email treasurysolicitor@governmentlegal.gov.uk

Clearing off

Disclaimer

5.99 In respect of deaths on or after 1 February 2012 where a person disclaims an inheritance either under a will or under the law of intestacy the inheritance devolves as if that person has died immediately before the deceased. The Estate of Deceased Persons (Forfeiture Rule and Law of Succession) Act 2011 amends the Wills Act 1837 and Administration of Estates Act 1925 to this effect; see para **5.194** ff below. For an example of a disclaimer, see Form No 52B (**A6.57B**). On application for a grant of representation the oath (*witness statement of application*) should clear off the person disclaiming by citing the facts and the probate papers should include the original disclaimer. If the disclaimer is required for some other purpose an examined copy should be should also be filed and the reason for the return of the original should be set out in writing. For forms of oath (*or as adapted, witness statement of application*) for letters of administration (with will) see Nos 155 and 162 (**A6.160** and **A6.167**). These may be adapted to suit the particular circumstances of the application. See also para **8.166** as to the effect of a disclaimer with regard to inheritance tax.

TO WHOM GRANTED

Rule 20, Class (c)

Any other residuary legatee or devisee, including one for life, or a person entitled to share in undisposed-of estate

5.111 Subject to the preference of vested to contingent interests and of persons of full age to guardians of minors (see the following paragraphs) all persons in this class are equally entitled to a grant. Thus:

(a) a residuary legatee and a residuary devisee have an equal right to the grant, irrespective of the nature of the estate[1];
(b) if there is a residuary gift of personalty but not of the immoveable estate, persons entitled to share in the estate not disposed of have an equal title to that of the residuary legatee, and similarly in the converse case;
(c) if the residuary estate was given to two or more persons in specified shares (and not as joint tenants) and the share of one of them has lapsed by his pre-decease, the surviving residuary legatees have a title equal to that of the persons entitled to share in the undisposed-of estate. (As to lapse of gifts, see paras **5.164** ff).

1 In the event of a dispute, however, if other considerations are equal the practice is to prefer the person having the predominating interest (see paras **14.25** and **14.26**).

Preference of persons of full age

5.130 Under NCPR SI 1987/2024 r 27(5), unless otherwise directed by a district judge or registrar, administration (with will) is to be granted to a person not under disability in preference to a guardian of a minor entitled in the same degree. When it is desired that a grant should be made to guardians of a minor residuary legatee or devisee (having attained a vested interest notwithstanding the minority) in preference to a person of full age entitled in the same degree, the facts should be placed before the district probate registrar or the probate manager. It is advisable to do this before the preparation of the papers to lead the grant.

Residuary legatee or devisee

Death by murder or manslaughter

DEATHS AFTER 31 JANUARY 2012

5.196 The Estates of Deceased Persons (Forfeiture Rule and Law of Succession) Act 2011[1] gives effect to the Law Commission's recommendations. Where a testator dies on or after 1 February 2012, s 2 of the Act which deals with disclaimer or forfeiture of a gift under a will amends the Wills Act 1837 by inserting a new s 33A. This provides in part that where the forfeiture rule precludes a person from taking a devise or bequest made in a will that person is, unless a contrary intention is expressed in the will, to be treated as having died immediately before the testator. Accordingly such person should be cleared off in the oath (*witness statement of application*) to lead the grant of letters of administration (with will) by setting out the facts and the details of the conviction of murder or manslaughter and confirming that: the conviction remains in force, no appeal is pending nor in the case of manslaughter was an application made within three months from the date of conviction to modify the effect of the forfeiture rule. For form of oath see No 163 (**A6.168**) which may be adapted to suit the circumstances of the application. An official copy of the conviction certificate should be filed with the probate papers.

1 See para **A1.685A**.

Persons entitled to share in undisposed-of estate

Where deceased left a surviving spouse or (after 5 December 2005) surviving civil partner

5.205 Where the net value of the estate not disposed of, arrived at as aforesaid, exceeds the appropriate statutory figure applicable for a death occurring after 1952, or the sum of £1,000 where the death occurred before 1953, a grant may be made to any person entitled to share in the residue[1] not disposed of. Where the deceased died after 1952 leaving a spouse or (from 5 December 2005) civil partner and issue, or before 1953 leaving a spouse, a life interest arises in these circumstances, and the grant must accordingly be made to not less than two individuals or to a trust corporation with or without an individual, unless the court thinks it expedient in all the circumstances to appoint a sole administrator[2]. (As to grants to trust corporations, see Chapter 9.)

[1] This is the wording of the rule, but in practice the normal order of priority would operate, and, for example, a grant would not be made to children of the deceased without clearing off the surviving spouse or civil partner.

[2] Supreme Court Act 1981, s 114(2) (see para **A1.333**).

No surviving spouse or civil partner

5.209 Where the residuary estate is wholly or partly not disposed of, or has lapsed, and the deceased died leaving no spouse or civil partner, the order of priority of right to a grant is that applicable in cases of total intestacy (see para **6.40** Table B), and is not affected by the amount of the estate not disposed of. The grant may be made to any person entitled to share in the estate not disposed of, or, if every such person has since died or is otherwise cleared off, to the personal representative of any such person who has since died. (Form of oath (*or as adapted, witness statement of application*), No 154 (**A6.159**)).

Disposition of residue not ascertainable

5.215 Where the residuary estate is not wholly disposed of by the will, a grant may be made to any person entitled to share in the residue not disposed of, or, if every such person has since died or is otherwise cleared off, to the personal representative of any such person who has died.

Notice to Treasury Solicitor

5.217 Where the residuary estate is wholly or partly undisposed of and the deceased died without kin entitled to share in the estate not disposed of, or without known kin entitled to share, notice of the application for the grant must be given to the Treasury Solicitor in accordance with NCPR SI 1987/2024 r 38, and an acknowledgment of such notice filed with the papers to lead the grant. Under the same rule the district judge or registrar may direct that no grant shall issue within 28 days after the notice has been given. Notice of the application should be sent to: The Government Legal Department (BVD), PO Box 2119, Croydon CR90 9QU, *or* DX 123240 Kingsway. Tel 020 7210 4700. Email bvestates@governmentlegal.gov.uk

Virtual disposition of residue

5.219 This provision does not derogate from the right of a person entitled to the estate not disposed of to obtain a grant if he applies for it, but it frequently facilitates the issue of a grant to a legatee or devisee who has the sole, or a substantial, interest under the terms of the will where the deceased left kin who, although having little or no interest in the estate, would otherwise have to be cleared off.

5.222 If it is clear from the papers that there are kin who would be entitled to share in any estate not disposed of, the Crown need not be regarded as interested. Unless this is clear, however, the applicant should either provide evidence that there are such kin, or give notice to the Treasury Solicitor (see para **5.211** for address) in accordance with NCPR SI 1987/2024 r 38 (even though the whole of the ascertained estate is disposed of). Where such notice is to be given, the district judge or registrar may direct that no grant shall issue within 28 days after notice has been given in order to give the Treasury Solicitor the opportunity of opposing the making of the grant if he wishes.

5.223 If any person who would be entitled to, or to share in, any estate not disposed of is a minor it is necessary (unless the court thinks it expedient in all the circumstances to appoint a sole administrator) for the grant to be made to not less than two individuals or to a trust corporation with or without an individual, even though the whole of the known estate has been disposed of.

5.224 In the event of a dispute between a legatee and a person entitled to the estate not disposed of, the matter is one for decision upon issue of a summons under NCPR SI 1987/2024 r 27(6) (see paras **14.08** ff).

Rule 20, Class (e)

Estate not wholly disposed of by the will

5.228 Where the residuary estate is partly or wholly undisposed of, all persons taking any part of the residue disposed of by the will, and in addition, all persons entitled to share in the undisposed-of estate, or the personal representatives of any that have died, must be similarly cleared off before the grant can be made to a legatee, devisee or creditor.

Estate not disposed of vested in spouse who has since died

5.230 Where the whole of the estate not disposed of has vested in the surviving spouse of the deceased, who has since died intestate, a child of the deceased who is also the child of the spouse should constitute himself personal representative of the surviving spouse by taking a leading grant in that estate, and then apply in that capacity for a grant in the estate of the first to die.

Rule 20, Class (f)

Persons having no interest under the will

5.235 It should be noted that the NCPR SI 1987/2024 r 20, unlike the previous rules, do not include provision for a grant to be made to a member of the nearest class of kin of the deceased having no interest under the will (except where that class is entitled to the estate undisposed of by the will, in respect of which see paras **5.110** ff).

Miscellaneous grants of administration (with will)

Grant to assignee

5.253 The Finance Act 2003 introduced Stamp Duty Land Tax which came into effect on 1 December 2003. The effect of this tax does away with the requirement of the Stamp Duty Act 1891 to original deeds unless they relate to the transfer of shares and securities. The Stamp Taxes enquiry line (tel. 0300 200 3510) will provide assistance about particular deeds or transactions.

REQUIREMENTS ON OBTAINING ADMINISTRATION (WITH WILL)

Practice as to will

5.269 The practice as to proof of the will and codicils, alterations, incorporation, etc is the same as in applications for probate. (See Chapter 3 and Chapter 4.)

5.269A The current programme for modernisation of the courts has led to the Non-Contentious Probate (Amendment) Rules 2016 and 2017 (SI 2016/972 and SI 2017/1034 respectively). These amend the Non-Contentious Probate Rules 1987 to provide new rules 4A and 5A. A personal applicant (SI 2016/972 with effect from 1 November 2016) or a solicitor or probate practitioner (together referred to as a probate practitioner in this work) (SI 2017/1034 with effect from 20 November 2017) may apply for a grant of probate or administration online at any registry if invited to do so by that registry. The amendment rules for the new alternative online process are introduced on a pilot basis. The Non-Contentious Probate Rules 1987 as amended are set out in Appendix II.

5.269B At the time of publication the pilot has begun and is being trialled for personal applicants in the District Probate Registry at Oxford. The procedure for making online applications will extend and be trialled for applications from solicitors and probate practitioners at the District Probate Registry at Birmingham during 2018 and migrate to other registries in due course. At present the criteria for personal applications are as follows:

- applications for probate by up to four executors;
- the original will and codicils are in existence; and
- the deceased died domiciled in England and Wales.

The criteria in applications for letters of administration (with will) should be broadly similar. When invited to do so, a probate practitioner makes the application by completing and sending an online application form in accordance with instructions given by the registry. The applicant must verify the application by a statement of truth in the online application form. As well as completing the online form, the will and any codicils, inheritance tax forms and any supporting documents such as renunciations must be posted to the registry. At the present time the online project is in its infancy and the amendment rules have not been supplemented by any explanatory practice direction. It would seem that in individual cases the registry gives directions about the provision of evidence to support the application in matters such as evidence of identity or in support of execution of a will or codicil. This online process will begin in other probate registries for applications for grants of letters of administration as the pilot scheme works out difficulties and improves the online process.

5.269C The following paragraphs set out the requirements in an order corresponding to the usual form of oath for persons entitled to the estate of the deceased. Similar care should be taken when completing an online application form together with any modifications required by the registry. In this work references to executor's witness statement include a statement of truth contained in an online application form.

Chapter 6
LETTERS OF ADMINISTRATION

Note: In anticipation of the revision of the Non-Contentious Probate Rules, the expression 'witness statement' where it is used in this work refers to the form of application or evidence required with reference to any rule in force at the time of the application.

IN WHAT CIRCUMSTANCES GRANTED

Representative grants

6.15 The papers in respect of both applications may be lodged at the registry simultaneously, a note that this has been done being made in the oaths (*witness statement of application*). If the applications are in order the grants will be made successively, usually on the same day.

Application by attorney administrator for representative grant

6.16 An attorney administrator may obtain a grant in another estate to which he is entitled as personal representative of the deceased without any further authority from the donor of the power being necessary[1]. If it is known that a further grant will be required, the power of attorney may, if so desired, be so worded as to authorise the attorney to obtain both grants (see para **11.76** and Form No 190 (**A6.195**) for a precedent for such a power of attorney).

1 Registrar's Direction (1974) 11 October.

TO WHOM GRANTED

6.17 The general rule applicable to the grant of letters of administration is that where possible administration is granted to one or more of the persons taking a beneficial interest in the estate of the deceased, but the court may also exercise discretion to pass over the rights of these persons in suitable circumstances (see the reference to the probate rules in s 116(1) of the Senior Courts Act 1981[1] and NCPR SI 1987/2024 r 22(1)[2]).

1 See para **A1.335**.
2 See para **A2.61**.

Assignment of life interest or reversion

6.27 In a consultation paper entitled the Forfeiture Rule and the Law of Succession [2003] EWLC 172(1) (30 September 2003) and subsequent Report No 295 the Law Commission in reviewing the problems associated with disclaimers recommended a reform of the law so that where a person has disclaimed an interest whether under a will or intestacy the property is distributed as if that person had died immediately before the deceased. The Estate of Deceased Persons (Forfeiture Rule and the Law of Succession) Act 2011[1] gives effect to the Law Commission's recommendation. The Act amends the Administration of Estates Act 1925 so that where the deceased dies on or after 1 February 2012 intestate and the person who would be entitled to the residuary estate disclaims it, that person is treated as having died immediately before the intestate. Accordingly, issue of the person disclaiming acquire title to the estate to which the disclaimer would otherwise be entitled. For an example of a disclaimer on intestacy, see Form No 52A (**A6.57A**). Form of oath, No 115 (**A6.120**).

1 See para **A1.685A** ff.

Marriage same sex couples

6.31A The Marriage of Same Sex Couples (Conversion of Civil Partnership) Regulations 2014 (SI 2014/3181) sets out the procedure for converting a civil partnership into a same sex couple's marriage.

DISTRIBUTION OF AN INTESTATE'S ESTATE WHERE THE DEATH HAS OCCURRED ON OR AFTER 1 JANUARY 1926

Husband or wife or civil partner: (a) Death on or after 1 January 1953[1]

Note.—

See note under heading above table A in para **6.40** *about deaths on or after 1 January 1996.*

1 Section 46, Administration of Estates Act 1925, as amended by the Intestates' Estates Act 1952 and the Family Provision Act 1966 and Civil Partnership Act 2004, Sch 4, Pt 2: see paras **A1.119** and **A1.615**.

6.48 The several amendments to the Administration of Estates Act 1925 introduced by the Intestates Act 1952, the Family Provision Act 1966 and the Civil Partnership Act 2004 affect the distribution of an intestate's estate as follows:

(1) If the intestate dies leaving a husband or wife or civil partner, but no issue[2] or parent[3], or brother or sister of the whole blood[4], or issue of brother or sister of the whole blood[4], he or she is entitled to the whole estate, whatever its value.

(2) If the intestate dies leaving a husband or wife or civil partner and issue[2], the husband or wife or civil partner is entitled to the personal chattels absolutely[5] and a charge on the residuary estate for a fixed net sum (£250,000 with effect from 1 February 2009[6]) free of death duties and costs, with interest thereon at the appropriate rate per annum from the date of death until paid or appropriated[7].

(3) If the intestate dies on or after 1 October 2014 leaving a husband or wife or civil partner but no issue, he or she is entitled to the whole estate[7A].

(4) If the intestate dies before 1 October 2014 leaving a husband or wife or civil partner and one or more of the following: a parent[3], brother or sister of the whole blood[4], or issue of brother or sister of the whole blood[4], but leaves no issue[2], the husband or wife or civil partner is entitled to the personal chattels and a charge on the residuary estate for a fixed net sum (£450,000 with effect from 1 February 2009[8]), free of death duties and costs; and

(i) *where death was before 1 October 2014*, with interest thereon at the rate of 6% per annum;

(ii) *where death was on or after 1 October 2014*, with simple interest at the Bank of England rate that had effect at the end of the day on which the deceased died;

from the date of death until paid or appropriated[7].

(5) And as to the residue of the estate the husband or wife or civil partner is entitled to:

(a) a life interest in one half *where there is issue*[2] *surviving* (on failure of the statutory trusts[9] as to the issue[2] the residue and any statutory accumulations go as though the intestate had left no issue);

(b) an absolute interest in one half *where there is no issue*[2], but there is a parent[3], or brother or sister of the whole blood[4], or issue of a brother or sister of the whole blood[4], surviving.

2 See para **6.54** ff for meaning of the expression 'issue'.

3 In relation to deaths occurring on or after 1 January 1970, the expression 'parents' includes natural parents (Family Law Reform Act 1969, s 14: see para **A1.195**). See also, para **6.73** ff.

4 See para **6.43**.

5 *Death before 1 October 2014:* Personal chattels mean carriages, horses, stable furniture and effects (not used for business purposes), motor cars and accessories (not used for business purposes), garden effects, domestic animals, plate, plated articles, linen, china, glass, books, pictures, prints, furniture, jewellery, articles of household or personal use or ornament, musical and scientific instruments and apparatus, wines, liquors and consumable stores, but do not include any chattels used at the death of the intestate for business purposes nor money or securities for money.
Death from 1 October 2014: Personal chattels means tangible movable property, other than any such property which consists of money or securities for money, or was used at the death of the intestate solely or mainly for business purposes, or was held at the death of the intestate solely as an investment (Administration of Estates Act 1925, s 55(1)(x), (as amended), para **A1.134**).

6 See para **6.42** for earlier figures and dates.

7 Intestate Succession (Interest and Capitalisation) Order 1977 (SI 1977/1491) (Amendment) Order 1983 (SI 1983/1374); but see fn 3 to para **6.40**, as to the need to calculate the interest payable at different rates for different periods, and the Inheritance and Trustees' Powers Act 2014, s 1.

7A As amended by the Inheritance and Trustees Powers Act 2014, s 1.

8 See para **6.42** for earlier figures and dates.

9 See 'Statutory trusts for issue', paras **6.66** ff.

Additional rights of surviving spouse or civil partner

6.50A Where death has occurred on or after 1 October 2014, a life interest in favour of the surviving spouse or civil partner does not arise. With effect from that date s 47A has no application and is omitted from the Act[1].

1 Inheritance and Trustees' Powers Act 2014, Sch 4, art 1(3).

Statutory trusts for issue

6.67 If the intestate dies leaving issue, then, subject to the rights of the husband or wife or civil partner of the intestate (if any), the residuary estate is to be held in trust, in equal shares if more than one, for all or any of the legitimate or illegitimate children of the intestate, living at the death of the intestate, who attain the age of 18 years or marry under that age, and for all or any of the issue of such children who predeceased the intestate (ie lawful issue where the intestate died before 4 April 1988 or lawful or illegitimate issue where he died on or after that date) who are living at the death of the intestate and who attain the age of 18 years or marry under that age, such issue to take through all degrees, according to their stocks, in equal shares if more than one, the share which their parent would have taken if living at the death of the intestate, and so that no issue shall take whose parent is living at the death of the intestate and so capable of taking[1]. However this is subject to s 46A of the Administration of Estates Act 1925 as amended by the Estates of Deceased Persons (Forfeiture Rule and Law of Succession) 2011[2]. The effect of this is that in respect of the intestate who dies on or after 1 February 2012 a person who is entitled to the residuary estate but disclaims it or is a person who would be entitled if he was not excluded by the forfeiture rule (unlawful killing of the intestate) is to be treated as having died immediately before the deceased so that his issue takes in his place. See oath forms Nos 52A, 95 and 115 (**A6.57A**, **A6.100** and **A6.120**). In cases of this type the applications papers should include an official copy of the conviction certificate or deed of disclaimer as is appropriate. Further if any issue fail to attain an absolutely vested interest because such issue has died without having reached the age of 18 years, without having married or forming a civil partnership and left a child, such issue is to be treated as having died immediately before the intestate. See oath form No 123 (**A6.128**).

1 Administration of Estates Act 1925, s 47(1)(i), as amended by Family Law Reform Act 1969, s 3(2) (para **A1.192**) and Family Law Reform Act 1987, s 18; para **A1.418** and see fn 2 below.

2 See paras **A1.114** ff.

Parents of illegitimate child

6.75 It is, however, provided by s 14(4) of the Family Law Reform Act 1969 that for the purposes of s 14(2), and of Pt IV of the Act of 1925, an illegitimate child is to be presumed not to have been survived by his father unless the contrary is shown. A statement in the oath by the child's father confirming that he is the father is a sufficient contrary indicator for the purposes of an application for a grant of administration.

6.79 As to an application for letters of administration of the estate of an illegitimate person, see paras **6.300** ff.

Failure of statutory trusts

6.90 In its report entitled 'Intestacy and Family Provision Claims on Intestacy' (Law Com No 331) dated 17 November 2011, the Law Commission recommended that if immediately before adoption a child has any contingent interest in the estate of his or her deceased parent, other than an interest in remainder, that interest shall not be affected by the adoption. This recommendation was given effect in respect of death on or after 1 October 2014 by the Adoption and Children Act 2002, s 69(4)(c), as amended by the Inheritance and Trustees' Powers Act 2014, s 4(2). Accordingly, a child being a minor preserves the interest he has in his deceased parent's estate prior to his adoption.

RIGHT TO THE GRANT

Grant to surviving spouse or civil partner

Renunciation etc, of spouse or civil partner entitled to whole estate

6.112 Where the net value of the estate (after making the deductions referred to in para **6.106**) does not exceed the fixed net sum taken by the surviving spouse or civil partner (see para **6.42**), then if the spouse or civil partner is cleared off by renunciation or citation[1] or by death before taking a grant and his or her personal representative has renounced, the following are equally entitled to a grant:

(i) *where the intestate dies on or after 1 October 2014*, the issue of the deceased (to be described as the 'son *or* daughter of the deceased and the person who may have a beneficial interest in the event of an accretion');
(ii) *where the deceased died before 1 October 2014*, the nearest of kin[2] of the deceased (to be described in the oath as 'the lawful[3] . . . of the said deceased, and a person who may have a beneficial interest in the estate in the event of an accretion thereto') (Form of oath, No 86 (**A6.91**)); and (ii) creditors (NCPR SI 1987/2024 r 22(3)). As to grants to creditors, see para **6.343**.

1 As to citations, see Chapter 24.

2 Where the death occurred after 1925, but before 1953, 'nearest kin' includes all persons in their order under NCPR SI 1987/2024 r 22. But where the death occurred after 1952, it is limited to issue, parents, brothers or sisters of the whole blood, and issue of brothers or sisters of the whole blood who predeceased the intestate. See Administration of Estates Act 1925, s 46, as amended by Intestates' Estates Act 1952, pp 767 ff, and NCPR SI 1987/2024 r 22(1)(a)–(d).

3 Or, in the case of death on or after 1 January 1970 but before 4 April 1988, the natural son or daughter or natural father or mother (see paras **6.57** ff and **6.73** ff). In the case of death on or after 4 April 1988 the relationship of the kin need not be lawful and the word 'lawful' may be omitted.

Legitimated persons

Legitimation on marriage of parents

6.199 The parents of a legitimated person are under a duty to furnish to the Registrar-General within a specified time information with a view to obtaining the re-registration of birth[1].

1 Legitimacy Act 1926, s 1(4) and Sch which provisions are since repealed and re-enacted by the Legitimacy Act 1976, s 9; see also fn 1 to para **6.235**.

Adopted persons

Requirements on obtaining grant

6.285 Other degrees of relationship should be described in similar terms. All persons may be described (if so entitled) as being 'entitled to (share in) the estate'. Forms of oath (*witness statement of application*), Nos 99 and 100 (**A6.104** and **A6.105**).

6.286 Where it is necessary to clear off a person who, because of his adoption, has no interest in an estate in which he would otherwise have participated, the Forms of oath (*witness statement of application*) Nos 97 (**A6.102**) or 98 (**A6.103**) may be used. It is not necessary to exhibit or produce the adoption order, and the adopted person should be referred to throughout the documents by the name under which he was known prior to the adoption[1].

1 Registrar's Circular, 2 March 1966.

'Overseas adoptions'

6.292 Adoptions effected in, and in accordance with the law[1] of, the following places have been specified as 'overseas adoptions'. This applies to any adoption effected before 1 February 1973 in any place which, at that date, formed part of a country or territory listed below. It applies also to any adoption effected on or after that date, in a place which forms part of a country or territory so listed[2].

1 The expression 'law' in this context does not include customary or common law (Adoption (Designation of Overseas Adoptions) Order 1973, art 3(3)).
2 Adoption (Designation of Overseas Adoptions) Order 1973, art 3(2) and Adoption (Recognition of Overseas Adoptions) Order 2013 (SI 2013/1801), art 2 and Sch.

COMMONWEALTH COUNTRIES AND UNITED KINGDOM DEPENDENT TERRITORIES:

Australia	Bahamas	Barbados
Bermuda	Botswana	British Honduras
British Virgin Islands	Canada	Cayman Islands
The Republic of Cyprus	Dominica	Fiji
Ghana	Gibraltar	Guyana
Hong Kong	Jamaica	Kenya
Lesotho	Malawi	Malaysia
Malta	Mauritius	Montserrat

New Zealand	Nigeria	Pitcairn
St Christopher, Nevis and Anguilla	St Vincent	Seychelles
Singapore	Southern Rhodesia (now Zimbabwe)	Sri Lanka
Swaziland	Tanzania	Tonga
Trinidad and Tobago	Uganda	Zambia

Other countries and territories

Albania	Finland	The Netherlands (including the Caribbean part of the Netherlands (the islands of Bonaire, Sint Eustatius and Saba) New Zealand
Andorra	Fiji Finland France	Norway
Armenia	Georgia	Panama
Austria	Germany	Paraguay
Azerbaijan	Greece	Peru
Belarus	Guinea	Philippines
Belgium	Hungary	Poland
Belize	Iceland	Portugal
Bolivia	India	Romania
Brazil	The Republic of Ireland	Rwanda
Bulgaria	Israel	San Marino
Burkina Faso	Italy	Senegal Seychelles
Burundi	Kazakhstan Kenya	Slovakia
Cape Verde	Latvia	Slovenia
Chile	Lesotho	South Africa
The People's Republic of China	Liechtenstein	Spain Sri Lanka Swaziland
Colombia	Lithuania	Sweden
Costa Rica	Luxembourg	Switzerland
Cuba	The Former Yugoslav Republic of Macedonia	Thailand
The Republic of Cyprus	Madagascar	Togo
Czech Republic	Mali Malta Mauritius	Turkey
Denmark (including the Faroe Islands and Greenland)	Mexico	The United States of America
Dominican Republic	The Republic of Moldova	Uruguay
Ecuador	Monaco	Venezuela
El Salvador	Mongolia	Vietnam

Estonia	Montenegro

Grant to parents

Adoptive parents

6.310 In the case of death on or after 1 January 1950, and after the making of an adoption order, s 16(1) of the Adoption Act 1958, or s 39 of the Adoption Act 1976, or s 67 of the Adoption and Children Act 2002 (as the case may be, depending upon the date of death) has the effect of placing an adoptive parent or, in the case of a joint adoption, both the adoptive parents, in the position of lawful parents for the purpose of succession on intestacy to the real and personal estate of the adopted person; accordingly, the adoptive parent has the same priority of right under NCPR SI 1987/2024 r 22 to a grant of administration of the estate of an adopted child who dies intestate on or after 1 January 1950 as if he had been a child of the adoptive parent born in lawful wedlock. See paras **6.282–6.285**, as to the practice in obtaining a grant where the entitlement arises by virtue of an adoption. Form of oath, No 100 (**A6.105**).

REQUIREMENTS ON OBTAINING ADMINISTRATION

Administrator's oath (witness statement)

6.379A The current programme for modernisation of the courts has led to the Non-Contentious Probate (Amendment) Rules 2016 and 2017 (SI 2016/972 and SI 2017/1034 respectively). These amend the Non-Contentious Probate Rules 1987 to provide new rules 4A and 5A. A personal applicant (SI 2016/972 with effect from 1 November 2016) or a solicitor or probate practitioner (together referred to as a probate practitioner in this work) (SI 2017/1034 with effect from 20 November 2017) may apply for a grant of probate or administration online at any registry if invited to do so by that registry. The amendment rules for the new alternative online process are introduced on a pilot basis. The Non-Contentious Probate Rules 1987 as amended are set out in Appendix II.

6.379B At the time of publication the pilot has begun and is being trialled for personal applicants in the District Probate Registry at Oxford. The procedure for making online applications will extend and be trialled for applications from solicitors and probate practitioners at the District Probate Registry at Birmingham during 2018 and migrate to other registries in due course. At present the criteria for personal applications are as follows:

- applications for probate by up to four executors;
- the original will and codicils are in existence; and
- the deceased died domiciled in England and Wales.

The criteria in applications for letters of administration should be broadly similar. When invited to do so, a probate practitioner makes the application by completing and sending an online application form in accordance with instructions given by the registry. The applicant must verify the application by a statement of truth in the online application form. As well as completing the online form, the inheritance tax forms and any supporting documents such as renunciations must be posted to the registry. At the present time the online project is in its infancy and the amendment rules have not been supplemented by any explanatory practice direction. It would seem that in individual cases the registry gives directions about the provision of evidence to support the application in matters such as evidence of identity. This online process will begin in other probate registries for applications for grants of letters of administration as the pilot scheme works out difficulties and improves the online process.

6.379C The following paragraphs set out the requirements in an order corresponding to the usual form of oath for persons entitled to the estate of the deceased. Similar care should be taken when completing an online application form together with any modifications required by the registry. In this work references to executor's witness statement include a statement of truth contained in an online application form.

Description of applicant

Death on or after 5 December 2005

6.391 Otherwise than as described in para **3.390** persons applying for administration, where the death occurred after 5 April 1988, are to be described as follows:

A husband	'the lawful husband'
A wife	'the lawful widow and relict (*or* (if she has remarried) the lawful relict)'. (Where the net estate, after allowing the permissible deductions, does not exceed £250,000 (or £450,000 if the deceased left no issue)[1] the husband or relict should be further described as 'the only person *now* entitled to the estate'. It is only where it can be sworn that there are no kin within the degrees mentioned in the tables in para **6.40** (no issue nor parent nor brother nor sister of the whole blood nor issue of a brother or sister of the whole blood), that the spouse can be described as 'the only person entitled to the estate'.
Issue of marriage	'the son (or daughter), and only person entitled to the estate'; or
Note: A child or other issue who has acquired an alternative gender under the Gender Recognition Act 2004 at the death of the deceased is described as a child or issue in the acquired gender	'the son (or daughter), and one of the persons entitled to share in the estate'; 'the lawful adopted son *or* daughter' or 'the lawful legitimated son *or* daughter', as the case may be[2]. 'the grandson (or granddaughter), and only person entitled to the estate'; or

	'the grandson (or granddaughter), and one of the persons entitled to share in the estate'[3]. (In the case of grandchildren or more remote issue, the oath (*witness statement of application*) should establish that the applicant has a beneficial interest, ie it should show either that the deceased died without child, or that the applicant is 'the [*or* lawful adopted *or* lawful legitimated] son (or daughter) of A. B., the [lawful] [*or* natural *or* lawful adopted *or* lawful legitimated] son (or daughter) of the said intestate, who died in the lifetime of the said intestate.')
A father	'the father (or mother), and only person entitled to the estate'; or
or	'the father (or mother), and one of the persons entitled to share in the estate.'
a mother	
	Note: a parent who has acquired an alternative gender under the Gender Recognition Act 2004 retains the original status as father or mother of the intestate.
A brother	'the brother (or sister) of the whole blood, and only person entitled to the estate'; or
or	
a sister	'the brother (or sister) of the whole blood, and one of the persons entitled to share in the estate'. *If there be no brother or sister of the whole blood, nor any issue of such brother or sister*, then the half blood is described as 'the brother (or sister) of the half blood, and' etc.
	Note: a sibling who has acquired an alternative gender under the Gender Recognition Act 2004 at the death of death of the deceased is described as a sibling of the acquired gender.
Issue of a brother or sister	'the nephew, or great-nephew (or niece), of the whole blood, and only person entitled to the estate'; or
	'the nephew, or great-nephew (or niece), of the whole blood, and one of the persons entitled to share in the estate'.
	(The oath (*witness statement of application*) must also establish that the applicant has a beneficial interest, in a similar manner to that given under 'Issue of marriage', above.)
	If there be no brother or sister of the whole blood, or any issue of such brother or sister, then the half blood, if entitled to take a beneficial interest in the estate, is described as 'the nephew, or great-nephew (or niece), of the half blood, and' etc.
	Note: a person in this class who has acquired an alternative gender under the Gender Recognition Act 2004 at the death of death of the deceased is described as of the acquired gender.

A grandparent	'the grandfather (or grandmother), and only person entitled to the estate'; or 'the grandfather (or grandmother), and one of the persons entitled to share in the estate' *Note: A person in this class who has acquired an alternative gender under the Gender Recognition Act 2004 at the date of death of the deceased is described as of the acquired gender.*
An uncle or an aunt	'the uncle (or aunt) of the whole blood, and only person entitled to the estate'; or 'the uncle (or aunt) of the whole blood, and one of the persons entitled to share in the estate' *If there be no uncle or aunt (being brother or sister of the whole blood of a parent), or any issue of such uncle or aunt, such person shall be described as* 'the uncle (or aunt) of the half blood, and', etc. *Note: a person in this class who has acquired an alternative gender under the Gender Recognition Act 2004 at the death of death of the deceased is described as of the acquired gender.*
Issue of an uncle or aunt	'the cousin german of the whole blood, and only person entitled to the estate'; or 'the cousin german of the whole blood, and one of the persons entitled to share in the estate'. (The oath (*witness statement of application*) must also establish that the applicant has a beneficial interest: see above.) *If there be no uncle or aunt (being brother or sister of the whole blood of a parent), or any issue of such uncle or aunt, such person shall be described as* 'the lawful cousin german of the half blood, and' etc.

1 The values are applicable when the intestate died on or after 1 February 2009. For the relevant amounts for earlier dates of death, see para **6.42**.

2 As to a grant in the case of illegitimacy, adoption or legitimation, see paras **6.191** ff, **6.247** ff and **6.197** ff, respectively.

3 As to the practice under which, on the renunciation of the surviving spouse, the issue or other kin may apply as persons 'who may have a beneficial interest in the estate in the event of an accretion thereto', see para **6.112**.

Chapter 7

MINORITY OR LIFE INTERESTS AND SECOND ADMINISTRATORS

Note: In anticipation of the revision of the Non-Contentious Probate Rules, the expression 'witness statement' where it is used in this work refers to the form of application or evidence required with reference to any rule in force at the time of the application.

APPLICATION FOR ORDER JOINING CO-ADMINISTRATOR

7.19 The Human Rights Act 1998 (HRA 1998) came into force on 2 October 2000. Hearings in chambers are subject to the overriding considerations of the HRA 1998. In particular art 6 in Sch 1 to the Act allows everyone the right to a public hearing. This places on the district judge or registrar a duty to allow public access to any hearing or to a transcript of a judgement in chambers. CPR 39.2 and PD 39.1/39A.1 set out the matters which the court must have regard to in deciding whether to hold a public or private hearing. A hearing may be in private if it involves uncontentious matters arising in the administration of trusts or in the administration of a deceased person's estate (CPR 39.2(3)(g)).

ONLY ONE CHILD ETC OF FULL AGE

7.28 Where the deceased has left no spouse or civil partner, but several children, of whom only one is of full age, he or she is not entitled to nominate a co-administrator as this right is given only to a person who has parental responsibility for the minor children. An application without notice under NCPR SI 1987/2024 r 25(2), supported by affidavit (*witness statement*), should be made to the district judge or registrar for the appointment of the proposed second administrator for the purpose of joining with the child of full age in taking the grant. The consent of the proposed co-administrator may be either exhibited to the affidavit (*witness statement*) or submitted separately with the affidavit (*witness statement*). A person entitled to a grant in his own right may not and will not be appointed on behalf of the minor to enable him to nominate a co-administrator[1].

1 Registrar's Direction (1955) 7 November.

PRACTICE IN MINORITY OR LIFE INTERESTS AND SECOND ADMINISTRATORS

7.44 The application should be made without notice at the registry from which the grant issued by lodging an affidavit (*witness statement*) as to the facts, the consent of the proposed substituted or additional administrator and the original grant.

7.45 The affidavit (*witness statement*) in support of the application, in addition to giving the details of the grant, should show that there is still a minority or life interest, or, where the grant was originally made to a sole administrator, that such an interest has now arisen and give details of this.

7.46 Upon the making of the order, the grant and records are noted with the appointment of the substituted or additional administrator and the registry returns the grant.

Chapter 8

HMRC ACCOUNTS

NECESSITY FOR ACCOUNT

8.03 The Inheritance Tax Account Form IHT400 and all completed appropriate supplementary pages should be sent to the HMRC Trusts and Estates, Inheritance Tax, Ferrers House, PO Box 38, Castle Meadow Road, Nottingham, NG2 1BB. From 1 April 2016 that office ceased to use the Document Exchange [DX] system. This office was formerly known as the HMRC Inheritance Tax, IR Capital Taxes Office or the Capital Taxes Office and may be shown as such on some forms or accounts. The previous Form IHT200 will no longer be accepted by HMRC Inheritance Tax, Trusts and Estates.

Personal applications

8.05 Form PA1 should be sent with the other papers necessary to apply for a Grant to the Probate Registry. Form IHT422 should be sent to HMRC Trusts and Estates, Inheritance Tax to obtain a reference and an IHT payslip at least three weeks prior to the submission of Form IHT400. Alternatively, it is possible to apply for a reference number online using the Inheritance Tax website. A reference number will be provided by post together with a pre-referenced payslip. Form IHT400, all the supplementary pages including Form IHT421 and any documents requested should then be sent to HMRC Trusts and Estates, Inheritance Tax, ideally at the same time as the form PA1 is sent to the Probate Registry. If the applicant has calculated the tax, the appropriate payment should also be sent in a separate envelope with the reference number and payslip obtained under the IHT422 procedure. If, however, the applicant wishes HMRC Trusts and Estates, Inheritance Tax to calculate the tax, a calculation will then be sent to the applicant. It is only necessary to apply for an Inheritance Tax reference if the estate is liable to Inheritance Tax. Where tax is payable and is being paid by cheque or money order, which should be crossed and made payable to 'HMRC' or 'Her Majesty's Revenue and Customs', the cheque or money order and the payslip should be sent in a separate envelope to HMRC Banking, St Mungo's Road, Cumbernauld, Glasgow, G70 5WY or by DX to HM Revenue & Customs, DX 550100, Cumbernauld 2. If payment is to be made by way of the Direct Payment Scheme, Form IHT423 should be sent to the bank or building society at the same time as the submission of the Form IHT400. See para **8.205** for details of the appropriate methods of payments and relevant addresses. Once payment is received and all is in order, HMRC Trusts and Estates, Inheritance Tax will complete its part of the Form IHT421 and send it direct to the Probate

Registry. The Probate Registry will normally issue the Grant within 10 days of the interview. The Form IHT400 will be retained by HMRC Trusts and Estates, Inheritance Tax. Form IHT400 Calculation or form IHT430 Reduced Rate of Inheritance Tax should also be submitted if the simple Inheritance Tax calculation on page 11 of the account cannot be used.

8.07 *Form IHT205[2011]*. A revised version of the Form IHT205 is now available in respect of deaths on or after 6 April 2011, known as IHT205[2011]. The new form covers estates where the deceased had his or her main home in the UK and (a) the gross value of their estate was below the appropriate inheritance tax excepted estate limit, currently £325,000, or (b) the gross value of the estate was below £1,000,000 and no tax is payable due to spouse, civil partner or charity exemption only, or (c) below twice the excepted estate limit and form IHT217 'Claim to transfer unused nil rate band for excepted estates' is attached. There is a time limit of 24 months from the end of the month in which the death occurred to submit form IHT217 plus the important condition that none of the nil rate band was used by the earlier death. Other criteria are detailed in form IHT217. The Finance Act 2013 introduced revised ss 162A–C and 175A to IHTA 1984 relating to certain liabilities. These rules have been extended to excepted estates by way of the Inheritance Tax (Delivery of Accounts) (Excepted Estates) (Amendment) Regulations 2014 (SI 2014/488) in respect of deaths on or after 1 April 2014. It is important that joint assets passing by survivorship, whether to a spouse, a civil partner or otherwise should be included in the appropriate box. There are questions regarding changes or disposal of pension benefits in the two years prior to the date of death which affect the qualification for the estate to be considered within the 'excepted estate' legislation. A facility now exists for the form IHT205(2011) to be completed online. Details are online at 'Inheritance Tax: return of estate information' (IHT205(2011)). This facility is not available for solicitor applications.

INHERITANCE TAX AND CAPITAL TRANSFER TAX

Scope of the tax

8.20 The efficacy of the tax depends upon a tree of concepts at the root of which is the—undefined—'disposition'. A liability for tax becomes a possibility if a disposition is a 'transfer of value': that is to say it is made by a person and, as a result, the estate of that person is less than it otherwise would have been[1]. The amount by which the value of the estate is so decreased is known as the 'value transferred'[2]. Most dispositions are transfers of value but some are specifically provided not to be. Moreover no account is taken of 'excluded property'[3]. If a transfer of value is made by an individual (as distinct from a person) and is not an 'exempt transfer'[4] or a potentially exempt transfer[5] then it is a 'chargeable transfer' and tax is chargeable[6] upon the value transferred[7]. The 'exempt transfer' needs no elaboration here; but a 'potentially exempt transfer' would become a chargeable transfer upon the death of the transferor within seven years thereafter.

1 See fn 1 to para **8.16** as to the meaning of 'estate'.
2 IHTA 1984, s 3(1) [FA 1975, s 20(2)].
3 IHTA 1984, s 3(2) [FA 1975, s 20(3)]; IHTA 1984, s 6 [FA 1975, s 24(2) and Sch 7,

paras 3(1), 5(1) and 6)].
4 IHTA 1984, ss 18 ff [FA 1975, Sch 6].
5 IHTA 1984, s 3A in relation to events on and after 18 March 1986.
6 IHTA 1984, s 2 [FA 1975, s 20].
7 IHTA 1984, s 1 [FA 1975, s 19] (see para **A1.723**).

Pension death benefits

8.44 On the death of an individual under the age of 75, a transfer of a lump sum payment of the remaining or eligible pension pot will be (income) tax-free if paid out within two years. The transfer of any remaining annuity or drawdown income will also be (income) tax-free if taken as an annuity or income drawdown (if designated within two years). If the individual is aged 75 or over as at the date of death, any lump sum payment will attract income tax at the rate of 45% during the year 2015/16 and, it is currently proposed, at the beneficiary's rate of income tax in following years. Following the transfer, any future drawdown or annuity income by the beneficiary will be taxed at the beneficiary's rate of income tax. Under the provisions of the Finance Act 2016, s 94, where a member or dependant's pension drawdown fund, or a money purchase arrangement under a corresponding scheme, has not been used up prior to death, a deemed distribution will not have been made. This legislation has effect in respect of deaths on or after 6 April 2011. Where the drawdown relates to a flex-access fund for the member, dependant or nominee, the effective date becomes 6 April 2015.

Rates of tax

8.50 Tax is chargeable if the total for rate exceeds the contemporary threshold, presently £325,000. The total for rate is found by aggregating the value transferred by the instant transfer with the cumulative total of the values transferred by any chargeable transfers made by the transferor within the previous seven years[1]. This does not involve a series of fixed seven-year periods but a moving seven-year cumulation period from which successive transfers fall away as time passes. The rate of tax chargeable can be summarised as follows:

(a) For deaths on and after 15 March 1988 the rate of tax on values in excess of the contemporary threshold is 40% but there is a taper relief in the form of a percentage reduction in the tax payable in respect of any chargeable transfer which occurred more than three years but less than seven years before the date of death[2]. If the transfer was a chargeable transfer immediately (as distinct from being a potentially exempt transfer) then any tax paid at that time is allowed as a credit against the tax payable in connection with the death. (A chargeable transfer made before 18 March 1986, however, is chargeable at the death rate only if made within three years before the transferor's death.)

(b) For deaths before 15 March 1988 but on or after 18 March 1986 the position is at (a) save that in place of the flat rate of 40% there was a progressively banded table of rates[3].

(c) For deaths before 18 March 1986 but on or after 10 March 1981 the cumulation period was ten years. There were two rate tables and tax in respect of the deceased's estate and any chargeable transfers made within three years before the death were charged according to the first table[4]. All other lifetime chargeable transfers were chargeable according to the second table. Any tax paid under the second table was allowed as a credit pro tanto against tax payable by reason of the transferor's death within three years after the transfer.

(d) For deaths before 10 March 1981 but on or after 13 March 1975 the position was as at (c) save that instead of a moving cumulation period of ten years there was a fixed period which commenced on 27 March 1974.

(e) Under the provisions of s 10 and Sch 4 to the Finance Act 2008, the transfer of any unused nil rate band of the estate of a spouse or civil partner who died before the deceased (the deceased must have died on or after 9 October 2007) may be made subject to the completion of the claim Form IHT402. The deceased's nil rate band is increased by the percentage of the nil rate band that was unused when his or her spouse or civil partner died. More detailed instructions are incorporated in the notes section on Form IHT402.

(f) Section 109 and Sch 33 of the FA 2012 provides with effect from 6 April 2012 a reduction in the rate of Inheritance Tax charged on a component part of the estate if at least 10% of that component part passes to a charitable body. The rate of tax becomes 36% instead of 40% for the component part of the estate, subject to apportionment calculations. This new legislation provides a new Sch 1A to IHTA 1984. Form IHT430 must be completed and sent to HMRC Trusts and Estates, Inheritance Tax within two years following the date of death.

(g) Section 9, Finance Act (No 2) 2015 and s 93 and Sch 15 of the Finance Act 2016 provide, with effect from 6 April 2017, a potential addition to the nil-rate band in respect of the deceased's residence, subject to certain criteria. This legislation allows an additional figure of up to £100,000 from 6 April 2017, rising annually to £175,000 for the year 2020/21 and then to increase in line with the Consumer Prices Index for the year 2021/22. To qualify for this extra nil-rate addition, the property must be left to a child (including step-child, adopted child or foster child) of the deceased and/or their lineal descendants and must be a residential property. The relief is tapered for estates exceeding £2,000,000 and there are provisions in respect of downsizing of property prior to the date of death. Forms IHT435 and/or IHT436 as appropriate should be completed and incorporated into form IHT400 to claim the relief.

1 IHTA 1984, s 7 as amended by the FA 1986, s 101(1) and Sch 19, para 2 [FA 1975, s 37 as amended by the FA 1981, s 93(1)].

2 IHTA 1984, s 7 as amended by the FA 1986, Sch 19, para 2.

3 See Appendix IV, para **A4.01**.

4 See Appendix IV, para **A4.01**.

PRACTICE IN HMRC ACCOUNTS

Completion of account

8.108 If the deceased died domiciled outside the United Kingdom according to general law (notwithstanding that, by virtue of s 267 of the IHTA 1984 he or she might be treated for the purposes of the tax as having been domiciled in the UK – amended to 15 out of the previous 20 years by the Finance (No2) Act 2017 s 30 with effect from 6 April 2017), Schedule IHT401 must be annexed to the account[1]. An additional statement from one or two individuals who were related to or well acquainted with the deceased and who might speak with authority with regard to any domicile of choice outside the UK could usefully be furnished where the domicile of origin was in the UK or the deceased had lived there at the time of or before his or her death. The case of a married woman or civil partner (after 5 December 2005) has no distinguishing features save where a married woman had already acquired—and had retained—a domicile of dependence by reference to her husband's domicile before 1 January 1974[2]. In such a case it would be necessary to indicate the husband's domicile of origin and give brief particulars of his life in addition to those of the deceased married woman since January 1974.

1 Domicile is explained in Chapter 12: ordinary residence outside the United Kingdom is relevant for the 'exclusion' of Government securities: see para **8.138**. The 'ordinary residence' rules were removed by the Finance Act 2013, s 219 and Sch 46, for deaths on or after 6 April 2013 in connection with non-residents' bank accounts. The test was also removed for Free of Tax for Residents Abroad (FOTRA) securities acquired on or after 6 April 2013, but remains in place for FOTRA securities acquired before that date.

2 Domicile and Matrimonial Proceedings Act 1973, s 1: see para **A1.230**.

PRACTICE

Exemptions from tax

8.138 Where property, which forms part of the estate passing under the grant of probate or administration, is exempt from tax, its value should be included in the Inheritance Tax account, in order that the true value for the purpose of the grant may be shown, and detailed in the spaces provided in the account on pages 9 and 10 as property on which tax is either not payable at all or is not at present payable. In addition to the exemptions in respect of transfers between spouses or civil partners (from 5 December 2005)[1], to charities[2] and political parties, and gifts for national purposes, considered in para **8.49**, in connection with lifetime transfers, this applies, inter alia, to the following types of property, which are variously 'exempt', 'conditionally exempt', or 'excluded' from being included for the purpose of ascertaining the tax payable on the rest of the estate—in certain cases with the reservations stated:

(a) Heritage property. Objects of national, scientific, historic or artistic interest, land of scenic, historic or scientific interest; and historic buildings with their adjoining land and associated contents. A claim for conditional exemption must be made using Schedule IHT420 and accepted by the Commissioners of HMRC[3]. In addition, transfers to approved maintenance fund settlements for certain heritage property are exempt transfers[4]. Under the provisions of the Finance Act 2016, s 97, the estate duty conditional exemption afforded by the FA 1930, s 40 and the Finance Act (Northern Ireland) 1931, s 2, is cancelled if the objects under this section are lost or destroyed.

(b) Gifts of property of any kind to national heritage bodies such as national or local art galleries or museums, local authorities, government departments and universities. Under the provisions of the Finance Act 2016, s 96, the approval function for such bodies reverts to the Treasury, having previously transferred to the Commissioners of Inland Revenue under the FA 1985, s 95.

Gifts for public benefit to bodies not run for profit where the Treasury approves exemption. Such gifts are limited to objects and land as at item (a). In addition, a reasonable maintenance fund may be included[5].

(c) Property situate in the UK by UK law but treated as situate elsewhere by virtue of a double taxation convention or agreement where the deceased was domiciled outside the UK.

(d) Certain British Government securities which are excluded property where the deceased was domiciled and ordinarily resident abroad[6].

Under s 161 of the Finance Act 1998 which is effective for transfers on or after 6 April 1998, the excluded Government securities were expanded to include any gilt-edged security issued before 6 April 1998. Such securities are treated as if they were securities issued with the post-1996 Act conditions. The one exception to this exclusion relates to 3½% War Loan 1952 or after.

Under s 154 of the Finance Act 1996, with effect from 29 April 1996, provided the deceased was ordinarily resident outside the UK, the Treasury was empowered to issue securities which were excluded from the charge to Inheritance Tax. The Domicile qualification previously required for such exclusion was negated for such securities. The securities issued within this qualification are 8% Treasury Stock 2000, Floating Rate Treasury Stock 2001, 7% Treasury Stock 2001, 7% Treasury Stock 2002, 6½% Treasury Stock 2003, 7¼% Treasury Stock 2007, 8% Treasury Stock 2015, 8% Treasury Stock 2021 and 6% Treasury Stock 2028.

Details of the Government securities which were regarded as excluded property for earlier transfers are detailed below.

(e) Property of which the deceased was life tenant is exempt from tax if it would have been exempt from estate duty under the Finance Act 1894, s 5(2), duty having been paid thereon in connection with the death of the deceased's spouse, such death having occurred before 13 November 1974. Any apportionment of income received after his or her death to which the estate may be entitled is treated as covered by the exemption[7].

(f) Reversionary interests which have not been acquired by the deceased or by a person previously entitled to it for a consideration in money or money's worth are excluded property.

1 The restricted exemption to spouses or civil partners was increased to the equivalent of the nil-rate band threshold (currently £325,000) for deaths on or after 6 April 2013 and is to rise in line with future changes to the threshold.

2 For which form IHT408 is required in respect of household or personal goods.

3 Undertakings are required, inter alia, as to maintenance and retention of the objects in the UK. Reasonable access for the public must also be provided in all cases: IHTA 1984, s 30 [FA 1976, s 76 replacing, in relation to deaths on and after 7 April 1976, FA 1975, s 31]. A general requirement is that the access to the public must be on an open basis on a prescribed number

of days and will be discussed and agreed with HMRC. Tax will be chargeable when sold (unless the sale is by private treaty to a national heritage body or similar public body) or on failure to observe the terms of the undertaking imposed as a condition of relief. Claims for exemption or enquiries relating thereto are dealt with by HMRC Trusts and Estates, Inheritance Tax. Any claim for exemption is investigated after the issue of the grant, and inspection of the objects by Officers of the National Collections is usually necessary. The objects should therefore not be dispersed before inspection has taken place, without adequate notice to HMRC Trusts and Estates, Inheritance Tax. If any objects were exempted on the ground of national, etc, interest in connection with a previous death, further inspection of those objects may be waived, but the name and date of death of the former owner and, if known, the HMRC Trusts and Estates, Inheritance Tax reference to his or her estate should be mentioned.

4 IHTA 1984, s 27 (see also Sch 4) [FA 1982, s 95 replacing, in relation to deaths on and after 9 March 1982, the FA 1976, s 84 which applied to deaths on and after 3 May 1976 as amended with effect from 1 August 1980 by the FA 1980, s 88. (See also the FA 1982, s 93 and 94 and Sch 16 replacing, in relation to deaths on and after 9 March 1982, the FA 1976, s 84, amended as aforesaid.)]

5 IHTA 1984, ss 25 and 26 [FA 1975, Sch 6, paras 12 and 13]. There is no limit in value, but, as regards gifts for public benefit, undertakings are required, inter alia, as to maintenance, use or disposal and as to reasonable access for the public.

6 Viz 3½% War Loan; 13% Treasury Stock 1990; 8% Treasury Convertible Stock 1990; 8¼% Treasury Loan 1987–90; 11% Exchequer Loan 1990; 10% Treasury Convertible Stock 1991; 5¾% Funding Loan 1987–91; 2% Index Linked Treasury Stock 1992; 8% Treasury Loan 1992; 10½% Treasury Convertible Loan Stock 1992; 12¾% Treasury Loan 1992; 10% Treasury Loan 1993; 6% Funding Loan 1993; 12½% Treasury Loan 1993; 13¾% Treasury Loan 1993; 9% Treasury Loan 1994; 10% Treasury Loan 1994; 14½% Treasury Loan 1994; 12¾% Treasury Loan 1995; 9% Treasury Loan 1992–96; 13¼% Exchequer Loan 1996; 15¼% Treasury Loan 1996; 8¾% Treasury Loan 1997; 13¼% Treasury Loan 1997; 7% Treasury Convertible Loan 1997; 6¾% Treasury Loan 1995-98; 4⅝% Index-linked Treasury Stock 1998; 7¼% Treasury Stock 1998; 15½% Treasury Loan 1998; 6% Treasury Stock 1999; 9½% Treasury Loan 1999; 8½% Treasury Loan 2000; 9% Conversion Stock 2000; 9½% Conversion Loan 2001; 8% Treasury Stock 2003; 9¾% Conversion Loan 2003; 8% Treasury Loan 2002–06; 4⅜% Index-linked Treasury Stock 2004, 6¾% Treasury Stock 2004; 8½% Treasury Stock 2005; 7½% Treasury Stock 2006; 7¾% Treasury Stock 2006; 8½% Treasury Loan 2007; 9% Treasury Loan 2008; 6¼% Treasury Stock 2010; 9% Conversion Loan 2011; 5½% Treasury Stock 2008–12; 9% Treasury Stock 2012; 8% Treasury Stock 2013; 7¾% Treasury Loan 2012–15; 8¾% Treasury Stock 2017; 2½% Index-Linked Treasury Stock 2024; 4⅛% Index-linked Treasury Stock 2030.

7 IHTA 1984, Sch 6, para 2 [FA 1975, s 22(4)].

RELIEFS

Variations: changes in the distribution of the estate on death

8.172 *Settlements with no beneficial interest in possession*[1]—s 144. The legislation provides not only for taxation in connection with transfers between individuals and transfers on death but also in connection with transfers by trustees of settlements[2]. Provisions are made for a chargeable event to occur in relation to a settlement with no beneficial interest in possession when, inter alia, funds are dealt with by the trustees so that an individual becomes entitled to those funds absolutely or takes a qualifying interest in possession[3] in them. The scheme of relief in this case postulates that the funds have been settled under the deceased's will on trusts under which no beneficial interest in possession subsists; and it secures relief from the charge to tax under those provisions[4] provided that the event concerned occurs within two years after the death of the testator. Also, it provides that tax is to be charged in connection with the death as though the testator's will had provided for the property so dealt with to be held as it was after the event concerned[4]. Under the provisions of s 14 of the FA (No2) 2015, section 144 is amended in respect of deaths on or after 10 December 2014, so that where property is settled by will and an appointment is made before an interest in possession subsists in the property, the provisions of s 65(4) are ignored.

1 Ie, broadly, discretionary trusts.
2 IHTA 1984, Pt III.
3 IHTA 1984, s 102(1).
4 IHTA 1984, s 144(2).

ASSESSMENT, PAYMENT AND DELIVERY

Assessment

8.202 Interest on tax on property not entitled to the 'instalment option' is payable from the end of the sixth month after the date of death to the date of payment. The rates of interest for all outstanding tax and effective periods are tabled below. The adjustments after 1989 until 12 August 2009 were made in accordance with the Finance Act 1989, s 178(1). The Taxes and Duties (Interest Rate) (Amendment) Regulations 2009 (SI 2009/2032), took effect on 12 August 2009 and contained provisions that replaced the single rate of interest of Inheritance Tax, Capital Transfer Tax and Estate Duty with one rate for charging interest on unpaid tax and another, lower, rate for the repayment interest supplement that is added to repayments. The interest rates so calculated are linked to the Bank of England base rate and will move with base rate changes announced by the Bank's Monetary Policy Committee (MPC).

Interest rate	*Effective dates*	*Authority*
6%	Up to 31 December 1979	FA 1974, Sch 4, para 19
9%	1 January 1980 to 30 November 1982	SI 1979/1688
6%	1 December 1982 to 30 April 1985	SI 1982/1585 and Inheritance Tax Act 1984, s 233
9%	1 May 1985 to 15 December 1986	SI 1985/560
8%	16 December 1986 to 5 June 1987	SI 1986/1944
6%	6 June 1987 to 5 August 1988	SI 1987/887
8%	6 August 1988 to 5 October 1988	SI 1988/1280
9%	6 October 1988 to 5 July 1989	SI 1988/1623
11%	6 July 1989 to 5 March 1991	Board's Order June 1989
10%	6 March 1991 to 5 May 1991	Board's Order 18 February 1989
9%	6 May 1991 to 5 July 1991	Board's Order April 1991
8%	6 July 1991 to 5 November 1992	Board's Order 21 June 1991
6%	6 November 1992 to 5 December 1992	Board's Order 22 October 1992
5%	6 December 1992 to 5 January 1994	Board's Order 20 November 1992
4%	6 January 1994 to 5 October 1994	Board's Order 15 December 1993
5%	6 October 1994 to 5 March 1999	Board's Order 20 September 1994
4%	6 March 1999 to 5 February 2000	Board's Order 18 February 1999
5%	6 February 2000 to 5 May 2001	Board's Order 20 January 2000
4%	6 May 2001 to 5 November 2001	Board's Order 23 April 2001
3%	6 November 2001 to 5 August 2003	Board's Order 19 October 2001
2%	6 August 2003 to 5 December 2003	Board's Order 21 July 2003

3%	6 December 2003 to 5 September 2004	Board's Order 17 November 2003
4%	6 September 2004 to 5 September 2005	Board's Order 10 August 2004
3%	6 September 2005 to 5 September 2006	Board's Order 5 September 2005
4%	6 September 2006 to 5 August 2007	Revenue and Customs (Interest Rates) Order 2006, dated 22 August 2006
5%	6 August 2007 to 5 January 2008	Revenue and Customs (Interest Rates) Order 2007, dated 20 July 2007
4%	6 January 2008 until 5 November 2008	Revenue and Customs (Interest Rates) Order 2007, dated 7 December 2007
3%	6 November 2008 until 5 January 2009	Revenue and Customs (Interest Rates) Order (No 2) 2008, dated 21 October 2008
2%	6 January 2009 until 26 January 2009	Revenue and Customs (Interest Rates) Order (No 3) 2008, dated 16 December 2008
1%	27 January 2009 until 23 March 2009	Revenue and Customs (Interest Rates) Order 2009, dated 12 January 2009
3% for late payments; 0.5% for overpayments	29 September 2009 until 22 August 2016	HMRC announcement dated 29 July 2009. Recalculation of interest rates following September Monetary Policy meeting of Bank of England.
2.75% for late payments: 0.5% for overpayments	23 August 2016 until 20 November 2017	HMRC guidance announcement dated 15 August 2016.
3% for late payments; 0.5% for overpayments	21 November 2017 onwards	HMRC guidance announcement dated 13 November 2017

8.203 Interest on the tax on real property and other property entitled to the 'instalment option' is charged in the same way, except that in the case of business assets and unquoted shares in companies (excluding certain investment and dealing companies) and, in the case of deaths after 9 March 1981, property afforded agricultural relief, interest is only charged on each instalment as from the date it falls due (as regards chargeable transfers made before 10 March 1981 a limit of £250,000 is imposed on the value by reference to which tax may be paid by interest free instalments)[1]. Land and buildings held as business assets are entitled to this interest relief. The FA (No2) 2015, s 15, further defines the extent and start dates of interest charged, particularly regarding instalment option property and where tax becomes payable under the provisions of the IHTA 1984, s 147(4).

1 IHTA 1984, s 234 [FA 1975, Sch 4, para 16 as amended by FA 1981, ss 95 and 96].

Payment of tax

8.205 Where tax is payable, the assessed Inheritance Tax account IHT400 and the Form IHT421 should first be sent to the HMRC Trusts and Estates, Inheritance Tax, Ferrers House, PO Box 38, Castle Meadow Road, Nottingham, NG2 1BB for the Form IHT421 to be authorised and impressed by that office once payment has been made. A receipt will not be issued by HMRC Trusts and Estates, Inheritance Tax as part of their normal practice. See also paras **8.02** and **8.17** above.

8.207 Where tax is payable and is being paid by cheque or money order, which should be crossed and made payable to 'HMRC' or 'Her Majesty's Revenue and Customs', the cheque or money order and the payslip should be sent in a separate envelope to HMRC Banking, St Mungo's Road, Cumbernauld, Glasgow, G70 5WY. With effect from 23 July 2016, the payslip sort code should be 25-61-21 and refer to Barclays Bank. Payslips using sort code 62-40-03 and referring to NatWest are no longer valid, and will be rejected in bank clearing and remain in the suspense account of the bank they are paid into. The cheque should be made payable to 'HM Revenue and Customs only' followed by the Inheritance Tax reference and should be crossed 'Account payee'. The full name of the deceased and the date of death should be written on the back of the cheque. The Inheritance Tax reference number may be obtained online using the Inheritance Tax website, or by completing the Form IHT422 which is a supplementary form to the Inheritance Tax account. The Form IHT422 should be submitted to the HMRC Trusts and Estates, Inheritance Tax office at least three weeks before the expected submission of the Form IHT400. Alternatively, it is possible to apply for a reference number online using the HMRC website. A reference number will be provided by post together with a pre-referenced payslip. It is only necessary to apply for an Inheritance Tax reference if the estate is liable to Inheritance Tax.

8.210 It is also possible for Inheritance Tax to be discharged using the deceased's Government Stock. In the first instance, write to the registrars for British Government Stock and let them know that it is desired for funds to be transferred from British Government Stock to pay Inheritance Tax on the deceased's estate and let them know how much it is desired to transfer. The registrars are: British Government Stocks (Gilts), Computershare Investor Services plc, The Pavilions, Bridgwater Road, Bristol, BS99 6ZW. Telephone number 0370 703 0143. E-mail: gilts@computershare.co.uk. Computershare may require the stock reference number to help them find a particular investment. This number appears on the stock certificate and correspondence from the Bank of England. They aim to deal with requests within five days.

CORRECTIVE ACCOUNTS

Pre-owned assets

8.229 Under the provisions of the Finance Act 2016, s 95, a relief is now available for payments to victims of persecution during World War II in respect of deaths on or after 1 January 2015 where a payment has been received by an appropriate person or their personal representatives. The relief takes the form of a reduction in the tax which would have been charged on the qualifying payment or the equivalent of the relevant percentage of the qualifying payment, the relevant percentage being the rate of tax over the nil-rate threshold.

Chapter 11

LIMITED GRANTS

Note: In anticipation of the revision of the Non-Contentious Probate Rules, the expression 'witness statement' where it is used in this work refers to the form of application or evidence required with reference to any rule in force at the time of the application.

INTRODUCTORY NOTES

Settling oaths (witness statements)

11.07 Where the application is complex, the oath (*witness statement of application*) may be submitted in draft, for settling to the probate department of the Principal Registry or to the district probate registry at which the application for the grant is to be made. The nature of the complexity must be clearly set out.

GRANTS TO ATTORNEYS AND CONSULAR OFFICERS

Form of power of attorney

11.44 The Lasting Powers of Attorney, Enduring Powers of Attorney and Public Guardian Regulations 2007 prescribe forms of lasting powers of attorney (Sch 1, Parts 1 and 2). References to the forms mentioned in the Regulations include a Welsh version of the forms. A donor may execute an instrument intended to create a property and affairs lasting power of attorney or/and an instrument intended to create a personal welfare lasting power of attorney. Of these, only a lasting power of attorney in respect of property and (financial) affairs may be used for the purpose of obtaining a grant for the use and benefit of the donor. The donor of a lasting power of attorney may appoint more than one donee. A lasting power of attorney is not created and therefore unusable until the Public Guardian registers it irrespective of whether the donor lacks capacity within the meaning of the Mental Capacity Act 2005 or not. An application made under NCPR SI 1987/2024 r 31(1) that relies upon a registered lasting power of attorney should include a statement in the oath (*witness statement of application*) that the donor does not lack capacity within the meaning of the Act to manage his property and affairs and that the registered lasting power of attorney has not been revoked nor has the donee disclaimed his appointment. However, the practice now is that if this statement is not included, the probate registry will assume that the donor has capacity within the meaning of the Act. The registered lasting power of attorney stamped by the Office of the Public Guardian together with a copy should be submitted with the application. The registry returns the original stamped power after inspection. Equally acceptable is an office copy of the registered lasting power or a copy certified on each page pursuant to s 3 of the Powers of Attorney Act 1971.

Power filed in the registry

11.79 A probate practitioner lodging a *general* or an *enduring* or *lasting* power of attorney, which is required for other purposes, may lodge with it a copy, and request that the original be returned with the grant. The original power must be duly stamped if it was executed before 19 March 1985 (see para **11.46**). The examined copy is filed with the oath (*witness statement of application*), and the original returned with the grant. A power of attorney limited only for the purpose of obtaining a grant is not returnable[1].

1 Registrar's Direction (1952) 14 March.

Oath (witness statement of application) of attorney

11.82 The oath (*witness statement of application*) should contain all the particulars which would be necessary in the case of a direct grant to the donor of the power. Additionally an attorney acting under an enduring power must confirm that the power is not registered with the Public Guardian and that the donor remains mentally capable. See paras **11.265** ff below for practice where the power is registered. An attorney acting under a registered lasting power of attorney should confirm that the donor does not lack mental capacity within the meaning of the Mental Capacity Act 2005, but if this is omitted the probate registrar will assume this to be the case. The appropriate limitation must be included. A grant to an attorney is expressed to be for the use and benefit of the donor and the usual limitation required by r 31(1) is 'until further representation be granted' but, under that rule, the district judge or registrar may direct some other form of limitation. The usual form of limitation in a grant allows a further grant to issue not only to the donor of the original power of attorney, or another attorney appointed by him, but to any other person with an equal title to a grant. The district judge or registrar would not normally allow a further grant to issue to anyone other than the original donor, or an attorney appointed by him in substitution for the original attorney, without good reason being given and without the original attorney or donor being given an opportunity to be heard on the matter. Some other possible forms of limitation are dealt with in the following paragraphs. See forms of oath, Nos 116–118, 165 and 172 (**A6.121–A6.123**, **A6.170** and **A6.177**).

GRANTS FOR USE OF MINORS

Grant where person entitled is a minor

11.126 The Children Act 1989 as subsequently amended sets out which persons have parental responsibility for a child, the acquisition of parental responsibility and the meaning of parental responsibility[1]. The Adoption and Children Act 2002 has extended the classes or persons who may have parental responsibility for a minor. In addition the Human Fertilisation and Embryology Act 2008 defines the parent of a child born as a result of placing in a woman an embryo or sperm and eggs or her artificial insemination. Accordingly with effect from 5 December 2005 priority of right to a grant for the use and benefit of a minor is now given by the NCPR SI 1987/2024 r 32 equally to a parent (including an adoptive parent and from 6 April 2009 a parent by virtue of the Human Fertilisation and Embryology Act 2008[2]) with parental responsibility for him, a person who has parental responsibility by virtue of a residence order in his favour in respect of the minor, a step-parent who has acquired parental responsibility for the minor, a guardian with parental responsibility for him, a special guardian (appointed by order of the court), an adoption agency authorised to place the minor for adoption or a local authority with parental responsibility for him. In the absence of or in appropriate circumstances in spite of such persons, adoption agency or local authority having parental responsibility, other persons may be appointed by district judge's or registrar's order[3] to obtain administration for the use and benefit of the minor.

1 Children Act 1989, Pt 1, ss 2–6, and see para **11.152** ff.
2 Section 2, Children Act 1989 as amended consequential to the Human Fertilisation and Embryology Act 2008.
3 NCPR SI 1987/2024 r 32(2).

11.127 Briefly, the rule gives priority of right to a grant for the use and benefit of a minor to the following who have or have acquired parental responsibility: parent, guardian, step-parent, special guardian, adoption agency or local authority. In the absence of such a parent or any of the above persons or bodies r 32(2) allows a wide discretion to a district judge or registrar to appoint other persons to obtain administration for the use and benefit of the minor. The rule also allows the appointment of persons to act jointly with any persons who are entitled in priority to obtain administration for the use and benefit of the minor[1].

1 NCPR SI 1987/2024 r 32(2).

Persons of full age equally entitled with minors

11.130 By NCPR SI 1987/2024 r 27(5), unless a district judge or registrar otherwise directs, a person of full age entitled to a grant is to be preferred to a person with parental responsibility for a minor entitled in the same degree. Thus, normally, where one of the persons entitled to a grant is of full age, he or she should apply for the grant in preference to the person with parental responsibility for a minor. This does not apply where the only one of several persons entitled to apply is of age and the remainder are minors. As to the practice in such cases, see Chapter 7.

Grant to parents (including adoptive parents)

11.161 Where the father of a minor was not married to the mother at the time of the child's birth, but has parental responsibility in accordance with paras 4 or 6 of Sch 14 to the Children Act 1989 either (a) by virtue of an order under s 4(1) of the Family Law Reform Act 1987; or (b) by virtue of an order giving him custody or care and control of the child, in force immediately before the commencement of Pts I and II of the Children Act 1989, the oath must state that he is the father of the minor and a parent having parental responsibility by virtue of such an order which was in force immediately before the commencement of the Children Act 1989. A copy of the order must be produced in each instance[1]. The passage of time has now made this requirement redundant.

[1] Practice Direction, 26 September 1991 ([1991] 4 All ER 562, [1991] 1 WLR 1069).

Oath (witness statement of application) and supporting evidence

11.165A The current programme for modernisation of the courts has led to the Non-Contentious Probate (Amendment) Rules 2016 and 2017 (SI 2016/972 and SI 2017/1034 respectively). These amend the Non-Contentious Probate Rules 1987 to provide new rules 4A and 5A. A personal applicant (SI 2016/972 with effect from 1 November 2016) or a solicitor or probate practitioner (together referred to as a probate practitioner in this work) (SI 2017/1034 with effect from 20 November 2017) may apply for a grant of probate or administration online at any registry if invited to do so by that registry. The amendment rules for the new alternative online process are introduced on a pilot basis. The Non-Contentious Probate Rules 1987 as amended are set out in Appendix II.

11.165B See paras **5.296B** and **6.379B** for developments about making online applications for grants.

11.166 Otherwise, the applicant's oath (witness statement of application) should include details of the residence order or parental responsibility agreement. A copy of the order or of the sealed agreement must be produced with the oath together with any will to be proved. For form of agreement see para **A2.115** (Form C(PRA3)).

11.171 For form of oath see Form Nos 122–128 (**A6.127–A6.133**).

Nomination of co-administrator

11.239 It should be noted that a person apart from a spouse or civil partner entitled to a grant *in his or her own right* will not be appointed on behalf of a minor to enable him or her to nominate a co-administrator (see para **7.28**).

GRANTS FOR USE OF PERSONS UNDER DISABILITY

Other persons having equal right

11.253 Where one of several executors named in a will lacks capacity within the meaning of the Mental Capacity Act 2005 to manage his affairs, probate is granted to the other executors, power being reserved to the executor[1] who lacks capacity. The district judge's or registrar's power under r 35(1) does not enable a grant to be made on behalf of an executor who lacks capacity without clearing off other executors who are sui juris[2].

[1] *Evans v Tyler* (1849) 2 Rob Eccl 128 at 131.

[2] Registrar's Circular, 12 June 1967.

Notice to Court of Protection

11.262 The notice should be addressed to: The Court of Protection, PO Box 70185, First Avenue House, 42–49 High Holborn, London WC1A 9JA *or* DX 160013 Kingsway 7. The email address is: courtofprotectionenquiries@hmcts.gsi.gov.uk and the website is https://courttribunalfinder.service.gov.uk/courts/court-of-protection. The telephone number is: 0300 456 4600.

Lawful attorney acting under a registered lasting power of attorney

11.279A It should be noted that the appointment of an attorney ceases to have effect and is terminated by death or bankruptcy of the attorney or the making of a debt relief order in respect of the attorney. Where the attorney is a bankrupt because of an interim bankruptcy order, his appointment is suspended for so long as the order has effect[1].

[1] Mental Capacity Act 2005, s 13 (as amended).

Sole executor or residuary legatee or devisee in trust lacks capacity to manage his affairs: grant to residuary legatee

11.284 As to the position where there are two or more executors, one of whom lacks capacity to manage his affairs, see 'Other persons having equal right', paras **11.251–11.254**.

Only person entitled on intestacy lacks capacity to manage his affairs

11.287 In the case of an intestacy, where the only person entitled to the grant lacks capacity to manage his affairs within the meaning of the Mental Capacity Act 2005, administration (with will if appropriate) will be granted for his use and benefit and during his incapacity or lack of capacity (i) to the person authorised by the Court of Protection or, if none, (ii) to his lawful attorney acting under a registered enduring power of attorney or registered lasting power of attorney; or, if none, or if such attorney renounces administration (with will if appropriate) for the use and benefit of the person who lacks capacity (iii) to such other person as the district judge or registrar may by order direct (see paras **11.291–11.292**). For forms of oath (or as adapted, application witness statement), see Nos 132 to 134 (**A6.137** to **A6.139**) and, where there is a will, No 169A (**A6.174A**).

Grant to persons appointed by district judge or registrar

11.292 Application for the order of the district judge or registrar is made by lodging an affidavit (*witness statement*) of the facts at the probate department of the Principal Registry, or if the application for the grant is to be made at a district probate registry, at that registry. Unless it is submitted separately the affidavit (*witness statement*) should exhibit a medical certificate of the person who lacks capacity as detailed in para **11.266** above. The applicant should also confirm that notice has been given to the Court of Protection. The district judge or registrar may direct that the application be made on notice or summons (*application notice*) if it becomes apparent that it is being, or likely to be, opposed[1].

1 NCPR SI 1987/2024 r 61(1).

GRANTS LIMITED AS TO PROPERTY

Grant to part of estate only

Fee for grant to trust property only

11.315 The Non-Contentious Probate Fees Order 2004 makes no provision for a fee on an application for a grant to trust property. Consequently, being a nil estate for the purpose of the grant, no fee is payable on making such application.

ADMINISTRATION PENDING DETERMINATION OF PROBATE CLAIM

Order required

11.365 Application for the appointment of an administrator pending determination of a probate claim is made by application notice in the probate claim (CPR Pt 23). For practice, see para **38.01**.

Issue of grant

11.367 If an order is made appointing an administrator pending determination of the claim, the solicitor or probate practitioner should prepare and lodge at the Principal Registry of the Family Division[1] the papers to lead the grant, ie the administrator's oath (*witness statement of application*) (Form No 135 (**A6.140**)), an HMRC Inheritance Tax account summary (if required, see Chapter 8), and an office copy of the order of the Chancery Division appointing the administrator. No reference need be made in the oath to any will of the deceased or grant that has already been issued. The grant is this case is always one of administration. The grant pending determination of a probate claim will be silent as to will or intestacy and will be limited pending determination of the claim.

1 CPR PD 57.8.4. The practice direction directs that the application for the grant be made to the Principal Registry as the grant cannot be made by a district probate registrar because of the unresolved contention arising from the probate claim—NCPR SI 1987/2024 r 7(1)(a). In practice, the application for the grant is now referred to a district probate registrar, it is assumed under the delegated power of the Senior District Judge.

Practice

11.371 An office copy of the judgment or order in the probate claim must be obtained and lodged with the papers, and the oath (*witness statement*) must include particulars of the judgment (see also paras **4.180** and **4.181**), and of any previous grant pending determination of the probate claim.

MISCELLANEOUS

Grant limited to a claim

11.376 Difficulties can also arise in those cases where a dependant of a deceased person wishes to bring a claim under the Inheritance (Provision for Family and Dependants) Act 1975 for financial provision from the deceased's estate, but is prevented from bringing proceedings until a grant has issued and a personal representative has been constituted, and there is no person either entitled or (if entitled) willing to apply for a grant. In this event, the claimant may make a claim without naming a defendant and may apply for directions as to the representation of the estate[1]. As to claims under the Inheritance (Provision for Family and Dependants) Act 1975, and the position where the claimant is also the constituted personal representative, see Chapter 41.

1 CPR 57.12, 57.16(3A) and see paras **A2.181** and **11.379–11.380.**

Proceedings against a deceased's estate

11.379 An alternative method of bringing proceedings against the estate of a deceased person where a cause of action has survived but no personal representative has been constituted is provided by rules of court made under the Civil Procedure Rules 1998: see CPR 19.8.

Practice in obtaining grant

11.385 In all cases the oath (*witness statement of application*) in support of the grant application need not include any statement whether a will exists or whether the deceased died intestate, nor contain any of the usual clearings. It will, however, always be necessary to consider the existence of life or minority interests. It is suggested that the question as to whether any life or minority interest arises in the estate of the deceased be dealt with in the affidavit in support of the application for the order. Every grant ad colligenda bona (*collection grant*) shall be silent as to the will or the intestacy and the grant is limited 'to collecting, getting in and receiving the estate and doing such acts as are necessary for the preservation of the same and until further representation be granted'[1].

1 Registrar's Direction (1979) 12 October.

Chapter 12

GRANT WHERE DECEASED DIED DOMICILED OUT OF ENGLAND AND WALES

Note: In anticipation of the revision of the Non-Contentious Probate Rules the expression 'witness statement' where it is used in this work refers to the form of application or evidence required with reference to any rule in force at the time of the application.

DOMICILE

Domicile of choice

12.07 Residence in a country is not, of itself alone, sufficient to create a domicile of choice without evidence of volition to change domicile[1]. A domicile of choice is not acquired merely by accepting and holding a post of employment in a country[2]. A person whose residence in England is illegal is not barred thereby from acquiring a domicile of choice here[3].

1 *IRC v Bullock* [1976] 3 All ER 353, [1976] 1 WLR 1178, CA.
2 *Bowie (or Ramsay) v Liverpool Royal Infirmary* [1930] AC 588; *Cooney v Cooney* (1950) 100 L Jo 705.
3 *Mark v Mark* [2005] UKHL 42, [2006] 1 AC 98, [2005] 3 All ER 912.

GRANTS WHERE DECEASED DIED DOMICILED OUT OF ENGLAND AND WALES

Reference to law of nationality

12.31 When the law of the country in which a person dies domiciled (he being a national of some other country) provides that the law applicable to the validity of his will and the devolution of his estate is that of his nationality, it is sometimes necessary to ascertain with which part of the 'empire' of which the deceased was a national he was directly associated. For this purpose it may be necessary to ascertain his domicile of origin[1]. As regards persons dying on or after 1 January 1964, reference should be made to the Wills Act 1963 as to nationality and to confirmation of which of several systems of law in force in a territory or state is applicable where the formal validity of a will is to be decided. As to the Wills Act 1963, see paras **3.400** ff.

1 *Re O'Keefe, Poingdestre v Sherman* [1940] Ch 124, [1940] 1 All ER 216; *Re Ross, Ross v Waterfield* [1930] 1 Ch 377.

Chapter 13

GRANTS 'DE BONIS NON' – CESSATE GRANTS – DOUBLE PROBATE

Note: In anticipation of the revision of the Non-Contentious Probate Rules the expression 'witness statement' where it is used in this work refers to the form of application or evidence required with reference to any rule in force at the time of the application.

PARTICULAR CASES

Administration, with draft or copy of will annexed, 'de bonis non'

13.47 Where a will has been proved in a draft, copy or reconstruction, on the death of the sole or last surviving grantee who leaves part of the estate unadministered, the following practice applies. Provided that a chain of representation does not arise, letters of administration with the draft, copy or reconstructed will may be granted on the same terms as the original grant, it being confirmed that the original will has not been found. But if the original will has been found, the application is for a cessate grant (see paras **13.85** ff).

PRACTICE IN GRANTS 'DE BONIS NON'

Oath

13.64 Where the grant is required for making title only, it may be sworn that the grantee died 'without having completed the administration of the estate'. This situation may occur for example when the spouse or civil partner has appropriated the property to which he or she was entitled under the will or intestacy but did not assent to title of the property. The oath should confirm this fact.

CESSATE GRANTS

Grant for use of executor who lacks capacity to manage his affairs

13.96 If the incapable executor should die without recovering his capacity, administration (with the will annexed) de bonis non may be granted to the person next entitled in order of priority under NCPR SI 1987/2024 r 20. In this event, careful consideration should be given to interpretation of the appointment clause in the will. Depending on the particular circumstances of the case, a substituted appointment of executor may take effect.

Chapter 14

RIGHT OF THE COURT TO SELECT AN ADMINISTRATOR; 'COMMORIENTES'

Note: In anticipation of the revision of the Non-Contentious Probate Rules the expression 'witness statement' where it is used in this work refers to the form of application or evidence required with reference to any rule in force at the time of the application.

COMMORIENTES

Deaths in disasters

14.54 Circulars have been issued from time to time by the Principal Registry in connection with the loss of ships or aircraft or other disasters, listing the names of passengers and members of the crew or other persons involved in respect of whom the Senior District Judge is satisfied, from evidence produced to him, that there is uncertainty as to which of them survived the others. Where such a circular has been issued no further evidence relating to commorientes is normally necessary on application for a grant in the estate of a person whose name is listed. Any request for information whether such a circular has been issued in any particular case should be addressed to the Senior Operations Manager, Probate, Rm WG 09, Royal Courts of Justice, Strand, London WC2A 2LL.

Chapter 15

RENUNCIATION AND RETRACTION

Note: In anticipation of the revision of the Non-Contentious Probate Rules the expression 'witness statement' where it is used in this work refers to the form of application or evidence required with reference to any rule in force at the time of the application.

RETRACTION

Practice

15.75 Form of retraction, Form 197 (**A6.202**).

Form of retraction by members of a partnership, Form 198 (**A6.203**).

Chapter 16

AMENDMENT AND NOTATION OF GRANTS

Note: In anticipation of the revision of the Non-Contentious Probate Rules the expression 'witness statement' where it is used in this work refers to the form of application or evidence required with reference to any rule in force at the time of the application.

AMENDMENT OF GRANT

Error as to deceased

16.04 Amendment of a grant may be allowed where the error was in the Christian name, address, or date of death of the deceased. Where an amendment is desired in the name of the deceased, or in the date of death, the certificate of birth or death must be produced.

Address of deceased

16.09 An additional address may be inserted by amendment[1] where there is a sufficient and exceptional reason for it to be included. Permission is rarely given.

1 *Re Towgood's Goods* (1872) LR 2 P & D 408.

Errors as to grantee

16.11 An executor may have omitted a first or medial name of his own, which has been omitted in his appointment in the will, or he may have used the surname stated in the will, without the right to do so. If he can give a sufficient and reasonable explanation, the necessary amendment will be made.

16.14 The district judges and registrars have allowed the insertion of a limitation for the use and benefit of named minors until one of them attains 18 years etc and also a note as to reservation of power to make a grant to another executor.

ELECTION BY SPOUSE OR CIVIL PARTNER TO HAVE LIFE INTEREST REDEEMED

Right of surviving spouse or civil partner to redemption

16.36 Where the deceased dies intestate on or after 1 October 2014 leaving a spouse or civil partner and issue, and the value of the net estate exceeds the spouse's or civil partner's statutory legacy, a life interest in the deceased's estate no longer arises. The Administration of Estates Act 1925, s 46 as amended by the Inheritance and Trustees' Powers Act 2014, s 1, omits the previous requirement, if any, for a spouse's or civil partner's life interest.

ORDERS FOR PROVISION OUT OF ESTATE OF DECEASED

Inheritance (Provision for Family and Dependants) Act 1975

16.50 A copy of every final order made under the relevant provisions of these Acts[1] is to be sent to the Principal Registry of the Family Division for entry and filing, and a memorandum of the order must be endorsed on, or permanently annexed to, the probate or letters of administration under which the estate is being administered.

1 Other than an order made under s 15(1) of the Act, but including an order dismissing an application or a final order embodying a consent order or terms of compromise (Registrar's Direction (Divorce), 21 March 1962; *Practice Direction* (Chancery Division: Endorsement of Orders on Grants of Representation): [1978] 3 All ER 1032, [1979] 1 WLR 1); now CPR PD 57B(18.1)–(18.3).

Practice for recording orders

Principal Registry

16.51 The grant of probate, letters of administration (with will) or letters of administration and a copy of the order are sent to the Leeds Registry by the Chancery Master, Family Division district judge or county court district judge, as the case may be. If the grant was made in the Principal Registry a memorandum of the order is prepared by the probate department and photocopied. A copy of the memorandum is attached to the grant, and a further copy is sent to HMRC Inheritance Tax. The order and another copy of the memorandum are sent to the Birmingham Probate Registry for filing at the Probate record Centre with the original will, or if there is no will, with the oath to lead the grant of administration.

16.52 A marginal note is made on the grant, as follows: 'Memorandum of order dated   pursuant to section 19(3) of the Inheritance (Provision for Family and Dependants) Act 1975 (*or as the case may be*), annexed hereto' and a note is also made on the record of the grant. The grant, with the copy memorandum attached, is returned to the extracting solicitor, probate practitioner or grantee.

Chapter 17

REVOCATION AND IMPOUNDING OF GRANTS

Note: In anticipation of the revision of the Non-Contentious Probate Rules the expression 'witness statement' where it is used in this work refers to the form of application or evidence required with reference to any rule in force at the time of the application.

BY WHOM REVOCATION IS OBTAINED

Other documents required

17.52 If one of the grantees lacks capacity to manage his property and affairs within the meaning of the Mental Capacity Act 2005, evidence of his lack of mental capacity is required. The district judge or registrar will normally accept a certificate or affidavit by the Responsible Medical Officer in the form set out in para **11.266**, or a certificate by the patient's doctor. If the Responsible Medical Officer or doctor is unable to give such a certificate, the matter should be referred to the district judge or registrar for his directions[1].

[1] *Practice Note* [1962] 2 All ER 613, [1962] 1 WLR 738; Registrar's Direction (1969) 31 January.

Combined application for revocation of probate and new grant

17.57 Where a grant of probate has issued to two or more executors, one of whom subsequently lacks mental capacity to manage his affairs, and it is proposed to revoke it and obtain a new grant of probate to the remaining original grantee or grantees, one sufficient affidavit may be used both to lead the order for revocation and to serve as the oath (*witness statement*) on which the new grant issues. The will may be referred to as that already proved, and need not be re-marked nor need a copy be annexed. No further HMRC Inheritance Tax account need be lodged.

IMPOUNDING GRANTS

When grant impounded

17.67 Where a sole, or sole surviving, grantee subsequently lacks mental capacity within the meaning of the Mental Capacity Act 2005, and a new grant is made, the former practice of impounding the old grant has been abandoned[1].

1 *Registrar's Direction* (1985) 9 July.

Chapter 18

RESEALING

Note: In anticipation of the revision of the Non-Contentious Probate Rules the expression 'witness statement' where it is used in this work refers to the form of application or evidence required with reference to any rule in force at the time of the application.

COLONIAL GRANTS RESEALED IN ENGLAND AND WALES[1]

1 The term 'colonial' is used for convenience in this chapter, but the Colonial Probates Acts also authorise the resealing of grants issued by a number of former colonies, protectorates, etc which have attained independence within the Commonwealth, by South Africa while it was a Republic outside the Commonwealth and more recently by Hong Kong which is now a Special Administrative Region of the People's Republic of China (see paras **18.35–18.39**).

18.27 By s 1 of the Colonial Probates Act 1892[1] it is provided that:

> 'Her Majesty the Queen may, on being satisfied that the legislature of any British possession has made adequate provision for the recognition in that possession of probates and letters of administration granted by the courts of the United Kingdom, direct by Order in Council that this Act shall, subject to any exceptions and modifications specified in the Order, apply to that possession, and thereupon, while the Order is in force, this Act shall apply accordingly.'

1 For full text of the Act, see para **A1.45**. The term 'British possession' under s 1 of the Act means, by virtue of Sch 1 to the Interpretation Act 1978, 'any part of H.M. Dominions outside the United Kingdom', and is thereby not restricted to British dependent territories.

Changes in status of former colonies etc

18.37 In the case of South Africa, s 2 of, and the Second Schedule to, the South Africa Act 1962 specifically authorised the continued resealing of grants issued in South Africa notwithstanding that it became a Republic outside the Commonwealth. South Africa rejoined the Commonwealth in 1994.

Territories to which the Act applies

18.39 The Colonial Probates Acts now apply to permit the resealing of grants made in the following countries and territories:

[Aden]

On 30 November 1967 Aden ceased to form part of HM Dominions. Grants made in Aden after that date cannot be resealed (Secretary's Circular, 17 January 1968).

Alberta

Antigua

Australian Capital Territory

Bahamas

Barbados

Belize (formerly British Honduras)

Bermuda

Botswana (formerly Bechuanaland)

British Antarctic Territory

British Columbia

British Sovereign Base Areas in Cyprus

Brunei

Cayman Islands

Christmas Island (Australian)

Cocos (Keeling) Islands

Cyprus (Republic)

Only those grants issued by the courts under the jurisdiction of the recognised government of Cyprus may be resealed. Accordingly any document purporting to be a grant issued by a court of the 'Turkish Republic of Northern Cyprus', having only de facto jurisdiction, may not be resealed although such a document may be used to support an application for an order under NCPR SI 1987/2024 r 30(1)(c) (see paras **12.110–12.115**).

Dominica

Falkland Islands

Falkland Islands Dependencies

Fiji

Gambia

Ghana

Gibraltar

Gilbert and Ellice Islands

On 1 January 1976 the Ellice Islands separated from the Gilbert Islands and became a separate colony under the name of Tuvalu. On 1 October 1978 the colony of Tuvalu achieved independence within the Commonwealth. On 19 June 1979, by virtue of the Kiribati Act 1979, the former Gilbert Islands attained full independent status as the Republic of Kiribati. By that Act, the Colonial Probates Acts continue to apply to Kiribati.

Grenada

Guyana (formerly British Guiana)

Hong Kong

The United Kingdom's mandate to govern Hong Kong ended on 30 June 1997 and on 1 July 1997 the territory was renamed The Hong Kong Special Administrative Region of the People's Republic of China. The Hong Kong (Colonial Probates Act) Order 1997 applies the Colonial Probates Act 1892 to that region as it applied to Hong Kong immediately before 1 July 1997.

Jamaica

Kenya

Kiribati

See entry for Gilbert and Ellis Islands above

Lesotho (formerly Basutoland)

Malawi

Malaysia

See also entry for Singapore below

Manitoba

Montserrat

New Brunswick

[New Hebrides]

The Act of 1892 applied to the New Hebrides only to the extent of Her Majesty's jurisdiction there. The New Hebrides became an independent country (now known as Vanuatu) on 30 July 1980. Since Her Majesty from that date has no jurisdiction there, the Colonial Probates Acts only apply to grants issued before independence.

New Guinea Territory

New South Wales

New Zealand

Newfoundland

Nigeria

Norfolk Island

Northern Territory of Australia

North-West Territories of Canada

Nova Scotia

Ontario

Papua (New Guinea)

Prince Edward Island

Queensland

St Christopher (Kitts), Nevis and Anguilla

On 19 December 1980 Anguilla ceased to form part of the territory of the associated states of St. Christopher, Nevis and Anguilla: the Colonial Probates Acts continue to apply to these states.

St Helena

St Lucia

St Vincent

Saskatchewan

Seychelles (Republic)

Sierra Leone

Singapore

On 9 August 1965 Singapore seceded from the Federation of Malaysia and became an independent sovereign state. The Colonial Probates Acts continue to apply to Singapore (see Singapore Act 1966).

Solomon Islands

South Africa

The resealing of grants issued in South Africa, continues under the authority of the South Africa Act 1962, s 2 and Second Sch, including the period when South Africa was a Republic outside the Commonwealth. As to South African grants, see also para **18.60**.

South Australia

Southern Rhodesia (now Zimbabwe)

On 18 April 1980, Southern Rhodesia became an independent country known as Zimbabwe. Provision has been made in the Act granting such independence for the continued application of the Colonial Probates Acts to grants issued by its courts on and after that date. Furthermore, by virtue of an Ordinance enacted on 7 December 1979, provision was made for the recognition of any act done in Southern Rhodesia in reliance upon any law or purported law in operation in that country from 11 November 1965 onwards until its independence. One of the effects of this provision is that grants of representation issued by the courts in Southern Rhodesia, irrespective of the date of issue, may now be resealed in England and Wales under the Colonial Probates Act. (*Practice Direction* [1980] 2 All ER 324, [1980] 1 WLR 553).

Sri Lanka (formerly Ceylon)

Grants of probate and letters of administration in Sri Lanka during the period 1 January 1974 to 31 December 1977 were issued by the Public Trustee and not by a court of law. Such grants may be resealed under the Colonial Probates Act 1892 (Secretary's Circular, 14 June 1985).

Swaziland

Tanzania

The Colonial Probates Act (Application to Tanzania) Order 1969 provides that the Colonial Probates Act 1892 shall be deemed to have applied to Tanganyika from 9 December 1961 (the date on which Tanganyika attained independence within HM Dominions) until immediately before 26 April 1964 (the date on which it entered into a union with Zanzibar).

Tasmania

Tortola (formerly Virgin Islands)

Trinidad and Tobago (Republic)

Turks and Caicos Islands

Tuvalu (formerly Ellice Islands)

See entry for Ellice and Gilbert Islands above

Uganda

Victoria

Western Australia

Zambia

Zimbabwe (formerly Southern Rhodesia)

See Southern Rhodesia above

Grantee not qualified under rule 30

18.51 Application for such leave should be made through the probate manager in the Probate Department of the Principal Registry or a district registry.

18.55 Such elections may be resealed under the Colonial Probates Acts, on it being certified on behalf of the trustee company that the election is still in force and an undertaking given that, in the event of further estate in New Zealand being discovered which would place the estate beyond the statutory limit for the election procedure, no further step will be taken in the administration of the estate in England without obtaining further representation in New Zealand: see also 'New Zealand. Public Trust', paras **18.81** ff.

Copy will to be lodged

18.60 Grants issued in certain countries, notably South Africa, are described as letters of administration or letters of executorship whether the deceased died testate or intestate, and no copy of the will is annexed to the grant. When preparing applications to reseal grants made in such countries it should be ascertained whether or not the deceased left a will, so that the copies of the will required by NCPR SI 1987/2024 r 39(5) can be lodged. The use of the expression 'executor testamentary' to describe the grantee is an indication that the deceased died testate and appointed an executor: on the other hand, the term 'executor dative' used as in the case of South African grants may apply both to cases of testacy and intestacy where the grantee is other than an executor named in the will.

New Zealand. Public Trust

18.81 The effect of certain provisions in the New Zealand statute the Public Trust Act 2001 is as follows:

(a) the Public Trust of New Zealand may in various circumstances obtain from the New Zealand court either a grant or an order to administer, which, while in force, has the full effect of a grant;

(b) if the estate in New Zealand is within certain limits (estate out of New Zealand is irrelevant for this purpose), the Public Trust of New Zealand may file an election to administer. This, while in force, has the full effect of a grant.

18.83 In the case of elections, the document produced should be an official copy showing that the election itself has been filed in the New Zealand court; and the Public Trust should certify that the election is still in force, and undertake that in the event of further estate in New Zealand beyond the statutory limitation being discovered he will not act further in the administration of the estate in England and Wales without obtaining further representation there[1].

1 Registrar's Direction (1958) 24 March.

18.84 A general power of attorney has been filed in the Principal Registry by the Public Trust of New Zealand appointing as his attorney the Public Trustee of England and Wales for the purposes of applying for resealing under the Colonial Probates Acts.

Australia. Public Trustee

18.85 The principles which apply to the resealing of orders to administer in favour of, and elections to administer by, the Public Trust of New Zealand as set out in the previous section apply equally to orders obtained and elections given by the Public Trustee of Queensland, Australia (formerly known as the Public Curator of Queensland)[1].

1 Registrar's Direction (1979) 18 June.

Chapter 21

SEARCHES AND COPIES – EXEMPLIFICATIONS – DUPLICATE GRANTS

SEARCHES AND COPIES

Wills proved since 11 January 1858

Public online searches

21.09 Facilities are now in place to search and order probate records online at www.probatesearch.service.gov.uk.

In order to search for and order a copy of a grant and any will, the site requires the surname and year of death of the deceased. A successful search displays the name of the deceased, the date of the grant, the probate number, the date of death, the record available to order, the grant and will if any, and the probate registry which issued the grant. The fee is £10 payable by credit or debit card following which the site informs the applicant when the probate record will be available to download and print (about ten days). In this context, the probate record is the grant and any testamentary papers that were proved.

Standing search for grant of representation

21.14 Postal applications should be addressed to the Probate Department, Principal Registry of the Family Division, 42–49 High Holborn, London WC1V 6NP *or* DX 941 London/Chancery Lane or to any district probate registry (see para **2.60** for addresses). Remittances for fees may be by credit or debit card in the Principal Registry but otherwise should be by crossed cheque or postal order payable to 'HMCTS' or 'HM Courts and Tribunals Service'.

Copies of wills, grants and other documents

21.17 As from 31 January 2000 the majority of probate records are kept at the Probate Records Centre in Birmingham which is privately managed. The records remain under the control and possession of the Family Division of the High Court. There is no public access to the Centre for the purpose of obtaining copies of or inspecting probate records. Record copies of all grants and wills are scanned and held as computer data at the Centre and the most registries have online access to the Centre for the purpose of retrieving copies by facsimile transmission (see para **21.07**). The general public now have online access to record copies of all grants and wills (see para **21.09**). When any notation is made to an original grant as a result of amendment, revocation or other notice of this is sent to Birmingham District Registry which is assigned the responsibility for replacing or noting the record copy.

EXEMPLIFICATIONS AND SPECIAL CERTIFICATES

21.38 An exemplification is a document sometimes required by foreign courts. It contains an exact copy of the will (if any), and a copy of the grant. A testimonium clause is signed by a district judge or registrar, and in the case of a special certificate or copy it is countersigned by the President of the Family Division and the seal of the Family Division is added. The name and address of the probate practitioner who extracted the grant are placed in the margin.

Chapter 22

AFFIDAVITS, AFFIRMATIONS AND STATUTORY DECLARATIONS

RULES

22.05A In the meantime, the Non-Contentious Probate (Amendment) Rules 2016 and 2017[1] which came into force on 1 November 2016 (for personal applicants) and 30 October 2017 (for solicitors and probate practitioners) allow online applications for grants of representation. The amendment rules are being rolled out on a pilot basis and a party may make an application online if it meets certain criteria and if invited to do so by the probate registry. The online application incorporates a statement of truth. If there is a requirement for supplementary evidence it is anticipated that this may be given in a statement of truth. The project is in its infancy and continues to be tested at the time of publication.

1 SI 2016/972 and SI 2017/1034. See Appendix II, para **A2.39** ff of this supplement for the incorporated rule amendments.

22.08 As to the description of the deponent, see under *Executor's oath*, paras **4.114–4.115**. The requirement that a female deponent's occupation or status should be given[1] is no longer rigidly enforced.

1 Secretary's Circular, 12 May 1967.

Chapter 23

CAVEATS (OBJECTIONS)

Note: In anticipation of the revision of the Non-Contentious Probate Rules the expression 'witness statement' where it is used in this work refers to the form of application or evidence required with reference to any rule in force at the time of the application.

NATURE

Definition

23.01 A caveat is a notice in writing by a person wishing to show cause against the sealing of a grant, that no grant is to be sealed in the estate of the deceased named without notice to that person (NCPR SI 1987/2024 r 44). *Note*—If the person does not wish to prevent a grant issuing but requires to know when a grant issues, so that he may pursue a claim against the estate or for any other reason, instead of entering a caveat he should enter a standing search under r 43—see paras **21.11–21.14**.

ENTRY OF CAVEAT (OBJECTION)

Date and duration

23.15 The life of a caveat is also extended beyond the normal period of six months by the issue of a summons for directions pursuant to r 44(6) (see paras **23.67** ff) until that summons is disposed of or the district judge or registrar gives a direction, on the summons, for the caveat to cease to have effect (r 44(8)). Before this happens the caveat may be withdrawn under r 44(11), but in the event of a caveat being withdrawn before such a summons has been finally disposed of, no grant will be sealed without reference to a district judge or registrar[1]. This allows for the resolution of any issues which a party has raised following the entry of the caveat and which may have a bearing on the administration of the estate.

1 Registrar's Circular, 12 June 1967.

Commencement of probate claim

23.17 The commencement of a probate claim operates to prevent the sealing of any grant (other than a grant of administration pending determination of the probate claim) until application for a grant is made by the person shown to be entitled thereto by the decision of the court in such claim. This is subject to the proviso that a district judge may direct that a grant issue on an application made by summons. On the application for a grant after the conclusion of a probate claim, any caveat (*objection*) entered by the claimant in the claim, and any caveat (*objection*) in respect of which notice of the claim has been given, ceases to have effect (r 45(4)).

Form of caveat

23.22 Care should be taken to include in the entry all alternative or alias names for the deceased to ensure that a grant does not issue in any of these names.

Index of caveats

23.24 The Non-Contentious Probate (Amendment) Rules 1998 introduced new rules and amendments as a result of computerisation of probate records including the index of pending applications and caveats. NCPR SI 1987/2024 r 44(4) is as follows:

> (4) An index of caveats entered in any registry or sub-registry shall be maintained and upon receipt of an application for a grant, the registry or sub-registry at which the application is made shall cause a search of the index to be made and the appropriate district judge or registrar shall be notified of the entry of a caveat against the sealing of a grant for which the application has been made.'

Further, under NCPR SI 1987/2024 r 57(1) the Senior District Judge is directed to maintain an index of every pending application for a grant in any registry or sub-registry. All the records are kept in one database with the result that each probate registry is able immediately to update the index when a caveat is entered. The caveat is instantly matched against pending applications.

Extension of caveat

23.29 The proviso to NCPR SI 1987/2024 r 44(1) (which provides that a caveat (*objection*) is not effective to prevent the sealing of a grant on the day of entry) is not expressly attached to an application for the extension of a caveat (*objection*) with the result that a successful application for extension made, or received in the registry, on the date upon which the caveat is due to expire will operate to prevent the sealing of a grant. In all other respects, the procedures relating to the entry of a caveat (*objection*) apply to applications for extension[1].

1 Registrar's Circular, 15 September 1976.

Restriction on entry of further caveat

23.33 Where leave of a district judge of the Principal Registry for the entry of a further caveat is granted, the further caveat is effective for six months from the date of its entry and not (as in the case of an application for extension of an existing caveat) from the date of expiry of the first caveat[1].

1 Registrar's Direction (1958) 28 January.

Search for caveat

23.36 An application may also be made by post or email to the Principal Registry or any district registry asking for a search to be made and it will be answered by a letter or email stating whether or not there is an effective caveat (*objection*), and, if there is one, a copy of it will be posted to the applicant[1].

1 Secretary's Circular, 11 August 1988.

WARNING OF CAVEATS – CURRENT PRACTICE

Caveats warned at the nominated registry—currently Leeds District Probate Registry

23.39 Caveats can be warned only at the nominated registry (NCPR SI 1987/2024 r 44(5)). 'Nominated registry' is defined by r 44(15). It is the registry nominated by the Senior District Judge for the purpose of r 44, and in the absence of such nomination it is the Leeds District Probate Registry – see para **23.41**.

23.42 The person warning the caveat must set out in the warning his interest in the estate including the date of any will or codicil under which he claims title to a grant (eg executor or residuary legatee, etc), or, in the case of intestacy, his interest in the estate of the deceased, and must also give an address within the jurisdiction, which is his address for service (NCPR SI 1987/2024 r 49).

APPEARANCE TO WARNING

How entered

23.60 To enter his appearance, a caveator may either attend in person or by his probate practitioner at the Leeds District Probate Registry and complete a form of memorandum of appearance, which may be obtained at the registry, or he may send at his own risk the completed form of appearance by post to that registry. Form of appearance, No 39 (**A6.44**).

Chapter 24

CITATIONS (NOTIFICATIONS)

Note: In anticipation of the revision of the Non-Contentious Probate Rules, the expression 'witness statement' where it is used in this work refers to the form of application or evidence required with reference to any rule in force at the time of the application.

OBJECT OF CITATIONS

Kinds of citations

(A) To accept or refuse a grant

24.04 The citation, therefore, answers two purposes:

(a) it compels those who are primarily entitled to take a grant to decide whether they will do so or not; and
(b) where such parties refuse either to take a grant or to renounce, it provides an alternative grantee.

24.11 *Alternative to citation* (*or notification*). Where it is sought to pass over persons entitled who cannot be traced, in favour of a lower title, and a citation served by advertisement would normally be required, a district judge or registrar may make an order, if he thinks fit, under s 116(1) of the Senior Courts Act 1981 after, in appropriate cases, requiring the publication of a suitable advertisement for the person who would normally be cited. This course may be adopted where costs associated with the citation procedure would deplete a small estate.

24.19 *Will must be filed*. Before any citation (*notification*) can issue every will referred to in it must whenever possible be lodged in the Principal Registry or a district probate registry[1]. This confirms the existence of the will and allows the probate registrar to establish that the will, the subject of the citation, is or appears to be valid and that in due course it may be proved.

1 NCPR SI 1987/2024 r 46(5).

(C) To propound a will

24.36 *Will already proved in common form*. If a will has been proved in common form, procedure by citation to propound is inappropriate. A person disputing such a will and wishing to compel the grantee to prove it in solemn form should take steps to have the grant called in, and himself commence proceedings for revocation: the Non-Contentious Probate Rules have no application in such circumstances[1]. The proceedings are begun by a probate claim in the Chancery Division.

1 *Re Jolley, Jolley v Jarvis* [1964] P 262, [1964] 1 All ER 596.

REQUIREMENTS ON EXTRACTING CITATIONS

Postal application

24.57 The procedure is as follows:

(a) Drafts of the citation and supporting affidavit should be sent for settling and perusal to the probate registry where the citation is to be issued, together with the originals of any relevant will and codicil. In the event of an original will or codicil being sent, registered post should be used and the registry will retain them unless their return is requested or necessary by reason of the intention to exhibit them to the affidavit.

(b) After the citation has been settled the papers (but not the original wills and codicils except in the circumstances set out in (a) above) will be returned to the probate practitioner who should then, if he has not already done so, enter a caveat (by post to any probate registry in respect of which a fee of £20[1] is payable: cheques or postal orders should be drawn in favour of 'HMCTS' or 'HM Courts and Tribunals Service'. In the Principal Registry payment may be by debit or credit card). The probate practitioner should return to the registry the settled draft citation, an engrossment of the citation, the draft affidavit, the sworn affidavit, any relevant wills and codicils in the solicitor's possession at this stage (eg if the draft citation has been provisionally settled in reliance on photographic copies, where the originals were not readily available and it would have been unreasonable to delay the matter until they were produced) and the receipt for the entry of the caveat. A payment for £12, being the fee for settling the citation, should also be sent.

(c) A signed and sealed citation will be returned to the probate practitioner. The receipt for the caveat will be returned at the same time.

(d) Details of the caveat are entered in the probate computer. These are automatically cross-referenced to the caveat filed under the rules.

It is anticipated that a similar procedure will continue to apply when the new rules come into force.

1 NC Probate Fees Order 2004 (SI 2004/3120) (as amended), Fee 4.

Chapter 25

APPLICATIONS TO DISTRICT JUDGE, REGISTRAR OR HIGH COURT JUDGE (NON-CONTENTIOUS BUSINESS)

Note: In anticipation of the revision of the Non-Contentious Probate Rules, the expression 'witness statement' where it is used in this work refers to the form of application or evidence required with reference to any rule in force at the time of the application.

APPLICATIONS WITHOUT NOTICE

Leave to swear death

25.20 The Presumption of Death Act 2013 came into force on 1 October 2014. Under s 3(1) of the Act, but subject to sub-ss (3) and (4) (which deal with appeals against a declaration), a declaration of presumed death is conclusive of the presumed death and the date and time of death, and under s 3(2) the declaration is effective against all persons for the purpose of the acquisition of an interest in any property and the ending of the marriage or civil partnership to which the missing person was a party. Section 1 of the Act lays down the following qualifications and conditions:

– the person who is missing is thought to have died or has not been known to be alive for a period of at least seven years;
– any person may apply to the High Court for a declaration that the missing person is presumed to be dead;
– the person was domiciled in England and Wales on the day on which he or she was last known to be alive or the person was habitually resident in England and Wales throughout the period of one year ending with that day; or
– on an application by a spouse or civil partner, the applicant is domiciled in England and Wales on the date of the application or has been habitually resident in England and Wales throughout the period of one year ending with that day;
– the court must refuse the application by someone other than the missing person's spouse, civil partner, parent, child or sibling and if the court considers that the applicant does not have a sufficient interest in the determination of the application.

25.20A *Applications to district judge, registrar or High Court judge*

25.20A An application for a declaration of presumed death of a person under the Presumption of Death Act 2013 may be made either to the Family Division or the Chancery Division. The Civil Procedure Rules apply to the proceedings in this regard save that in the Family Division the Family Procedure Rules apply to the drawing up and service of orders.

25.20B While limited in nature, an application may be made under NCPR SI 1987/2024 r 53 to a district judge or probate registrar for leave to swear to the death of a person. Where the applicant for a grant cannot swear in his oath to the death of the deceased, and there is no direct evidence of his being dead[1], but only evidence from which his death may be presumed to have taken place, application must be made for an order giving him leave to swear to the death[2]. Such a presumption may arise: (1) from the disappearance of the presumed deceased at or after a given time, and from the circumstances attending such disappearance, or from his not having been heard of for a prolonged period by those with whom he might reasonably have been expected to communicate[3]; or (2) from his having been on board a ship, which, from its non-arrival in port within a reasonable time, from the absence of tidings of any of those on board, and from other circumstances, is supposed to have been lost at sea; and similarly in the case of a missing or totally destroyed aeroplane.

1 But where death can be sworn to have occurred between two dates, and the fact is not in doubt, the grant can be made in the registry without order (*Re Long-Sutton's Estate* [1912] P 97). In this case the oath should state that the deceased 'was last seen alive [or last known to be alive] on the day of 19 and that his dead body was found on the day of 19 '.

2 It must be always remembered in these cases that the court does not presume the death of the deceased; it merely gives the applicant leave to swear the death (*Re Jackson's Goods* (1902) 87 LT 747).

3 The fact that the family or friends of a man whose habit was to communicate with them received no communication from or news of him for seven years leads to the presumption of his death at some time during the seven years, but not at the beginning or at the end of the seven years (*Re How's Goods* (1858) 1 Sw & Tr 53, 31 LTOS 26), provided that there is no assignable cause for the cessation of his communications. The mere fact, however, that he has not been heard of for seven years, where it was not his practice to communicate, does not lead to such an inference, but it may, coupled with other circumstances, induce the court to act on the presumption of his death.
Where application was made for an order on the ground that a man had not been heard of for nearly seven years, there being also a Chancery suit, it was ordered that the letters of administration were not to be given out (*except for the purposes of the suit*) till the end of the seven years (*Re Winstone's Goods* [1898] P 143).

Decree under Matrimonial Causes Act

25.37 A decree of presumption of death and dissolution of marriage made before 1 October 2014 by virtue of s 19 of the Matrimonial Causes Act 1973[1] does not remove the necessity of applying for an order for leave to swear to the death of the missing former spouse. Section 19 of the MCA 1973 was repealed by the Presumption of Death Act 2013, s 16(3), Sch 2, para 1. See paras **25.20** ff.

1 27 Halsbury's Statutes (4th edn) 720.

Person found to be living after order giving leave to swear death

25.50 A claim for a declaration of presumed death under the Presumption of Death Act 2013, s 1 is issued in the High Court in either the Family Division or the Chancery Division in accordance with CPR Pt 57 and PD 57B.

Grant 'ad colligenda bona' (collection grant)

25.182 The application must be supported by an affidavit (*witness statement*) setting out the grounds of the application, and provided that it is not opposed should be made without notice at the registry at which the application for the grant is to be made[1]. A district probate registrar may, if he considers it necessary, obtain the directions of a district judge of the Principal Registry on any application made to him[2].

1 NCPR SI 1987/2024 rr 2(1), 52(b); see also *Ghafoor v Cliff* [2006] EWHC 825 (Ch), [2006] 2 All ER 1079, [2006] 1 WLR 320.

2 NCPR SI 1987/2024 r 7.

Subpoena to bring in a testamentary document

25.194 Application for the issue of a subpoena (*witness statement*) under s 123 of the Senior Courts Act 1981[1] is made by lodging at a probate registry an affidavit (*witness statement*) setting out the grounds of the application (NCPR SI 1987/2024 r 50(2)) (see Form No 35 (**A6.40**)), together with two copies of the form of subpoena (*witness summons*) (Form No 200 (**A6.205**)), duly completed. If the district judge or registrar directs the issue of the subpoena (*witness summons*) one of the copies is sealed and returned to the solicitor or probate practitioner, the affidavit (*witness statement*) being indorsed with the district judge's or registrar's direction and filed in the registry.

1 See para **A1.342**.

APPLICATIONS BY SUMMONS (APPLICATION NOTICE)

Discontinuance of proceedings arising from caveat

25.221 When an appearance has been entered to the warning of a caveat, no grant can issue until the decision of the court in the proceedings (by probate claim) arising from the appearance to warning. But if, prior to the commencement of a probate claim the caveator abandons his opposition to the issue of a grant, application may be made by summons to a district judge of the Principal Registry for an order for discontinuance of the caveat and for the issue of a grant notwithstanding the caveat, warning and appearance (NCPR SI 1987/2024 r 44(13)). If the parties come to terms an application for discontinuance of the caveat is made by consent under the same rule to a district judge in the Principal Registry or to the registrar of the district probate registry to which the application for the grant has been, or is to be, made. It should be noted that an order by consent of a district judge or registrar may not include the pronouncing for or against the validity of a will as these are properly matters for Chancery. Form of summons, No 203 (**A6.208**).

25.223 As to the right of a caveator who has not appeared to a warning to withdraw his caveat and practice, see paras **23.48–23.51**. As to caveats generally, see Chapter 23.

PRACTICE AS TO SUMMONSES (APPLICATION NOTICES)

Where reference to be made to Hansard

25.238 Unless the judge otherwise directs, where any party intends to refer at a hearing, as an aid to construing legislation, to the reports of parliamentary proceedings as reported in *Hansard*, that party must not less than five clear working days before the first date of the hearing serve upon all other parties and the court copies of any such extract together with a brief summary of the argument intended to be based upon such extract. Service on the court is to be in accordance with RSC Ord 65, r 5 to (a) in the Family Division in cases to be heard in London, the Clerk of the Rules, Floor 1M, Queens Building, Royal Courts of Justice, Strand, London WC2A 2LL; in cases to be heard out of London the manager of the relevant district registry, and (b) in the Principal Registry of the Family Division, the Probate Manager, First Avenue House, 42–49 High Holborn, London WC1V 6NP *or* DX 920 London/Chancery Lane. Service upon other parties is also to be effected in accordance with RSC Ord 65, r 5 or as otherwise agreed between the parties (*Practice Direction* [1995] 1 All ER 234, sub nom *Practice Direction* [1995] 1 WLR 192).

When heard

25.245 The Human Rights Act 1998 (HRA 1998) came into force on 20 October 2000. It gives effect to rights and freedoms guaranteed under the European Convention on Human Rights. In this regard the matter of hearings in chambers is subject to the overriding considerations of the Act. In particular HRA 1998, Sch 1, art 6 allows everyone the right to a public hearing. This places on the district judge or registrar a duty to allow public access to any hearing or to transcript of judgment in chambers. CPR 39.2 and PD 39.2 set out the matters which the court must have regard to when deciding whether to hold a public hearing. CPR 29.2(3)(f) provides that a hearing, or any part of it, may be private if it involves non-contentious matters arising in the administration of trusts or in the administration of a deceased person's estate.

Orders

25.252 Orders are drawn up in the registry, and normally bear the date of the day on which they are made. Sealed copies of orders are sent by post to the applicant and respondent.

Part II

CONTENTIOUS BUSINESS

Chapter 26

INTRODUCTION

JURISDICTION OF THE COURT

High Court

26.16 Contentious probate business in the High Court is by statute assigned to the Chancery Division[1]. Since 2 October 2017 the Chancery Division operates as part of the Business and Property Courts ('B&PCs'). The B&PCs are made up of a number of specialists, lists and sub-lists. The appropriate list for probate claims is the Property, Trusts and Probate List (ChD). For the title of claims in the B&PCs, see para **29.02**.

A probate claim in the High Court must be begun by claim form issued out of Chancery Chambers (that is, the offices of the Chancery Division in the Royal Courts of Justice, 7 Rolls Building, Fetter Lane, London, EC4A 1NL) or out of one of the Chancery district registries (that is, one of the district registries of Birmingham, Bristol, Caernafon, Cardiff, Leeds, Liverpool, Manchester, Mold, Newcastle upon Tyne and Preston)[2]. Five of these Chancery district registries, Birmingham, Bristol, Cardiff, Leeds and Manchester, are also B&PCs. They are known as the B&PCs District Registries. For the title of claims issued in one of the B&PCs District Registries, see para **29.02**.

A probate claim in the High Court may only be transferred to the Chancery Division at the Royal Courts of Justice or to one of the Chancery district registries[3].

1 The Senior Courts Act 1981, s 61(1) and Sch 1, para 1(h).
2 CPR 57.3(a) and 57.1(2)(b)(i) and (ii).
3 CPR 30.2(8).

26.18 Procedure and case management in the Chancery Division are set out in the Chancery Guide (February 2016). The Guide is regularly updated and amended on the court website: www.gov.uk/courts-tribunals/chancery-division-of-the-high-court. The process of implementation of the Chancery Modernisation Review Report published in December 2013 has led to a significant number of recent changes to Chancery practice and it is essential to refer to the updated and amended online version. Probate procedure is summarised between paras 29.47 and 29.58 of the Chancery Guide.

THE PRACTICE: HIGH COURT AND COUNTY COURT

Pre-action steps

(1) Larke v Nugus

26.31 The Law Society Practice Note '*Disputed Wills*' (6 October 2011) sets out what is good practice on receipt of a request for information by a solicitor and the consequences of the failure to provide full information. It refers to the issue of privilege and to where there is a possibility of negligence. See www.lawsociety.org.uk/support-services/advice/practice-notes/disputed-wills.

A refusal by an executor to provide a full response to a reasonable request for information contained in a *Larke v Nugus* letter or to provide disclosure of the central documents is likely to have serious costs consequences and may result in his being deprived of part of his costs[1].

1 *Watton v Crawford* [2016] NICh 14 in which a previous will and medical notes and records were not disclosed in response to a request for information.

Chapter 27

CLAIMS

(1) CLAIMS FOR PRONOUNCING FOR OR AGAINST A WILL IN SOLEMN FORM

When proof in solemn form may be required

27.10 The above persons may put an executor, or other person interested under a will, to proof in solemn form either before or after probate has been taken in common form, but the following two, by reason of their particular status, can only do so before, and not after, probate in common form has issued, namely:

(4) *A creditor.* A creditor to whom administration has been granted[1].

(5) *An appointee of the court.* Any other person in possession of a grant of administration, as appointee of the court, eg, by order under the Senior Courts Act 1981, s 116, but not having a beneficial interest in the estate.

This should not be regarded as an exhaustive list of the circumstances in which persons have been found to be entitled to require proof of a will in solemn form. Paragraph 28.01(ff) is expressed very broadly. It states that the rules of the probate court as to standing have always been flexible. This is in line with the new procedural code introduced by the Civil Procedure Rules 1998 with their overriding objective of enabling the court to deal with cases justly and at proportionate expense[2].

1 *Menzies v Pulbrook and Kerr* (1841) 2 Curt 845 at 851. The decision in *Menzies v Pulbrook and Kerr* was stated still to be good law by the Court of Appeal in *Randall v Randall* [2016] EWCA Civ 494, [2017] Ch 77, [2016] 3 WLR 1217 but it was held to be wrong to assimilate the position of a creditor of a beneficiary of an estate with that of a creditor of an estate. The interests of the two types of creditor were held to be fundamentally different. The interest of the creditor of a beneficiary is to ensure that the beneficiary receives what is due to him or her under the will or on an intestacy. The interest of a creditor of an estate is to ensure that there is due administration of the estate: see the judgment of the Master of the Rolls at [22].

2 *Randall v Randall* [2016] EWCA Civ 494, [2017] Ch 77, [2016] 3 WLR 1217 at [28] per the Master of the Rolls and at [36] per McCombe LJ.

(2) INTEREST ACTIONS

27.22 The decision in an interest action may involve an issue of pedigree or of legitimacy, but a prayer for a declaration of legitimacy may not be included in the claim form. Applications for declarations as to legitimacy or legitimation are now made under s 56 of the Family Law Act 1986 (as substituted by s 22 of the Family Law Reform Act 1987) and any such declaration may be made only under that section (Family Law Act 1986, s 58(4)). Any application for a declaration under s 56 of the Act of 1986 must be made in the form prescribed by rules of court (Family Law Act 1986, s 60(1)) and the Family Procedure Rules 2010 r 8.20 sets out what should normally be contained in an application for such a declaration. The proceedings should be brought in the Family Court. An interest action may arise from a dispute as to whether a person claiming to be a beneficiary and entitled to administer the estate was married to the deceased or whether the marriage was valid[1]. It might also arise in the context of an issue such as whether adopted children were included within the testator's description of 'children' for the purposes of his will.[2]

1 For a recent example see: *Adepoju v Akinola* [2016] EWHC 3160 (Ch). The issue was tried within the framework of a probate claim.

2 An issue of this type arose in *Hand v George* [2017] EWHC 533 (Ch), [2017] 3 WLR 559, [2017] WTLR 495 in which it was decided that the failure to ensure that s 5(2) of the Adoption Act 1926 had no continuing effect was in breach of art 14 of the European Convention of Human Rights, and that the Adoption Act 1976, Sch 2, para 6 had to be read down pursuant to s 3 of the Human Rights Act 1998 in order to bring it into compliance with the claimants' Convention rights. For the position of adopted persons under English domestic law in the context of the right to a grant, see paras **6.247** ff.

(3) CLAIMS FOR REVOCATION OF GRANTS

Claims for revocation when a will has been proved

27.26 A claim under the Inheritance (Provision for Family and Dependants) Act 1975 was held to give the claimant an interest in the estate within the meaning of CPR 57.7 sufficient to bring a claim for revocation of a grant in circumstances where it was conceded that the claim under the 1975 Act would be more valuable under intestacy than if a previous will admitted to probate in common form were upheld[1]. A claim by a former husband to challenge the validity of a will made by his wife following divorce was held to give sufficient standing in circumstances where if the will was invalid the husband stood to be entitled to an additional £75,000 as part of a divorce settlement[2]. In both cases there was in practice held to be no other route by which the will in question would be brought before the court to be proved in solemn form or for the grant to be revoked.

1 *O'Brien v Seagrave* [2007] EWHC 788 (Ch), [2007] 3 All ER 633, [2007] 1 WLR 2002. The broad construction of the meaning of 'interest' adopted by Judge Mackie QC was adopted and applied by the Court of Appeal in *Randall v Randall* [2016] EWCA Civ 494, [2017] Ch 77, [2016] 3 WLR 1217.

2 *Randall v Randall* [2016] EWCA Civ 494, [2017] Ch 77, [2016] 3 WLR 1217.

Claims for revocation of letters of administration

27.27 A claim for the revocation of letters of administration is instituted: (1) On the allegation that they were granted to a person without sufficient title to the grant[1]. The object of such a claim is to compel the party who has obtained the grant of administration to establish such a degree of relationship with the deceased as will entitle him to the grant, and in the result it becomes an interest suit. (2) On the discovery of a will, the validity of which is not admitted by the grantee. This may necessitate a claim for the revocation of the grant and for a pronouncement in favour of the will. A defendant administrator who with knowledge of a will applied for a grant of letters of administration was held liable to pay costs on the indemnity basis and to account on the footing of wilful default.[2]

1 A grant to the Crown, and the order authorising it, may be revoked by a district judge's or a registrar's order, if kin are discovered. See para **24.88**. See also Chapter 17, as to the jurisdiction of the district judge or registrar to revoke a grant.

2 *Morris v Browne* [2017] EWHC 631 (Ch).

Lodgment of grant

27.29 No copy of the grant may issue, without leave, after the claim form has been issued until the claim has been concluded. For a form of order, see: CP13A (**A6.223A**): Chapter 28.

ASSOCIATED CLAIMS

27.41 The following claims or applications are not, strictly, contentious probate claims, but they have sufficient connection to the subject matter of a contentious probate claim to warrant mention in this book. They are:

(1) a claim for the rectification of a will;
(2) a claim or application for the substitution and removal of a personal representative;
(3) a claim under the Inheritance (Provision for Family and Dependants) Act 1975[1]; and
(4) an application for a declaration under the Presumption of Death Act 2013.

The first two such proceedings (claims for rectification of a will and claims or applications for the substitution and removal of a personal representative) are contained in CPR Pt 57 as 57.12 Section II and as 57.13 Section III and the corresponding sections in Practice Direction 57A. Claims under the 1975 Act are governed by the rules in CPR 57 Part IV and the corresponding section in Practice Direction 57A.

CPR 57 Section V and Practice Direction 57B concern proceedings under the Presumption of Death Act 2013. The 2013 Act assists the problems of families trying to resolve the affairs of missing persons: see Chapter 25 at paras **25.49–25.50** and see also paras **41.42** ff.

1 See Chapter 41.

Chapter 28

PARTIES TO CLAIMS

WHO MAY BE A PARTY

28.01 The foundation of title to be a party to a probate claim is *interest*—so that whenever it can be shown that it is competent to the court to make a decree in a claim for probate or administration, or for the revocation of probate or of administration, which may affect the interest, or possible interest, of any person, such person has a right to be a party to such a suit[1].

Such was the rule in the Prerogative Court of Canterbury as to the foundation of title to be a party to a cause in that court.

1 *Kipping and Barlow v Ash* (1845) 1 Rob Eccl 270; *Crispin v Doglioni* (1860) 2 Sw & Tr 17. This passage was quoted in *Randall v Randall* [2016] EWCA Civ 494, [2017] Ch 77, [2016] 3 WLR 1217 in support of adopting a flexible approach to issues of standing and interest entitling a person to bring a probate claim.

28.02 In a claim for the revocation of a grant every person who is or claims to be entitled to administer the estate under that grant must be made a party to the claim[1].

1 CPR 57.6(1). This is by way of exception to the normal rule that executors are not necessary parties to a probate claim.

28.03 The question whether a person has a sufficient *interest* to be permitted to bring a probate claim is a procedural issue and not a matter of substantive law. The nature of an interest adequate to found a probate claim is a matter of practice and procedure. It is decided on a pragmatic basis from case to case. There is no rigidity about the test[1]. A claim under the Inheritance (Provision for Family and Dependants) Act 1975 was on particular facts a sufficient interest for the purposes of bringing a probate action. The claimant's motivation for challenging the will was that her Inheritance Act claim would be more likely to succeed on intestacy than under the will[2]. A divorced husband was allowed to proceed with a probate revocation claim to challenge the validity of a will made by his deceased ex-wife in circumstances where if the will was held to be invalid he would stand to receive an additional sum under their divorce settlement[3].

1 *Randall v Randall* [2016] EWCA Civ 494, [2017] Ch 77, [2016] 3 WLR 1217 at [27] per the Master of the Rolls and at [32] per McCombe LJ.

2 *O'Brien v Seagrave* [2007] EWHC 788 (Ch), [2007] 3 All ER 633, [2007] 1 WLR 2002, approved in *Randall v Randall* [2016] EWCA Civ 494, [2017] Ch 77, [2016] 3 WLR 1217. In *O'Brien*, a claimant with a prospective claim under the 1975 was held to have standing to challenge a will where the only surviving relation by blood or marriage was an elderly brother who did not wish to be a party to any proceedings. In *Randall*, the CA held there to be a

distinction between the position of a creditor of a beneficiary of an estate with that of a creditor of an estate. The interests of the two types of creditor were said to be 'fundamentally different'. The interest of the creditor of a beneficiary is to ensure that the beneficiary receives what is due to that beneficiary under the will or on intestacy. The interest of a creditor is limited to ensuring that there is due administration of the estate; at [22] per the Master of the Rolls.

3 *Randall v Randall* [2016] EWCA Civ 494, [2017] Ch 77, [2016] 3 WLR 1217.

PARTIES GENERALLY

Defendants

28.07 In certain cases it may be appropriate to apply for a representation order under CPR 19.6 (representation of parties with same interest) or CPR 19.7 (representation of interested parties who cannot be ascertained etc). These are matters to which the master or district judge will give consideration at a case management conference[1]: see CPR Pt 57 PD57A, para 4(1) and (2). For a recent review of the scope of CPR 19.6 in a non-probate context see: *Emerald Supplies Ltd v British Airways plc* [2010] EWCA Civ 1284, [2011] Ch 345, [2011] 2 WLR 203. If, for example, in a probate claim, there are very large numbers of persons who would be interested under intestacy were a will to be held invalid, including a significant number resident out of the jurisdiction, the appointment of a representative beneficiary may be easier than having to give individual notices under CPR 19.8A.

1 See para **37.08**.

Chapter 29

CLAIM FORM

ISSUE OF CLAIM FORM

Rules applicable

29.02 A probate claim in the High Court must be begun by a claim form issued out of the Chancery Division of the High Court either at the Rolls Building in London at 7 Rolls Building, Fetter Lane, London EC4A 1NL or out of one of the Chancery district registries (that is, one of the district registries of Birmingham, Bristol, Cardiff, Caernafon, Cardiff, Leeds, Liverpool, Manchester, Mold, Newcastle upon Tyne and Preston)[1]. A probate claim must be commenced by using the procedure in CPR Pt 7[2]. The appropriate claim form is N2 Claim Form Probate.

Since 2 October 2017 the Chancery Division forms part of the Business and Property Courts ('B&PCs'). The B&PCs are made up of a number of specialist courts, list and sub-lists. The appropriate list for probate claims is the Property, Trusts and Probate List (ChD).

Probate claims issued in the High Court in London should be headed:

IN THE HIGH COURT OF JUSTICE

BUSINESS AND PROPERTY COURTS OF ENGLAND AND WALES

PROPERTY, TRUSTS AND PROBATE LIST (ChD)

Probate claims issued in one of the Business and Property Courts District Registries[3] ('the B&PCs District Registries') should be headed:

IN THE HIGH COURT OF JUSTICE

BUSINESS AND PROPERTY COURTS IN [   ]

PROPERTY, TRUSTS AND PROBATE LIST (ChD)

All of the B&PCs District Registries are located in centres which are also Chancery District Registries. Preston, Mold and Caernarfon are the only Chancery District Registries which are not also designated as one of the B&PCs District Registries.

1 CPR 57.3(a) and 57.1(b)(i) and (ii).

2 CPR 57.3(b).

3 Birmingham, Bristol, Cardiff, Leeds and Manchester. Newcastle and Liverpool either are or are expected shortly to be added as B&PCs District Registries.

Heading of claim form and other court documents

29.06 The claim form in a probate claim and all subsequent court documents must be marked at the top 'In the estate of [name] deceased (Probate)'[1]. Practice Form N2 (**A6.216**) is to be used for a claim form in a probate claim. That form, and the forms entitled Notes for claimant on completing a claim form and Notes for defendant are set out in Appendix VI. For the heading of claim forms in the Business and Property Courts, see para **29.02** above. The Advisory Note 'The Business and Property Courts of England and Wales' contains further useful information about the courts, lists and sub lists, titles of claims and transfer of proceedings[2].

1 CPR Pt 57 PD para 2.1.

2 The Advisory Note 'Business and Property Courts of England and Wales' is available online at https://www.gov.uk/courts-tribunals/chancery-division-of-the-high-court.

STATEMENTS OF INTEREST

Forms of statement

29.11 See Forms CP14 ff (**A6.224** ff).

Chapter 31

TESTAMENTARY DOCUMENTS

GENERAL MATTERS CONCERNING TESTAMENTARY DOCUMENTS

31.01 The requirement for each party to file evidence about testamentary documents and lodge the documents at court (as set out below) is most important.[1] It allows the Master or district judge, initially, and later the judge to satisfy himself that the relief sought is correct (and that the claimant has not, for example, mistakenly asked the court to pronounce against will 'A' (an alleged last will) and in favour of will 'B' (an earlier will) without realising that there existed a valid intermediate will, which would be the valid will if will 'A' failed). The requirements as to testamentary documents also assists the Master when considering the question which parties should be added (or notified of proceedings).

1 The importance of compliance with CPR 57.5(2) was stressed by Henderson LJ in *Payne v Payne* [2018] EWCA Civ 985. In that case the original of an earlier will had not been lodged and was not available to the judge or the parties at trial. This was 'a serious procedural error which should never have been allowed to happen'.

INSPECTION OF TESTAMENTARY DOCUMENTS

Loan of testamentary documents for examination

31.12 If a party wishes his expert to examine a testamentary document, his solicitor should attend the master at the time for oral applications without notice to give a written undertaking (as to safekeeping and return) against loan of the testamentary document for a specified time. For a form of order, see CP4A (**A6.214A**): CH27 Handing out Testamentary Documents for examination.

Verification of testamentary documents

31.14 When the court orders trial on written evidence it is normally necessary for an attesting witness to sign a witness statement or swear an affidavit of due execution of the will or codicil sought to be admitted to probate, but the will or codicil is lodged at court and cannot be handed out of court for use as an exhibit to the witness statement or affidavit. Either the attesting witness can attend at the court and sign or swear his evidence before an officer of the court or, if he is unable to do so, his solicitor may request from the court a photocopy of the will or codicil. This will be certified as authentic by the court and may be exhibited to the witness statement or affidavit of due execution in lieu of the original. The witness statement or affidavit must state that the exhibited document is an authenticated copy of the document signed in the witness' presence[1].

1 Chancery Guide paras 29.53 and 29.54; see para **26.18**.

Transmission of scripts in cases tried outside London

31.15 When a probate claim in the Royal Court of Justice is listed for trial at a Chancery District Registry the solicitor for the party responsible for preparing the court bundle must write to the Masters' Appointments (Ground Floor, Rolls Building), Chancery Chambers, Royal Courts of Justice, 7 Rolls Building, Fetter Lane, London EC4A 1NL and request that the testamentary documents be forwarded to the appropriate Chancery District Registry[1].

1 Chancery Guide para 29.55; see para **26.18**; and see CPR Pt 57 PD(A) para 2.2.

Chapter 32

STATEMENTS OF CASE GENERALLY

PRACTICE AS TO STATEMENTS OF CASE

Statements of interest and denial of interest

32.07 The claim form must contain a statement of the nature of the interest of the claimant and of each defendant in the estate[1]. If a party disputes another party's interest in the estate he must state this in his statement of case and set out his reasons[2]. The nature of an interest adequate to found a right to bring or defend probate proceedings falls to be determined on a case by case basis. The issue is one of practice and procedure rather than substantive law. A creditor of an estate does not have a sufficient interest in an estate to bring a probate claim. A creditor of a beneficiary on the other hand may do so depending on the circumstances[3].

1 CPR 57.7(1).

2 CPR 57.7(2).

3 In *O'Brien v Seagrave* [2007] EWHC 788 (Ch), [2007] 1 WLR 2002, [2007] 3 All ER 633 and in *Randall v Randall* [2016] EWCA Civ 494, [2017] Ch 77, [2016] 3 WLR 1217 sufficient interests to bring a probate claim were shown. In *Randall* the claimant was classified as being a creditor of a beneficiary. There will of course be cases in which on looking at all the circumstances it will be apparent that a person has no interest in bringing a claim. For that reason the parties are required to lodge testamentary documents at the outset of their involvement in a probate claim.

Chapter 34

DEFENCE AND COUNTERCLAIM

COUNTERCLAIM

34.04 It is possible to counterclaim for probate in other proceedings[1]. A probate counterclaim must contain a statement of the nature of the interest of the defendant and the claimant in the estate of the deceased to which the counterclaim relates[2]. If the action is not in the Chancery Division the court will, if necessary of its own motion, transfer the action to the Chancery Division and to either the Royal Courts of Justice or a Chancery district registry (if it is not already proceeding in one of those places)[3]. Application may however be made within seven days after the service of a probate counterclaim for the counterclaim to be dealt with in separate proceedings (under CPR 3.1(2)(e) or to be struck out (under CPR 3.4)[4]. If an order is made that the probate counterclaim be dealt with in separate proceedings the order shall order the transfer of the probate counterclaim (if not already proceeding there) to the Chancery Division and to either the Royal Courts of Justice or to a Chancery District Registry[5].

1 CPR 57.9.
2 CPR 57.9(3).
3 CPR 57.9(4).
4 CPR 57.9(4).
5 CPR 57.9(5).

(1) WANT OF DUE EXECUTION

Forgery

34.12 The charge that the signature or mark of the testator is a forgery is also raised by this plea, but forgery itself must also be specifically pleaded[1].

Allegations of forgery were not upheld in *Fuller v Strum* [2001] WTLR 677 or *Wyniczenko v Plucinska-Surowka* [2005] EWHC 2794 (Ch), 8 ITELR 385 but succeeded in *Supple v Penter* [2007] EWHC 829 (Ch), [2007] WTLR 1461 (account of the execution and attestation of a will given by an attesting witness not believed). The normal civil standard of proof on the balance of probabilities applies to forgery allegations in probate claims but with the inherent probability or improbability of the allegation falling to be taken into account[2].

1 CPR 16.5 and 57.7(4).
2 *Patel v Patel* [2017] EWHC 133 (Ch) applying the guidance of Lord Nicholls in *Re H (Minors)* [1996] AC 563 at 586 D-G, [1996] 1 All ER 1. In *Patel v Patel* the claimant was found to have

forged his mother's will. The claimant and the witnesses to the forged will were subsequently found to have been in contempt of court 'of the most serious kind'. The claimant was given an immediate custodial sentence of twelve months and the witnesses three months.

Notice under CPR 57.7(5)

34.13 Where it is proposed merely to put the executors to proof and only to cross-examine their witnesses, the notice as to such cross-examination must be given in the defence[1]. A notice under CPR 57.7(5) will not provide costs protection to a defendant who did not have reasonable grounds for opposing a will. This follows from the wording of CPR 57(5)(b)[2]. Once a defendant is in a position to make a proper assessment as to whether there were reasonable grounds to oppose a will, he is at risk for costs incurred from that date[3]. The notice will no longer provide costs protection.

1 CPR 57.7(5)(a).

2 CPR 57(5)(b) provides that if a defendant gives such a notice, the court will not make an order for costs against him 'unless it considers that there was no reasonable ground for opposing the will.'

3 *Elliott v Simmonds* [2016] EWHC 962 (Ch), [2016] WTLR 1375 at [14] and [17].

Summary of reported cases as to due execution

E *Subscription by witnesses*

34.21 NB *In respect of wills of testators* dying on or after 1 January 1983, *s 9 of the Wills Act 1837, as substituted by the Administration of Justice Act 1982, s 17 (see* para **A1.05**), *now allows a witness to acknowledge his earlier signature.*

May be by mark (*Re Ashmore's Goods* (1843) 3 Curt 756; *Re Amiss' Goods* (1849) 2 Rob Eccl 116); see also *Hindmarsh v Charlton* (1861) 8 HL Cas 160; or by description of himself (*Re Duggins' Goods* (1870) 39 LJP & M 24; *Re Sperling's Goods* (1863) 3 Sw & Tr 272); but not by signing the name of another person (*Re Leverington's Goods* (1886) 11 PD 80); another person may write name or mark of witness so long as he holds the pen (*Lewis v Lewis* (1861) 2 Sw & Tr 153; *Bell v Hughes* (1880) 5 LR Ir 407); but another person cannot subscribe for witness at his desire (*Re Cope's Goods* (1850) 2 Rob Eccl 335; *Re Duggins' Goods*); nor is it sufficient if witness's name is affixed by means of a rubber stamp affixed by the other witness in his presence but without any physical act or participation on his part (*Re Bulloch's Estate* [1968] NI 96, applying dictum in *Bell v Hughes*); signature of witness cannot be acknowledged afterwards by any means as can that of a testator, nor is it sufficient to re-write, with a dry pen, a signature written before acknowledgment by the testator in the presence of *both* witnesses (*Re Maddock's Goods* (1874) LR 3 P & D 169; *Hindmarsh v Charlton*; *Horne v Featherstone* (1895) 73 LT 32); if witness is unable to complete signature the execution is invalid (*Re Maddock's Goods* (1874) LR 3 P & D 169; *McConville v McCreesh* (1879) 13 ILTR 35); the signatures of the witnesses need not appear on any particular part of the instrument (*Re Davis' Goods* (1843) 3 Curt 748; *Re Chamney's Goods* (1849) 1 Rob Eccl 757; *Roberts v Phillips* (1855) 4 E & B 450); but if not on same sheet as signature of testator, the sheets must be physically connected at time of execution (*Re Braddock's Goods* (1876) 1 PD

433); and the court must be satisfied that witnesses intended to attest the signature of the testator (*Re Streatley's Goods* [1891] P 172; *Re Taylor's Goods* (1851) 2 Rob Eccl 411; *Phipps v Hale* (1874) LR 3 P D 166; *Re Denning, Harnett v Elliott* [1958] 2 All ER 1, [1958] 1 WLR 462 (signatures of witnesses upside down on reverse of paper on which will written: see also para **3.103**)); the signature of third person at end of will may be omitted from probate upon proof that it was not written for purpose of attesting (*Re Sharman's Goods* (1869) LR 1 P & D 661): see also paras **3.104–3.106**. See also *Re White, Barker v Gribble* [1991] Ch 1, [1990] 3 All ER 1 (witnesses only attested alterations). An attesting witness may validly sign a will at the direction of the testator and as attesting witness without signing a second time when it is clear that the witness had intended to perform the dual function of both signing the will on behalf of the testator and of witnessing the direction to do so (*Re Elsie Marsden Deceased* LTL 21/3/2006, an appeal from the Registrar's refusal to admit the will to probate).

The requirement since 1982 for an attesting witness to 'sign' the will should be construed as meaning the same as the previous requirement that the witness should 'subscribe' the will. The change should not be interpreted as requiring a 'signature' in the sense of an identifiable and probably unique personal mark.[1] The use of 'sign' instead of 'subscribe' was not intended to be a change of any substance. The points of principle which the 1982 amendments were intended to deal with were quite different. The changes arose from recommendations made in the 22nd Report of the Law Reform Committee on the Making and Revocation of Wills (Cmnd 7902, May 1980).[2]

1 *Payne v Payne* [2018] EWCA Civ 985 at [31] per Henderson LJ.

2 *Payne v Payne* at [30] per Henderson LJ citing *Tristram and Coote's Probate Practice* (31st edn), para **3.60**. This is consistent with the view expressed in para **3.61** that in all other respects the former requirements of s 9 of the Wills Act 1837 continue to apply and that the former case law in general remains relevant.

(2) INCAPACITY

Testamentary capacity: an overview

34.28 In *Perrins v Holland* [2009] EWHC 1945 (Ch) Lewison J referred to the common law test having been superseded by the Mental Capacity Act 2005. A different conclusion was reached by Mr N Strauss QC (sitting as a deputy judge of the High Court) in *Walker v Badmin* [2014] EWHC 71 (Ch), [2014] Lexis Citation 237 who after a full review of the case law and full argument concluded that the correct and only test for testamentary capacity is the common law test[1].

1 See also *James v James* [2018] EWHC 43 (Ch) (Judge Paul Matthews) where the test of mental capacity in *Banks v Goodfellow* (1870) LR 5 QB 549, [1861–73] All ER Rep 47 was stated as remaining the sole test for judging will-making capacity in retrospect.

The nature of the inquiry by the court

34.32 A will which is drawn up in accordance with instructions given by a testator at a time when he had full testamentary capacity but executed at a time when he no longer had such capacity will be upheld provided the testator knew that the document he was signing conformed with the instructions he had given and approved it by executing it in those terms[1]. The rule in *Parker v Felgate* 8 PD 171 does not displace the requirement for full testamentary capacity; it merely displaces the ordinary requirement that the testator should have had such capacity at the time he executed the will[2]. The rule has been held to apply in the case of inter-vivos dispositions[3].

For precedent of defence, see Form CP33 (**A6.243**).

1 *Perrins v Holland* [2011] Ch 270, [2011] 2 WLR 1086 approving *Parker v Felgate* (1883) 8 PD 171.

2 Per Moore-Bick LJ at [54] in *Perrins v Holland.*

3 *Singellos v Singellos* [2010] EWHC 2353 (Ch), [2011] Ch 324; *Re Smith (decd)* [2014] EWHC 3926 (Ch), [2015] 4 All ER 329.

Summary of reported cases

What constitutes undue influence

34.47 To be undue influence there must be coercion (*Wingrove v Wingrove* (1885) 11 PD 81); or fraud (*Boyse v Rossborough* (1857) 6 HL Cas 2 at 45; *Williams v Goude* (1828) 1 Hag Ecc 577 at 581); a testator may be led but not driven; his will must be the offspring of his own volition and not the record of someone else's (*Hall v Hall* (1868) LR 1 P & D 481). See also *Mountain v Bennet* (1787) 1 Cox Eq Cas 353 at 355. The relevant principles of law were summarised by Lewison J in *Re Edwards (dec'd)* [2007] EWHC 1119 (Ch), [2007] All ER (D) 46 (May) as:

'(i) In a case of a testamentary disposition of assets, unlike a lifetime disposition, there is no presumption of undue influence;

(ii) Whether undue influence has procured the execution of a will is therefore a question of fact;

(iii) The burden of proving it lies on the person who asserts it. It is not enough to prove that the facts are consistent with the hypothesis of undue influence. What must be shown is that the facts are inconsistent with any other hypothesis. In the modern law, this is, perhaps no more than a reminder of the high burden, even on the civil standard, that a claimant bears in proving undue influence as vitiating a testamentary disposition;

(iv) In this context undue influence means influence exercised by coercion, in the sense that the testator's will must be overborne, or by fraud;

(v) Coercion is pressure that overpowers the volition without convincing the testator's judgment. It is to be distinguished from mere persuasion, appeals to ties of affection or pity for future destitution, all of which are legitimate. Pressure which causes a testator to succumb for the sake of a quiet life, if carried to an extent that overbears the testator's free judgment discretion or wishes, is enough to amount to coercion in this sense;

(vi) The physical and mental strength of the testator are relevant factors in determining how much pressure is necessary in order to overbear the will. The will of a weak and ill person may be more easily overborne than that of a hale and hearty one. As was said in one case simply to talk to a weak and feeble testator may so fatigue the brain that a sick person may be induced for quietness' sake to do anything. A "drip drip" approach may be highly effective in sapping the will;

(vii) There is a separate ground for avoiding a testamentary disposition on the ground of fraud. The shorthand used to refer to this species of fraud is "fraudulent calumny". The basic idea is that A poisons the testator's mind against B, who would otherwise be a natural beneficiary of the testator's bounty, by casting dishonest aspersions on his character, then the will is liable to be set aside;

(viii) The essence of fraudulent calumny is that the person alleged to have been poisoning the testator's mind must either know that the aspersions are false or not care whether they are true or false. In my mind if a person believes that he is telling the truth about a potential beneficiary then even if what he tells the testator is objectively untrue, the will is not liable to be set aside on this ground alone;

(ix) The question is not whether the court considers that the testator's testamentary disposition is fair because, subject to statutory powers of intervention, a testator may dispose of his estate as he wishes. The question, in the end, is whether in making his dispositions, the testator has acted as a free agent.'

In *Re Edwards*, undue influence and fraud were established where a son was found to have deliberately poisoned his mother's mind by making untruthful accusations against another son and his wife, causing her to change her will.

What is not undue influence

34.48 Appeals to affection, ties of kindred, gratitude for past services, or pity for future destitution are legitimate; but not pressure if so exerted as to overpower the volition without convincing the judgment (*Hall v Hall* (1868) LR 1 P & D 481). Even immoral considerations do not amount to undue influence unless the testator is in such a condition that if he could speak his wishes to the last, he would say, 'This is not my wish, but I must do it' (*Baudains v Richardson* [1906] AC 169 at 184). See also *Cowderoy v Cranfield* [2011] EWHC 1616 (Ch), [2011] WTLR 1699, *Wharton v Bancroft* [2011] EWHC 3250 (Ch), [2012] WTLR 693 and *Nesbitt v Nicholson* [2013] EWHC 4027 (Ch) in which undue influence claims failed. A plea of undue influence failed in *Edkins v Hopkins* [2016] EWHC 2542 (Ch). The main beneficiary had had a significant level of control over the testator, his business and personal financial affairs, but that level of control was given by the testator and not taken by the main beneficiary. The main beneficiary had encouraged the testator to change his will but the testator had acted out of his own judgment.

Fraudulent calumny

34.52A This provides a separate ground for avoiding a testamentary disposition on the ground of fraud where A poisons the testator's mind against B who would otherwise be a natural beneficiary of the testator's bounty, by casting dishonest aspersions on his character[1]. The requirements of fraudulent calumny are: (i) that A made a false representation (ii) to the testator (iii) about B's character (iv) for the purpose of inducing the testator to alter his or her testamentary disposition and that (v) A made such a representation knowing it to be untrue or being reckless as to its truth and (vi) the will was only made because of the fraudulent calumny[2].

1 See (vii) and (viii) of the principles of law summarised by Lewison J (as he then was) in *Re Edwards (dec'd)* [2007] EWHC 1119 (Ch), [2007 All ER (D) 46 (May) at para **34.47** above.

2 *Christodoulides v Marcou* [2017] EWHC 2632 (Ch), Morgan J.

(5) WANT OF KNOWLEDGE AND APPROVAL

Summary of reported cases

Burden of proof

34.64 Suspicious circumstances may arise where the testator is mentally or physically frail or where beneficiaries have been part of the process of drawing up the will. In such cases the judge must consider whether the suspicion has been dispelled (*Hawes v Burgess* [2013] EWCA Civ 74 at [12] per Mummery LJ). It may be obvious that the burden has not been dispelled (*Poole v Everall* [2016] EWHC 2126 (Ch), [2016] WTLR 1621 where a person on whom the testator depended had received the great bulk of the estate through a will drafted by him).

It is not the law that in no circumstances can a solicitor or other person who has prepared a will for a testator take a benefit under it; but that fact creates a suspicion that must be removed by the person propounding the will. In all cases the court must be vigilant and jealous. The degree of suspicion will vary with the circumstances of the case. It may be slight and easily dispelled; it may, on the other hand, be so grave that it can hardly be removed (*Wintle v Nye* [1959] 1 All ER 552, [1959] 1 WLR 284, HL). A solicitor beneficiary under a will has a personal obligation to see that the testator was separately advised before he could benefit (*Re a Solicitor* [1975] QB 475, [1974] 3 All ER 853).

(7) REVOCATION

Summary of reported cases

III. By burning, tearing, or otherwise destroying (Wills Act 1837, s 20[1]*)*

[1] See para **A1.20**.

34.87 *(i) Generally:*

(a) *Intention to revoke.* The intention to revoke must accompany the act (*Bibb v Thomas* (1775) 2 Wm Bl 1043; *Clarke v Scripps* (1852) 2 Rob Eccl 563 at 567; *Giles v Warren* (1872) LR 2 P & D 401). Therefore a person of unsound mind cannot revoke his will by destruction (*Brunt v Brunt* (1873) LR 3 P & D 37 at 38; *Re Taylor's Estate, National and Provincial and Union Bank of England v Taylor* (1919) 64 Sol Jo 148). As to standard of capacity required, see *Re Sabatini* (1969) 114 Sol Jo 35. Where the destruction is not with consent of the testator, he cannot subsequently ratify such destruction so as to effect a revocation (*Mills v Millward* (1889) 15 PD 20; *Gill v Gill* [1909] P 157), and subsequent acquiescence does not constitute revocation (*Re Booth, Booth v Booth* [1926] P 118). If there is an express revocation clause in a later will which is not in accord with the testator's instructions there is no rule of law that the testator is bound by the draftsman's mistake. The burden of proving on the balance of probabilities that the testator had not intended to revoke the earlier will is on the party seeking to prevent the express clause having effect. The standard of proof is no higher than the usual balance of proof, but the existence of the revocation clause is strong evidence that needs to be overcome (*Lamothe v Lamothe* [2006]

EWHC 1387 (Ch), [2006] WTLR 1431). For a later lost will to revoke an earlier will there must be clear, stringent and conclusive evidence that there was either a revocation clause in the lost will or that its provisions were inconsistent with those of the earlier will (*Broadway v Fernandes* [2007] EWHC 684 (Ch), [2007] All ER (D) 485 (Mar)).

(b) *Presumption as to will not forthcoming at testator's death*. Where a will is traced into the testator's custody, and there is no evidence of its having subsequently left his custody, and it is not forthcoming at his death—this will be prima facie evidence of its destruction by him animo revocandi (*Patten v Poulton* (1858) 1 Sw & Tr 55; *Welch v Phillips* (1836) 1 Moo PCC 299 at 302), and it is not necessary for those alleging revocation to show how, in fact, it was lost or destroyed (*Patten v Poulton* (1858) 1 Sw & Tr 55). The presumption may be rebutted by surrounding circumstances, eg declaration of unchanged affection or intention (*Patten v Poulton* (1858) 1 Sw & Tr 55; *Welch v Phillips* (1836) 1 Moo PCC 299 at 302; *Re Mackenzie's Estate* [1909] P 305; *Re Sykes, Drake v Sykes* (1906) 22 TLR 741; affd (1907) 23 TLR 747, CA); *Re Wilson's Estate, Walker v Treasury Solicitor* (1961) 105 Sol Jo 531. The strongest proof of the improbability of revocation by destruction arises from the contents of the document itself (*Saunders v Saunders* (1848) 6 Notes of Cases 518 at 522). Where a will which has been in the custody of a testator at a time when he has been of unsound mind as well as of sound mind, is found torn, or is not forthcoming at his death, the burden of showing that it was revoked by him while of sound mind lies on the party who sets up the revocation (*Harris v Berrall* (1858) 1 Sw & Tr 153). See also *Sprigge v Sprigge* (1868) LR 1 P & D 608 (the presumption of destruction animo revocandi does not apply where the testator became of unsound mind after execution of the will and continued so until his death. The burden of showing that the will was revoked before he became of unsound mind lies on the party asserting revocation); *Re Yule's Estate* (1965) 109 Sol Jo 317 (the presumption of destruction animo revocandi and the contrary presumption, in the case where the testator had lost testamentary capacity, that the will was destroyed unintentionally, were not intended to be rigid rules but as indications of the inferences which would always be drawn from a given state of evidence. But the court was not entitled to depart from *Sprigge v Sprigge*, above). In *Re Dickson* [1984] LS Gaz R 3012, CA; [2002] WTLR 1395 the presumption that a missing will had been destroyed animo revocandi was rebutted where the only reasonable inference from declarations by the testator and other evidence was that he had intended the missing will to be effective and had intended to benefit the beneficiaries thereunder. If the deceased has passed the will to a third party for safe custody no presumption arises (*Chana v Chana* [2001] WTLR 205). In *Rowe v Clarke* [2006] WTLR 347 the presumption was rebutted on the facts, which pointed to the testator having lost or destroyed the will in his lifetime without intending to revoke it. In *Wren v Wren* [2006] EWHC 2243 (Ch), [2007] WTLR 531, the will was not found at death, however, the deceased's clear post-will testamentary declarations rebutted the presumption of revocation. In *Nicholls v Hudson* [2006] EWHC 3006 (Ch), 150 Sol Jo LB 1333 the will made by the deceased was found to have been lost through mistake, accident or inadvertence with no intention of revoking it and a copy of the will was admitted to probate. In *Singh and McDonald v Vozniak* [2016] EWHC 114 (Ch) a wife's assertion that her husband had torn up his will was rejected in circumstances in which the deceased had repeatedly confirmed to one of the executors named in the will, after his wife had found out about the will, that his testamentary wishes were unchanged.

(c) *Revocation by partial destruction*. Where a testator signed his name, which was attested by both the witnesses, on each of the sheets of his will, and at his death only two of the middle sheets were found among his papers, it was held that the will must be presumed to be revoked (*Re Gullan's Goods* (1858) 1 Sw & Tr 23); so, too, where the testator had replaced the three middle sheets of his will (consisting of five sheets) by three other sheets, and the original sheets could not be found (*Treloar v Lean* (1889) 14 PD 49); see also *Clarke v Scripps* (1852) 2 Rob Eccl 563 (the question is whether the portion destroyed is so important as to raise a presumption that the remainder cannot have been intended to stand without it, or whether it is unimportant and independent of the remainder of the will); *Leonard v Leonard* [1902] P 243. Where part of a will is destroyed, but the part preserved contains the signatures of testator and the witnesses, the onus is normally on the party alleging revocation to prove the necessary animus. But if the part preserved is so mutilated as to be unworkable as a testamentary instrument this raises a presumption that the testator could not have intended it to stand as his will (*Re Green's Estate, Ward v Bond* (1962) 106 Sol Jo 1034). In *Re Adams* [1990] Ch 601, [1990] 2 All ER 97 it was held that the obliteration of his signature by the testator, so that it could not be read with a magnifying glass was by itself sufficient evidence of intention to revoke the whole will.

(d) *Revocation of duplicate wills*. Where a will is executed in duplicate the revocation of one is the revocation of both (*Boughey v Moreton* (1758) 3 Hag Ecc 191). But there must be evidence that the will was, in fact, executed in duplicate—subsequent declarations by the testator to this effect are inadmissible (*Atkinson v Morris* [1897] P 40, CA; *Eyre v Eyre* [1903] P 131 at 137). See para **3.209**.

AVOIDANCE OF GIFTS TO ATTESTING WITNESSES OR THEIR SPOUSES

34.103 Section 15 of the Wills Act 1837 makes gifts to an attesting witness or the spouse of an attesting witness 'utterly null and void'. The operation of s 15 is restricted by the Wills Act 1968, s 1. Section 1 provides that the operation of s 15 is to be disregarded if the will is duly executed without his attestation and without that of any other such person.

Section 28(4)(a) of the Trustee Act 2000 provides that any payments to which a trustee is entitled in respect of services are to be treated as remuneration for services (and not as a gift) for the purposes s 15 of the Wills Act 1837. This exemption applies where there is a charging clause in the will.

34.104 Section 15 will apply in the case of a marriage of a same sex couple which has the same effect in relation to same sex couples as it has in relation to opposite sex couples[1], and in relation to the attestation of a will by a person to whose civil partner there is made a gift of a kind described by s 15[2]. Section 15 cannot be extended to persons signing at the direction of the testator who receive a gift under the will[3], but the Court of Appeal has said that it is plainly undesirable that beneficiaries should be permitted to execute a will in their favour in any capacity and Parliament should consider changing the law to ensure this cannot happen.[4]

1 See the Marriage (Same Sex Couples) Act 2013, ss 1(1) and 11(1).
2 Civil Partnership Act 2004 s 71, Sch 4, Pt 1, para 3(a).
3 *Barrett v Bern* [2012] Ch 573 per Vos J at 597 (reversed on a different point).
4 *Barrett v Bern* [2012] Ch 573 at 612. This topic is included in the Law Commission's Consultation Paper 'Making a Will' (Law Com no 231).

Chapter 36

DISCLOSURE

DNA TESTING

36.27 The High Court has inherent jurisdiction to direct DNA testing in the case of a sample of a deceased's DNA. The power is one that is to be used sparingly[1].

1 *Spencer v Anderson (Paternity Testing: Jurisdiction)* [2016] EWHC 851 (Fam), [2016] 3 WLR 905, [2016] Fam Law 808.

PATERNITY

36.28 The High Court has inherent jurisdiction to direct that a party to proceedings where paternity is in issue give a saliva sample by way of mouth swabs for the purposes of establishing paternity and, if consent is refused, the court is able to draw an adverse inference[1].

1 *Nield-Moir v Freeman* [2018] EWHC 299 (Ch).

Chapter 37

COSTS AND CASE MANAGEMENT OF PROBATE CLAIMS

DIRECTIONS QUESTIONNAIRE AND DIRECTIONS

Directions

37.07 The parties are expected to endeavour to agree proposals for the management of the case at the directions stage and submit agreed directions, or their respective proposals, to the court at least seven days before any case management conference in accordance with CPR 29.4 and CPR 29 PD paras 4.6 to 4.8. If the directions are suitable the court may use them as the basis of making an order. Unless both directions and costs budgets are agreed, the claim is likely to be listed for a costs and case management conference. Case and Costs Management is dealt with in Chapter 17 of the Chancery Guide (2016).

37.09 For draft orders commonly made by the Master on allocation and case management conference see the justice.gov website at http://hmctsformfinder.justice.gov.uk/HMCTS/FormFinder.do. The costs and case management conference requires preparation well in advance of the hearing and if this has not been done the hearing may be adjourned and adverse costs orders made[1].

1 Chancery Guide Ch 17 para 17.6.

OTHER PRE-TRIAL MATTERS

Trial timetable

37.20 Trial timetables have become essential following the introduction of trials with a fixed end date in the Chancery Division. The judge at trial, or at the pre-trial review, will determine the timetable of the trial. The advocates for parties should be ready to assist the court in this respect if so required. The time estimate given for the trial at the case management conference stage should be based on an approximate forecast of the trial timetable, and must be reviewed by each party at the stage of the pre-trial review and as preparation for trial proceeds thereafter[1]. If that review requires a change in the estimate the other parties' advocates and the court must be informed. When a trial timetable is set by the court, it ordinarily fixes the time for the oral submissions and factual and expert evidence, in greater or lesser detail. Trial timetables are always subject to further order by the trial judge[2].

1 Chancery Guide Ch 17 para 17.25.
2 Chancery Guide Ch 20 para 20.7.

Pre-trial review

37.21 In cases estimated to take more than five days, a pre-trial review will be directed. The date for the pre-trial review is fixed at the time when the trial date is given[1]. The pre-trial review will, where possible, be heard by the trial judge. This requires the trial judge to have been nominated in advance of the trial. The pre-trial review is usually held between four and eight weeks before the trial date[2].

1 Chancery Guide Ch 20 para 20.1.
2 Chancery Guide Ch 20 para 20.3.

37.22 A pre-trial review should be attended by advocates who are to represent the parties at the trial[1].

1 Chancery Guide Ch 20 para 20.4.

37.23 Not less than seven days before the dated fixed for the review the claimant or some other party if the court so directs must circulate a list of matters to be considered to the other parties who must respond with their comments at least two days before the review[1].

1 Chancery Guide Ch 20 para 20.5.

37.24 The claimant or another party if so directed should deliver a bundle containing the matters to be considered and the proposals from other parties and the trial timetable and the results of inter party discussions and any other necessary documents to the Listing Officer by 10am on the day before the day fixed for the hearing[1].

1 Chancery Guide Ch 20 para 20.6.

37.25 At the review the court will review the state of the case and deal with outstanding matters, and give any necessary directions as to how the case is to be tried[1]. Interim applications should not be stored up for the pre-trial review, which is intended primarily to review the issues in the case and the proposed trial timetable.

1 Chancery Guide Ch 20 para 20.6.

Trial bundle

37.26 Unless the court otherwise orders the claimant must file the trial bundle made as provided in CPR Pt 39 PD paras 3.2–3.9 and Chancery Guide paras 21.34–21.72 not more than seven days nor less than three days before the start of the trial.

Skeleton arguments and reading lists

37.27 As a general rule for the purpose of all hearing before a judge skeleton arguments should be prepared. For trials and applications by order they should be delivered not less than two clear days before the date or first date on which the application or trial is due to come on for hearing. For guidelines see Chancery Guide paras 21.73–21.81 (skeleton arguments) and 21.82 (reading lists). *Practice Direction on the Citation of Authorities*[1] lays down rules as to the citation of cases. Excessive citation of authority should be avoided and practitioners must have full regard to *Practice Direction (Citation of Authorities)* [2012] 1 WLR 780.

1 [2001] 1 WLR 1001.

37.28 *Practice Direction (Reading Lists and Time Estimates)*[1] requires that a reading list and an estimated length of reading time and an estimated length of hearing signed by all advocates must be prepared in all matters where the lodging of bundles is required. Time estimates must make a realistic estimate for pre-reading by the judge. All trials in the Chancery Division in London, following practice and procedure successfully adopted in Manchester and elsewhere, are now conducted on a fixed-end trial basis[2].

1 [2000] 1 All ER 640.
2 Chancery Guide Ch 21 paras 21.20–21.26.

Chapter 39

TRIAL

LISTS AND DURATION

Estimate of duration

39.06 With the introduction of fixed-end trials, estimates need to be kept under constant review. If after a case is listed in the Royal Courts of Justice the estimated length of the hearing is varied, or if the case is settled, withdrawn or discontinued, the solicitors for the parties must forthwith inform the Chancery Listing Officer in writing. Failure to do so may result in an adverse costs order being made[1].

The parties must inform the court immediately of any material change in a time-estimate[2].

1 Chancery Guide Ch 21 para 21.11.
2 Chancery Guide Ch 21 para 21.22.

Time limits

39.08 All cases in the Chancery Division are now to be given fixed-end dates. The court may, either at the outset of the trial or at any other time thereafter fix time limits for oral submissions, speeches and the examination and cross-examination of witnesses[1].

1 Chancery Guide Ch 21 paras 21.20, 21.29 and 21.30.

THE HEARING

Opening oral submissions

39.09 Generally the claimant opens, unless the burden of proof of all issues in the case lies on the defendant, in which case the defendant has the right to begin. In general and subject to any direction to the contrary by the trial judge there should be a short opening statement on behalf of the claimant, at the conclusion of which the judge will invite short opening statements on behalf of the other parties[1]. Unless notified otherwise advocates should assume that the judge will have read the skeleton arguments and the principal documents referred to in the reading list lodged in advance of the hearing. The judge will state at an early stage how much he or she has read and what arrangements are to be made about reading documents not already read. If additional documents need to be read by the judge a list should be provided during the opening[2].

1 Chancery Guide Ch 21, para 21.90.
2 Chancery Guide Ch 21 para 21.91.

Witness statements

39.10 Chapter 19 of the Chancery Guide lays down guidelines for the preparation of witness statements.

Closing oral submissions

39.15 After the evidence is concluded, and subject to contrary directions by the judge, the claimant will make closing oral submissions followed by the defendant(s) in the order they appear on the claim form, followed by a reply on behalf of the claimant[1]. This differs from the traditional order of speeches where the defendant made his submissions before the claimant. In a lengthy and complex case each party should provide written summaries of their closing submissions. The court may require the written summaries to set out the principal findings of fact for which a party contends[2].

1 Chancery Guide Ch 21 para 21.93.
2 Chancery Guide Ch 21 para 21.94.

Chapter 40

COSTS

COSTS OF PARTIES OPPOSING PROBATE

(a) Where the litigation has been caused by the testator, or those interested in the residuary estate

Where conduct of beneficiary under the will caused the litigation

40.30 An unsuccessful party is usually given his costs where one of the principal beneficiaries under a will has been actively engaged in its preparation, and has not shown by disinterested evidence that its dispositions were read over or explained to and approved of by the testator before its execution[1]. The mere fact that someone can be said to be responsible for a will having been executed otherwise than in front of a solicitor cannot make it appropriate to view him as the cause of litigation about it[2].

1 *Dale v Murrell* (March 1879, unreported). See also *Orton v Smith* (1873) LR 3 P & D 23; and *Wilson v Bassil* [1903] P 239, 72 LJP 89.

2 *Breslin v Bromley* [2015] EWHC 3760 (Ch), [2015] 6 Costs LR 1115 per Newey J at [4].

(b) Where the circumstances lead reasonably to an investigation

40.35 Where the circumstances led reasonably to an investigation, the court by reviewing all the facts and state of knowledge of the parties may consider the stage down to which this exception to the general rule that costs follow the event should be treated as applying. In *Kostic v Chaplin*[1] this exception to the general rule was treated as being applicable down to the date on which the expert reports were exchanged. From that point on, the losing party stood to be condemned in costs since there were no longer reasonable grounds for continuing with the investigation. The court declined to relieve a losing party of the costs of his unsuccessful opposition where that party had failed to show reasonable grounds for challenging a will on the ground of want of knowledge and approval[2].

1 [2007] EWHC 2909 (Ch), [2008] 2 Costs LR 271.

2 *Inchbald v Inchbald* [2017] EWHC 616 (Ch).

(c) Where the opposing party gives notice to cross-examine under CPR 57.7(5)

40.37 Under CPR 57.7(5), in probate claims the party opposing a will may give notice in his defence that he does not raise any positive case but insists on the will being proved in solemn form and, for that purpose, will cross-examine the witnesses who attested the will. If a defendant gives such a notice, the court will not make an order for costs against him unless it considers there was no reasonable ground for opposing the will. It does not follow, because a defendant fails, that there was no reasonable ground for opposing the will[1]. On the other hand, once a defendant has sufficient material to form a view as to whether there were any reasonable grounds for opposing a will, he or she becomes at risk for costs incurred from that date and is no longer protected by rule CPR 57.7(5)[2].

1 *Davies v Jones* [1899] P 161 at 164. For a case under the rule where it was held that there had been no reasonable ground for opposing the will, see *Re Spicer, Spicer v Spicer* [1899] P 38. See also *Perry v Dixon* (1899) 80 LT 297.

2 *Elliott v Simmonds* [2016] EWHC 962 (Ch), [2016] WTLR 1375.

Chapter 41

ASSOCIATED ACTIONS

RECTIFICATION OF A WILL

41.01 An action for the rectification of a will under the Administration of Justice Act 1982, s 20 is not a probate claim within the meaning of CPR 57.1(2) but CPR 57.12 and CPR 57 PD(A) paras 9, 10 and 11 apply.

Under the section the court may order rectification to carry out the intentions of the testator if satisfied that the will fails to carry them out in consequence of a clerical error or of a failure to understand the instructions of the testator.

REMOVAL OF A PERSONAL REPRESENTATIVE

41.16 The test for removing an executor is the same as that for removing a trustee, and is not more stringent. Friction and hostility between an executor and a beneficiary will not, of itself, be a good reason for removing the executor. If however, such hostility is obstructing the administration of an estate, it is a factor to be taken into account. A testator's choice of executors is also capable of being of relevance.[1] There has to be a good reason to interfere and remove.[2] The additional cost of replacing some or all of the personal representatives is a material consideration, particularly where it is proposed to appoint professional persons. The size of the estate and the likely cost of the work needed will have to be considered.[3]

1 *Kershaw v Micklethwaite* [2010] EWHC 506 (Ch), [2011] WTLR 413.

2 *Alkin v Raymond* [2010] WTLR 1117, [2010] Lexis Citation 17 at [32].

3 *Harris v Earwicker* [2015] EWHC 1915 (Ch) at [9](vi).

FAMILY PROVISION

General

41.19 The law governing family provision is contained in the Inheritance (Provision for Family and Dependants) Act 1975[1]. Application is made to the High Court or to the county court[2]. The court conventionally treats claims under the Act as involving a two-stage process, namely: (i) has there been a failure to make reasonable financial provision, and, if so (ii) what order ought to be made? Section 3(1) of the Act introduces factors which fall to be considered at both stages. Thus, the two questions will usually become: (i) did the will/intestacy make reasonable financial provision for the claimant, and (ii) if not, what reasonable financial provision ought now to be made for him[3]?

If application is made in the High Court it can be made either to the Chancery Division or to the Family Division in the High Court[4] and the procedure in both Divisions is the same except for modifications dependant on the difference in organisation of the two Divisions.

The Masters in the Chancery Division and the district judges in the Family Division have power to hear applications under the Act. Hearings under the Act are, in the first instance, listed by the court as hearings in private under CPR 39.2(3)(c)[5].

1 As amended by the Law Reform (Succession) Act 1995, the Civil Partnership Act 2004 and by the Inheritance and Trustees' Powers Act 2014, s 6 and Sch 2. The Marriage (Same Sex Couples) Act 2013 provides that marriage of same sex couples is lawful and has the same effect in relation to same sex couples as it has in relation to opposite sex couples.

2 By virtue of the County Courts Act 1984, s 25 and the High Court and County Courts Jurisdiction Order 1991 (SI 1991/724), art 2(8) the county court has unlimited jurisdiction to hear and determine any application for an order under s 2 including any application for permission to apply for such an order.

3 *Ilott v The Blue Cross* [2017] UKSC 17, [2017] 4 All ER 545, [2017] WTLR 533 at [23] per Lord Hughes.

4 CPR 57.15(1).

5 CPR Pt 39 PD r 39.1.5(9).

Time limits

41.36 Applications for leave are usually heard by the Master or district judge prior to the main hearing and the evidence is normally limited to what is required for the application. The Inheritance (Provision for Family and Dependants) Act 1975, s 4 does not itself give guidance as to how the court should approach the application for permission. The correct approach is to be found in the case law under s 4.[1]

1 *Re Salmon, Coard v National Westminster Bank Ltd* [1981] Ch 167, [1980] 3 All ER 532 and *Re Dennis, Dennis v Lloyds Bank Ltd* [1981] 2 All ER 140. Permission to make a claim six years after the expiry of the time limit was refused in *Berger v Berger* [2013] EWCA Civ 1305. In *McNulty v Mc Nulty* [2002] WTLR 737 a claim by an elderly widow in relation to her husband's estate was permitted three and a half years out of time. Permission was refused in *Sargeant v Sargeant* [2018] EWHC 8 (Ch) to a widow to make a claim after ten years where no steps had been taken by the claimant to establish whether she could challenge a discretionary trust set up by her late husband's will.

General

41.39 On the hearing of a claim the personal representative must produce to the court the original grant of representation to the deceased's estate[1]. If the court makes an order under the Act, the original grant (together with a sealed copy of the order) must be sent to the Principal Registry of the Family Division for a memorandum of the order to be endorsed on or permanently annexed to the grant in accordance with the Inheritance (Provision for Family and Dependants) Act 1975, s 19(3)[2]. Every final order embodying terms of compromise made in proceedings under the Act with or without a hearing must contain a direction that a memorandum of the order should be endorsed on or permanently annexed to the probate or letters of administration and a copy of the order should be sent to the Principal Registry with the relevant grant of probate or letters of administration for endorsement[3]. An agreement settling a claim under the 1975 Act was held to be void for common mistake where it was subsequently discovered that the deceased had left a will under which the claimant obtained more than she had done under the agreement[4]. A claim under the Act abates on the death of the claimant. This is because the Act gives a personal right to bring a claim but that right is not itself a cause of action. It is a hope or a contingency. It cannot therefore be pursued by the personal representatives of a surviving spouse after her death[5].

1 CPR Pt.57 PD(A) 18.1.
2 CPR Pt.57 PD(A) 18.2.
3 CPR Pt.57 PD(A) 18.3.
4 *British Red Cross v Werry and Garcia* [2017] EWHC 875 (Ch), [2017] WTLR 441.
5 *Roberts v Fresco* [2017] EWHC 283 (Ch) applying *Whyte v Ticehurst* [1986] Fam 64, [1986] 2 All ER 158.

Costs management of 1975 Act claims

41.41 Claims pursuant to the Inheritance (Provision for Family and Dependants) Act 1975 are specifically referred to as one of the categories of Part 8 claims in which an order for the provision of costs budgets may be particularly appropriate with a view to a costs management order being made[1].

1 CPR Pt 3 PD 3E para 5(d).

PRESUMPTION OF DEATH

Applications under the Presumption of Death Act 2013

41.42 The Presumption of Death Act 2013 (PDA 2013) came into force on 1 October 2014. It enables applications to be made to the High Court for a declaration that a missing person is presumed to have died.

Jurisdiction

41.43 The court has jurisdiction to hear and determine an application if and only if: (i) the missing person was domiciled in England and Wales on the day on which he or she was last known to be alive; or (ii) the missing person had been habitually resident in England and Wales throughout the period of one year ending with that day; or (iii) if PDA 2013, s 1(4) is satisfied. That sub-section is satisfied if an application is made by the spouse or civil partner of the missing person, and the applicant is domiciled in England and Wales on the day on which the application is made or if the applicant has been habitually resident in England and Wales throughout the period of one year ending with that day. The sub-section cannot be relied on where the application is made by a parent, child or sibling of the missing person. In the case of such an application, jurisdiction must be founded on s 1(3).

The form of declaration made

41.44 Subject to jurisdiction being established, the court must make a declaration if it is satisfied that the missing person has died or has not been known to be alive for a period of at least seven years[1].

Where the court is satisfied that a missing person has died, but is uncertain at which moment during a period the missing person died, a declaration will be made pursuant to s 2(1)(a) that the missing person is presumed to have died at the end of that period.

Where the court is satisfied that the missing person has not been known to be alive for a period of at least seven years, but is not satisfied that the missing person has died, a declaration will be made pursuant to s 2(1)(b) that the missing person is presumed to have died at the end of the period of seven years beginning with the day after the day on which he was last known to be alive[2].

1 PDA 2013, s 1(3).

2 This was the form of declaration made in *Re Charles George Bingham* [2015] EWHC 226 (Ch) in relation to Lord Lucan, the Seventh Earl of Lucan.

The effect of a declaration

41.45 A declaration under the Act is conclusive of the missing person's presumed death and the date and time of death[1].

1 PDA 2013, s 3.

Procedure

41.46 CPR Part 57 Section V and PD 57B sets out detailed rules of court concerning the information to be provided in the claim form, giving of notice of the claim to others who would be entitled themselves to be the claimant, and for advertisement of the claim and for intervening in a claim.

Section 11 of the PDA 2013 permits the missing person's spouse, civil partner, child or sibling to intervene in proceedings on an application under the Act. The Attorney General may intervene. Any other person may only intervene with the permission of the court[1].

The rules provide for a first directions hearing and then a final hearing. If the matter is not opposed, an order may be made by a permanent Master.

1 An application for permission to intervene must be served on the claimant and must specify the applicant's relationship to the missing person or other interest in the proceedings and the reasons for seeking to intervene: CPR Pt 57 PD57B para 3.2. The prescribed form of advertisement requires any person seeking to intervene do so as soon as possible, and if possible within 21 days of the advertisement.

The Register of Presumed Deaths

41.47 The Act provides for the creation and maintenance by the Registrar General for England and Wales of the Register of Presumed Deaths. A certified copy of an entry in the Register of Presumed Deaths in relation to a person is to be received as evidence of the person's death without further or other proof, if it purports to be sealed or stamped with the seal of the General Register

Office[1].

1 PDA 2013, s 15 and Sch 1, para 4.

APPENDICES

Appendix I

STATUTES

Contents

Note.

The following text contains extracts from Acts of Parliament having a bearing on the probate practice. In general, those enactments, since repealed, which remain applicable in relation to cases where death occurred prior to the relevant date of repeal have been retained for the purpose of reference.

PART I – PROBATE BUSINESS

WILLS ACT 1837

(7 Will 4 & 1 Vict c 26) as amended

A1.01

1 Meaning of certain words in this Act: "Will": "Real estate": "Personal estate": Number: Gender

. . . the words and expressions herein-after mentioned, which in their ordinary signification have a more confined or a different meaning, shall in this Act, except where the nature of the provisions or the context of the Act shall exclude such construction, be interpreted as follows; (that is to say,) the word "will" shall extend to a testament, and to a codicil, and to an appointment by will or by writing in the nature of a will in exercise of a power, [and also to an appointment by will of a guardian of a child], [and also to an appointment by will of a representative under section 4 of the Human Tissue Act 2004 [or section 8 of the Human Transplantation (Wales) Act 2013],] . . . and to any other testamentary disposition; and the words "real estate" shall extend to manors, advowsons, messuages, lands, tithes, rents, and hereditaments, . . . whether corporeal, incorporeal, or personal, . . . and to any estate, right, or interest (other than a chattel interest) therein; and the words "personal estate" shall extend to leasehold estates and other chattels real, and also to monies, shares of government and other funds, securities for money (not being real estates), debts, choses in action, rights, credits, goods, and all other property whatsoever which by law devolves upon the executor or administrator, and to any share or interest therein; and every word importing the singular number only shall extend and be applied to several persons or things as well as one person or thing; and every word importing the masculine gender only shall extend and be applied to a female as well as a male.

Repealed in part, in relation to Northern Ireland, by the Statute Law Revision (Northern Ireland) Act 1954, the Statute Law Revision (Northern Ireland) Act 1976, and the Wills and Administration Proceedings (NI) Order 1994, SI 1994/1899, art 38, Sch 3.

First words omitted repealed by the Statute Law Revision Act 1893, s 1, Schedule.

Words from "and also to" to "of a child," in square brackets substituted by the Children Act 1989, s 108(5), (6), Sch 13, para 1, Sch 14, para 1.

Words from "and also to" to "," in square brackets inserted by the Human Tissue Act 2004, s 56, Sch 6, para 1. Date in force: 1 September 2006: see SI 2006/1997, art 3(2).

Words "or section 8 of the Human Transplantation (Wales) Act 2013" in square brackets inserted by the Human Transplantation (Wales) Act 2013, s 17. Date in force: 1 December 2015: see SI 2015/1679, art 3(e).

Second and third words omitted repealed by the Statute Law (Repeals) Act 1969, s 1, Schedule, Pt III.

Final words omitted repealed by the Trusts of Land and Appointment of Trustees 1996, s 25(2), Sch 4; for savings in relation to entailed interests created before the commencement of that Act, and savings consequential upon the abolition of the doctrine of conversion, see s 25(4), (5) thereof.

LAW OF PROPERTY (AMENDMENT) ACT 1926

(16 & 17 Geo 5, c 11)

A1.138

3 Meaning of 'trust corporation'

(1) For the purposes of the Law of Property Act 1925, the Settled Land Act 1925, the Trustee Act 1925, the Administration of Estates Act 1925, and the [Senior Courts Act 1981], the expression "Trust Corporation" includes the Treasury Solicitor, the Official Solicitor and any person holding any other official position prescribed by the Lord Chancellor, and, in relation to the property of a bankrupt . . . , includes the trustee in bankruptcy . . . , and, in relation to charitable ecclesiastical and public trusts, also includes any local or public authority so prescribed, and any other corporation constituted under the laws of the United Kingdom or any part thereof which satisfies the Lord Chancellor that it undertakes the administration of any such trusts without remuneration, or that by its constitution it is required to apply the whole of its net income after payment of outgoings for charitable ecclesiastical or public purposes, and

is prohibited from distributing, directly or indirectly, any part thereof by way of profits amongst any of its members, and is authorised by him to act in relation to such trusts as a trust corporation.
(2) For the purposes of this provision, the expression "Treasury Solicitor" means the solicitor for the affairs of His Majesty's Treasury, and includes the solicitor for the affairs of the Duchy of Lancaster.

Sub-s (1): words "Senior Courts Act 1981" in square brackets substituted by the Constitutional Reform Act 2005, s 59(5), Sch 11, Pt 1, para 1(2). Date in force: 1 October 2009: see SI 2009/1604, art 2(d).

Sub-s (1): first words omitted repealed by the Deregulation Act 2015, s 19, Sch 6, Pt 1, para 2(1), (5)(a); for effect see para 3. Date in force: 1 October 2015: see SI 2015/1732, art 2(e)(i).

Sub-s (1): second words omitted repealed by the Deregulation Act 2015, s 19, Sch 6, Pt 1, para 2(1), (5)(b); for effect see para 3. Date in force: 1 October 2015: see SI 2015/1732, art 2(e)(i).

PUBLIC RECORDS ACT 1958

(6 & 7 Eliz 2, c 51)

[23rd July 1958]

A1.165

5 Access to public records

* * * * *

(5) The [Secretary of State] shall as respects all public records in places of deposit appointed by him under this Act outside the Public Record Office require arrangements to be made for their inspection by the public comparable to those made for public records in the Public Record Office, ...

Sub-s (5): words "Secretary of State" in square brackets substituted by SI 2015/1897, art 9, Schedule, para 1(1), (3)(f). Date in force: 9 December 2015: see SI 2015/1897, art 1(2).

Sub-s (5): words omitted repealed by the Freedom of Information Act 2000, ss 67, 86, Sch 5, Pt I, para 2(1), (4), Sch 8, Pt III. Date in force: 1 January 2005: see SI 2004/3122, art 2.

A1.166

8 Court records

(1) The Lord Chancellor shall be responsible for the public records of every court of record or magistrates' court which are not in the Public Record Office or a place of deposit appointed by [the Secretary of State] under this Act and shall have power to determine in the case of any such records [other than records of the Supreme Court,] the officer in whose custody they are for the time being to be:

. . .

[(1A) Records of the Supreme Court for which the Lord Chancellor is responsible under subsection (1) shall be in the custody of the chief executive of that court.]

(2), (3) . . .

(4) Where any private documents have remained in the custody of a court in England or Wales for more than fifty years without being claimed, the Keeper of Public Records may, with the approval of the Master of the Rolls, require the documents to be transferred to the Public Record Office and thereupon the documents shall become public records for the purposes of this Act.

(5) Section three of this Act shall not apply to such of the records of ecclesiastical courts described in paragraph (n) of sub-paragraph (1) of paragraph 4 of the First Schedule to this Act as are not held in any office of the [Senior Courts] or in the Public Record Office, but, if the Lord Chancellor after consulting the President of the [Family

Division] so directs as respects any of those records, those records shall be transferred to such place of deposit as may be appointed by the [Secretary of State] and shall thereafter be in the custody of such officer as may be so appointed.
(6) The public records which at the commencement of this Act are in the custody of the University of Oxford and which are included in the index a copy of which was transmitted to the principal probate registrar under section two of the Oxford University Act 1860 shall not be required to be transferred under the last foregoing subsection but the Lord Chancellor shall make arrangements with the University of Oxford as to the conditions under which those records may be inspected by the public.

Sub-s (1): words "the Secretary of State" in square brackets substituted by SI 2015/1897, art 9, Schedule, para 1(1), (4). Date in force: 9 December 2015: see SI 2015/1897, art 1(2).

Sub-s (1): words "other than records of the Supreme Court," in square brackets inserted by the Constitutional Reform Act 2005, s 56(1), (2)(a). Date in force: 1 October 2009: see SI 2009/1604, art 2(b).

Sub-s (1): words omitted repealed by the Courts Act 1971, s 56(4), Sch 11, Pt II.

Sub-s (1A): inserted by the Constitutional Reform Act 2005, s 56(1), (2)(b). Date in force: 1 October 2009: see SI 2009/1604, art 2(b).

Sub-s (2): repealed by the Supreme Court Act 1981, s 152(4), Sch 7.

Sub-s (3): repealed by the Administration of Justice Act 1969, ss 27(2), 35(2), Sch 2.

Sub-s (5): words "Senior Courts" in square brackets substituted by the Constitutional Reform Act 2005, s 59(5), Sch 11, Pt 2, para 4(1), (3). Date in force: 1 October 2009: see SI 2009/1604, art 2(d).

Sub-s (5): words "Family Division" in square brackets substituted by the Administration of Justice Act 1970, s 1(6), Sch 2, para 19.

Sub-s (5): words "Secretary of State" in square brackets substituted by SI 2015/1897, art 9, Schedule, para 1(1), (3)(i). Date in force: 9 December 2015: see SI 2015/1897, art 1(2).

[SENIOR COURTS ACT 1981]

(1981, c 54)

[28th July 1981]

PART II
JURISDICTION

The Court of Appeal

* * * * *

A1.304

16 Appeals from High Court

(1) Subject as otherwise provided by this or any other Act (and in particular to the provision in section 13(2)(a) of the Administration of Justice Act 1969 excluding appeals to the Court of Appeal in cases where leave to appeal from the High Court directly to the [Supreme Court] is granted under Part II of that Act), [or as provided by any order made by the Lord Chancellor under section 56(1) of the Access to Justice Act 1999,] the Court of Appeal shall have jurisdiction to hear and determine appeals from any judgment or order of the High Court.
(2) An appeal from a judgment or order of the High Court when acting as a prize court shall not be to the Court of Appeal, but shall be to Her Majesty in Council in accordance with the Prize Acts 1864 to 1944.

Sub-s (1): words 'Supreme Court' in square brackets substituted by the Constitutional Reform Act 2005, s 40(4), Sch 9, Pt 1, para 36(1), (3). Date in force: 1 October 2009: see SI 2009/1604, art 2(d).

Sub-s (1): words from "or as provided" to "Access to Justice Act 1999," in square brackets inserted by SI 2016/917, art 9. Date in force: 3 October 2016: see SI 2016/917, art 1(2); for transitional provisions see art 8.

A1.305

17 Applications for new trial

(1) Where any cause or matter, or any issue in any cause or matter, has been tried in the High Court, any application for a new trial thereof, or to set aside a verdict, finding or judgment therein, shall be heard and determined by the Court of Appeal except where rules of court made in pursuance of subsection (2) provide otherwise.

(2) As regards cases where the trial was by a judge alone and no error of the court at the trial is alleged, or any prescribed class of such cases, rules of court may provide that any such application as is mentioned in subsection (1) shall be heard and determined by the High Court.

(3) Nothing in this section shall alter the practice in bankruptcy.

Sub-ss (1) derived from the Supreme Court of Judicature (Consolidation) Act 1925, s 30.

FORFEITURE ACT 1982

(1982, c 34)

[13 July 1982]

A1.359

2 Power to modify the rule

(1) Where a court determines that the forfeiture rule has precluded a person (in this section referred to as "the offender") who has unlawfully killed another from acquiring any interest in property mentioned in subsection (4) below, the court may make an order under this section modifying [or excluding] the effect of that rule.

(2) The court shall not make an order under this section modifying [or excluding] the effect of the forfeiture rule in any case unless it is satisfied that, having regard to the conduct of the offender and of the deceased and to such other circumstances as appear to the court to be material, the justice of the case requires the effect of the rule to be so modified [or excluded] in that case.

(3) In any case where a person stands convicted of an offence of which unlawful killing is an element, the court shall not make an order under this section modifying [or excluding] the effect of the forfeiture rule in that case unless proceedings for the purpose are brought before the expiry of the *period of three months beginning with his conviction* [relevant period].

[(3A) In subsection (3) above, the "relevant period" is the period of 6 months beginning with—

- (a) the end of the period allowed for bringing an appeal against the conviction, or
- (b) if such an appeal is brought, the conclusion of proceedings on the appeal.]

(4) The interests in property referred to in subsection (1) above are—

- (a) any beneficial interest in property which (apart from the forfeiture rule) the offender would have acquired—

(i) under the deceased's will (including, as respects Scotland, any writing having testamentary effect) or the law relating to intestacy or by way of ius relicti, ius relictae or legitim;

(ii) on the nomination of the deceased in accordance with the provisions of any enactment;

(iii) as a donatio mortis causa made by the deceased; or

(iv) under a special destination (whether relating to heritable or moveable property); or

(b) any beneficial interest in property which (apart from the forfeiture rule) the offender would have acquired in consequence of the death of the deceased, being property which, before the death, was held on trust for any person.

(5) An order under this section may modify [or exclude] the effect of the forfeiture rule in respect of any interest in property to which the determination referred to in subsection (1) above relates and may do so in either or both of the following ways, that is—

(a) where there is more than one such interest, by excluding the application of the rule in respect of any *(but not all)* [or all] of those interests; and

(b) in the case of any such interest in property, by excluding the application of the rule in respect of [all or any] part of the property.

(6) On the making of an order under this section [modifying the effect of the forfeiture rule], the forfeiture rule shall have effect for all purposes (including purposes relating to anything done before the order is made) subject to the modifications made by the order.

(7) The court shall not make an order under this section modifying the effect of the forfeiture rule in respect of any interest in property which, in consequence of the rule, has been acquired before the coming into force of this section by a person other than the offender or a person claiming through him.

(8) In this section—

"property" includes any chose in action or incorporeal moveable property; and

"will" includes codicil.

Sub-s (1): words "or excluding" in square brackets inserted by the Succession (Scotland) Act 2016, s 15(1), (2). Date in force: 1 November 2016: see SSI 2016/210, reg 2(1)(a), (2).

Sub-s (2): words "or excluding" in square brackets inserted by the Succession (Scotland) Act 2016, s 15(1), (3)(a). Date in force: 1 November 2016: see SSI 2016/210, reg 2(1)(a), (2).

Sub-s (2): words "or excluded" in square brackets inserted by the Succession (Scotland) Act 2016, s 15(1), (3)(b). Date in force: 1 November 2016: see SSI 2016/210, reg 2(1)(a), (2).

Sub-s (3): words "or excluding" in square brackets inserted by the Succession (Scotland) Act 2016, s 15(1), (4). Date in force: 1 November 2016: see SSI 2016/210, reg 2(1)(a), (2).

Sub-s (3): words "period of three months beginning with his conviction" in italics repealed and subsequent words in square brackets substituted by the Succession (Scotland) Act 2016, s 16(1), (2). Date in force: 1 November 2016: see SSI 2016/210, reg 2(1)(a), (2).

Sub-s (3A): inserted by the Succession (Scotland) Act 2016, s 16(1), (3). Date in force: 1 November 2016: see SSI 2016/210, reg 2(1)(a), (2).

Sub-s (5): words "or exclude" in square brackets inserted by the Succession (Scotland) Act 2016, s 15(1), (5)(a). Date in force: 1 November 2016: see SSI 2016/210, reg 2(1)(a), (2).

Sub-s (5): in para (a) words "(but not all)" in italics repealed and subsequent words in square brackets substituted by the Succession (Scotland) Act 2016, s 15(1), (5)(b). Date in force: 1 November 2016: see SSI 2016/210, reg 2(1)(a), (2).

Sub-s (5): in para (b) words "all or any" in square brackets inserted by the Succession (Scotland) Act 2016, s 15(1), (5)(c). Date in force: 1 November 2016: see SSI 2016/210, reg 2(1)(a), (2).

Sub-s (6): words "modifying the effect of the forfeiture rule" in square brackets inserted by the Succession (Scotland) Act 2016, s 15(1), (6). Date in force: 1 November 2016: see SSI 2016/210, reg 2(1)(a), (2).

CHILDREN ACT 1989

(1989, c 41)

[16th November 1989]

PART IV
CARE AND SUPERVISION

Care orders

A1.445

33 Effect of care order

(1) Where a care order is made with respect to a child it shall be the duty of the local authority designated by the order to receive the child into their care and to keep him in their care while the order remains in force.

(2) Where—

(a) a care order has been made with respect to a child on the application of an authorised person; but

(b) the local authority designated by the order was not informed that that person proposed to make the application,

the child may be kept in the care of that person until received into the care of the authority.

(3) While a care order is in force with respect to a child, the local authority designated by the order shall—

(a) have parental responsibility for the child; and

(b) have the power (subject to the following provisions of this section) to determine the extent to which[—

(i) a parent, guardian or special guardian of the child; or

(ii) a person who by virtue of section 4A has parental responsibility for the child,]

may meet his parental responsibility for him.

(4) The authority may not exercise the power in subsection (3)(b) unless they are satisfied that it is necessary to do so in order to safeguard or promote the child's welfare.

(5) Nothing in subsection (3)(b) shall prevent [a person mentioned in that provision who has care of the child] from doing what is reasonable in all the circumstances of the case for the purpose of safeguarding or promoting his welfare.

(6) While a care order is in force with respect to a child, the local authority designated by the order shall not—

(a) cause the child to be brought up in any religious persuasion other than that in which he would have been brought up if the order had not been made; or

(b) have the right—

(i) . . .

(ii) to agree or refuse to agree to the making of an adoption order, or an order under [section 84 of the Adoption and Children Act 2002], with respect to the child; or

(iii) to appoint a guardian for the child.

(7) While a care order is in force with respect to a child, no person may—

(a) cause the child to be known by a new surname; or

(b) remove him from the United Kingdom,

without either the written consent of every person who has parental responsibility for the child or the leave of the court.

(8) Subsection (7)(b) does not—

(a) prevent the removal of such a child, for a period of less than one month, by the authority in whose care he is; or

(b) apply to arrangements for such a child to live outside England and Wales (which are governed by paragraph 19 of Schedule 2 [in England, and section 124 of the Social Services and Well-being (Wales) Act 2014 in Wales]).

(9) The power in subsection (3)(b) is subject (in addition to being subject to the provisions of this section) to any right, duty, power, responsibility or authority which [a person mentioned in that provision] has in relation to the child and his property by virtue of any other enactment.

Sub-s (3): para (b)(i), (ii) substituted by the Adoption and Children Act 2002, s 139(1), Sch 3, paras 54, 63(a). Date in force: 30 December 2005: see SI 2005/2213, art 2(o).

Sub-s (5): words "a person mentioned in that provision who has care of the child" in square brackets substituted by the Adoption and Children Act 2002, s 139(1), Sch 3, paras 54, 63(b). Date in force: 30 December 2005: see SI 2005/2213, art 2(o).

Sub-s (6): para (b)(i) repealed by the Adoption and Children Act 2002, s 139(1), (3), Sch 3, paras 54, 63(c)(i), Sch 5. Date in force: 30 December 2005: see SI 2005/2213, art 2(o).

Sub-s (6): in para (b)(ii) words "section 84 of the Adoption and Children Act 2002" in square brackets substituted by the Adoption and Children Act 2002, s 139(1), Sch 3, paras 54, 63(c)(ii). Date in force: 30 December 2005: see SI 2005/2213, art 2(o).

Sub-s (8): in para (b) words from "in England, and" to "Social Services and Well-being (Wales) Act 2014 in Wales" in square brackets inserted by SI 2016/413, regs 55, 97. Date in force: 6 April 2016: see SI 2016/413, reg 2(1); for transitional provisions and savings see reg 325, Schedule.

Sub-s (9): words "a person mentioned in that provision" in square brackets substituted by the Adoption and Children Act 2002, s 139(1), Sch 3, paras 54, 63(d). Date in force: 30 December 2005: see SI 2005/2213, art 2(o).

PART XII
MISCELLANEOUS AND GENERAL

* * * * *

Jurisdiction and procedure etc

A1.451

105 Interpretation

(1) In this Act—

["activity condition" has the meaning given by section 11C;]

["activity direction" has the meaning given by section 11A;]

"adoption agency" means a body which may be referred to as an adoption agency by virtue of [section 2 of the Adoption and Children Act 2002];

[. . .]

"bank holiday" means a day which is a bank holiday under the Banking and Financial Dealings Act 1971;

["care home"—

(a) has the same meaning as in the Care Standards Act 2000 in respect of a care home in England; and

(b) means a place in Wales at which a care home service within the meaning of Part 1 of the Regulation and Inspection of Social Care (Wales) Act 2016 is provided wholly or mainly to persons aged 18 or over;]

"care order" has the meaning given by section 31(11) and also includes any order which by or under any enactment has the effect of, or is deemed to be, a care order for the purposes of this Act; and any reference to a child who is in the care of an authority is a reference to a child who is in their care by virtue of a care order;

"child" means, subject to paragraph 16 of Schedule 1, a person under the age of eighteen;

["child arrangements order" has the meaning given by section 8(1);]

"child assessment order" has the meaning given by section 43(2);

"child minder" has the meaning given by section 71;

["child of the family", in relation to parties to a marriage, or to two people who are civil partners of each other, means—

(a) a child of both of them, and

(b) any other child, other than a child placed with them as foster parents by a local authority or voluntary organisation, who has been treated by both of them as a child of their family;]

["children's home"—

(a) has the same meaning as it has for the purposes of the Care Standards Act 2000 in respect of a children's home in England (see section 1 of that Act); and

(b) means a place in Wales at which a care home service within the meaning of Part 1 of the Regulation and Inspection of Social Care (Wales) Act 2016 is provided wholly or mainly to children;]

["clinical commissioning group" means a body established under section 14D of the National Health Service Act 2006;]

"community home" has the meaning given by section 53;

[. . .]

[. . .]

. . .

"day care" [*(except in Part XA)*] has the same meaning as in section 18;

"disabled", in relation to a child, has the same meaning as in section 17(11);

. . .

"domestic premises" has the meaning given by section 71(12);

[dwelling-house" includes—

(a) any building or part of a building which is occupied as a dwelling;

(b) any caravan, house-boat or structure which is occupied as a dwelling;

and any yard, garden, garage or outhouse belonging to it and occupied with it;]

["education functions" has the meaning given by section 579(1) of the Education Act 1996;]

"education supervision order" has the meaning given in section 36;

"emergency protection order" means an order under section 44;

["enforcement order" has the meaning given by section 11J;]

"family assistance order" has the meaning given in section 16(2);

"family proceedings" has the meaning given by section 8(3);

"functions" includes powers and duties;

"guardian of a child" means a guardian (other than a guardian of the estate of a child) appointed in accordance with the provisions of section 5;

"harm" has the same meaning as in section 31(9) and the question of whether harm is significant shall be determined in accordance with section 31(10);

[. . .]

"health service hospital" [means a health service hospital within the meaning given by the National Health Service Act 2006 or the National Health Service (Wales) Act 2006];

"hospital" [*(except in Schedule 9A)*] has the same meaning as in the Mental Health Act 1983, except that it does not include a *special hospital within the meaning of that Act* [hospital at which high security psychiatric services within the meaning of that Act are provided];

"ill-treatment" has the same meaning as in section 31(9);

["income-based jobseeker's allowance" has the same meaning as in the Jobseekers Act 1995;]

[*"income-related employment and support allowance" means an income-related allowance under Part 1 of the Welfare Reform Act 2007 (employment and support allowance);*]

["independent hospital"—

(a) in relation to England, means a hospital as defined by section 275 of the National Health Service Act 2006 that is not a health service hospital as defined by that section; and

(b) in relation to Wales, has the same meaning as in the Care Standards Act 2000;]

"independent school" has the same meaning as in [the Education Act 1996];

"local authority" means, in relation to England . . . , the council of a county, a metropolitan district, a London Borough or the Common Council of the City of London[, in relation to Wales, the council of a county or a county borough] and, in relation to Scotland, a local authority within the meaning of section 1(2) of the Social Work (Scotland) Act 1968;

["local authority foster parent" means a person authorised as such in accordance with regulations made by virtue of—

(a) paragraph 12F of Schedule 2; or

(b) sections 87 and 93 of the Social Services and Well-being (Wales) Act 2014 (regulations providing for approval of local authority foster parents);]

. . .

["Local Health Board" means a Local Health Board established under section 11 of the National Health Service (Wales) Act 2006;]

"local housing authority" has the same meaning as in the Housing Act 1985;

. . .

. . .

["officer of the Service" has the same meaning as in the Criminal Justice and Court Services Act 2000;]

"parental responsibility" has the meaning given in section 3;

"parental responsibility agreement" has the meaning given in [sections 4(1)[, 4ZA(4)] and 4A(2)];

"prescribed" means prescribed by regulations made under this Act;

["private children's home" means a children's home in respect of which a person is registered under Part II of the Care Standards Act 2000 [or Part 1 of the Regulation and Inspection of Social Care (Wales) Act 2016] which is not a community home or a voluntary home;]

[. . .]

"privately fostered child" and "to foster a child privately" have the same meaning as in section 66;

"prohibited steps order" has the meaning given by section 8(1);

. . .

. . .

"registered pupil" has the same meaning as in [the Education Act 1996];

"relative", in relation to a child, means a grandparent, brother, sister, uncle or aunt (whether of the full blood or half blood or [by marriage or civil partnership)] or step-parent;

. . .

. . .

"responsible person", in relation to a child who is the subject of a supervision order, has the meaning given in paragraph 1 of Schedule 3;

"school" has the same meaning as in [the Education Act 1996] or, in relation to Scotland, in the Education (Scotland) Act 1980;

["section 31A plan" has the meaning given by section 31A(6);]

"service", in relation to any provision made under Part III, includes any facility;

"signed", in relation to any person, includes the making by that person of his mark;

"special educational needs" has the same meaning as in [the Education Act 1996];

["special guardian" and "special guardianship order" have the meaning given by section 14A;]

["Special Health Authority" means a Special Health Authority established under [section 28 of the National Health Service Act 2006 or section 22 of the National Health Service (Wales) Act 2006,];]

"specific issue order" has the meaning given by section 8(1);

[. . .]

"supervision order" has the meaning given by section 31(11);

"supervised child" and "supervisor", in relation to a supervision order or an education supervision order, mean respectively the child who is (or is to be) under supervision and the person under whose supervision he is (or is to be) by virtue of the order;

"upbringing", in relation to any child, includes the care of the child but not his maintenance;

"voluntary home" has the meaning given by section 60;

"voluntary organisation" means a body (other than a public or local authority) whose activities are not carried on for profit;

["Welsh family proceedings officer" has the meaning given by section 35 of the Children Act 2004].

(2) References in this Act to a child whose father and mother were, or (as the case may be) were not, married to each other at the time of his birth must be read with section 1 of the Family Law Reform Act 1987 (which extends the meaning of such references).

(3) . . .

[(4) References in this Act to a child who is looked after—

(a) in relation to a child who is looked after by a local authority in England, has the meaning given in section 22; and

(b) in relation to a child who is looked after by a local authority in Wales, has the meaning given in section 74 of the Social Services and Well-being (Wales) Act 2014 (child or young person looked after by a local authority).]

(5) References in this Act to accommodation provided by or on behalf of a local authority are references to accommodation so provided in the exercise of functions [of that or any other local authority which are social services functions . . .].

[(5A) *References in this Act to a child minder shall be construed—*

(a) . . . ;
(b) *in relation to . . . Wales, in accordance with section 79A.]*

[(5B) In subsection (5) "social services functions" means—
(a) in England, social services functions within the meaning of the Local Authority Social Services Act 1970, and
(b) in Wales, social services functions within the meaning of the Social Services and Well-being (Wales) Act 2014.]

(6) In determining the "ordinary residence" of a child for any purpose of this Act, there shall be disregarded any period in which he lives in any place—
(a) which is a school or other institution;
(b) in accordance with the requirements of a supervision order under this Act . . .
[(ba) in accordance with the requirements of a youth rehabilitation order under Part 1 of the Criminal Justice and Immigration Act 2008; or]
(c) while he is being provided with accommodation by or on behalf of a local authority.

(7) References in this Act to children who are in need shall be construed in accordance with section 17.

[(7A) References in this Act to a hospital or accommodation made available or provided pursuant to arrangements made by the Secretary of State under the National Health Service Act 2006 are references to a hospital or accommodation made available or provided pursuant to arrangements so made in the exercise of the public health functions of the Secretary of State (within the meaning of that Act).

(7B) References in this Act to arrangements made by the National Health Service Commissioning Board or a clinical commissioning group under the National Health Service Act 2006 include references to arrangements so made by virtue of section 7A of that Act.]

(8) Any notice or other document required under this Act to be served on any person may be served on him by being delivered personally to him, or being sent by post to him in a registered letter or by the recorded delivery service at his proper address.

(9) Any such notice or other document required to be served on a body corporate or a firm shall be duly served if it is served on the secretary or clerk of that body or a partner of that firm.

(10) For the purposes of this section, and of section 7 of the Interpretation Act 1978 in its application to this section, the proper address of a person—
(a) in the case of a secretary or clerk of a body corporate, shall be that of the registered or principal office of that body;
(b) in the case of a partner of a firm, shall be that of the principal office of the firm; and
(c) in any other case, shall be the last known address of the person to be served.

Sub-s (1): definition "activity condition" inserted by the Children and Families Act 2014, s 12(4), Sch 2, Pt 1, paras 1, 38(1), (2)(a). Date in force: 22 April 2014: see SI 2014/889, art 4(b), (f).

Sub-s (1): definition "activity direction" inserted by the Children and Families Act 2014, s 12(4), Sch 2, Pt 1, paras 1, 38(1), (2)(a). Date in force: 22 April 2014: see SI 2014/889, art 4(b), (f).

Sub-s (1): in definition "adoption agency" words "section 2 of the Adoption and Children Act 2002" in square brackets substituted by the Adoption and Children Act 2002, s 139(1), Sch 3, paras 54, 70(a). Date in force: 30 December 2005: see SI 2005/2213, art 2(o).

Sub-s (1): definition "appropriate children's home" inserted by the Care Standards Act 2000, s 116, Sch 4, para 14(1), (23)(a)(i). Date in force (in relation to England): 1 April 2002: see SI 2001/4150, art 3(3)(a); for transitional provisions see SI 2001/4150, arts 3(2), 4(1), (3), (4) and

SI 2002/1493, art 4 (as amended by SI 2002/1493, art 6). Date in force (in relation to Wales): 1 April 2002: see SI 2002/920, art 3(3)(d); for transitional provisions see arts 2, 3(2), (4), (6)–(10), Sch 1 thereto.

Sub-s (1): definition "appropriate children's home" (omitted) repealed by the Children and Young Persons Act 2008, ss 8(2), 42, Sch 1, para 3(1), (2), Sch 4. Date in force (in relation to England): 1 April 2011: see SI 2010/2981, art 4(a). Date in force (in relation to Wales): 6 April 2016: see SI 2016/452, art 2(b).

Sub-s (1): definition "care home" (as inserted by the Care Standards Act 2000, s 116, Sch 4, para 14(1), (23)(a)(ii)) substituted by SI 2018/195, regs 8, 12(a). Date in force: 2 April 2018: see SI 2018/195, reg 2(1).

Sub-s (1): definition "child arrangements order" inserted by the Children and Families Act 2014, s 12(4), Sch 2, Pt 1, paras 1, 38(1), (2)(b). Date in force: 22 April 2014: see SI 2014/889, art 4(b), (f).

Sub-s (1): definition "child minder" repealed by the Care Standards Act 2000, s 117(2), Sch 6. Date in force (in relation to Wales): 1 April 2002: see SI 2002/920, art 3(3)(g)(vi); for transitional provisions see arts 2, 3(2), (5)–(10), Schs 1, 2 thereto. Date in force (in relation to England): to be appointed: see the Care Standards Act 2000, s 122.

Sub-s (1): definition "child of the family" substituted by the Civil Partnership Act 2004, s 75(1), (3). Date in force: 5 December 2005: see SI 2005/3175, art 2(1), Sch 1.

Sub-s (1): definition "children's home" substituted by SI 2018/195, regs 8, 12(b). Date in force: 2 April 2018: see SI 2018/195, reg 2(1).

Sub-s (1): definition "clinical commissioning group" inserted by the Health and Social Care Act 2012, s 55(2), Sch 5, paras 47, 56(1), (2)(a). Date in force: 1 April 2013: see SI 2013/160, art 2; for transitional provisions and savings see arts 5–7 thereof.

Sub-s (1): definition "contact activity condition" (omitted) inserted by the Children and Adoption Act 2006, s 15(1), Sch 2, paras 7, 11. Date in force: 8 December 2008: see SI 2008/2870, art 2(2)(e).

Sub-s (1): definition "contact activity condition" (omitted) repealed by the Children and Families Act 2014, s 12(4), Sch 2, Pt 1, paras 1, 38(1), (2)(c). Date in force: 22 April 2014: see SI 2014/889, art 4(b), (f).

Sub-s (1): definition "contact activity direction" (omitted) inserted by the Children and Adoption Act 2006, s 15(1), Sch 2, paras 7, 11. Date in force: 8 December 2008: see SI 2008/2870, art 2(2)(e).

Sub-s (1): definition "contact activity direction" (omitted) repealed by the Children and Families Act 2014, s 12(4), Sch 2, Pt 1, paras 1, 38(1), (2)(c). Date in force: 22 April 2014: see SI 2014/889, art 4(b), (f).

Sub-s (1): definition "contact order" (omitted) repealed by the Children and Families Act 2014, s 12(4), Sch 2, Pt 1, paras 1, 38(1), (2)(c). Date in force: 22 April 2014: see SI 2014/889, art 4(b), (f).

Sub-s (1): in definition "day care" words "(except in Part XA)" in square brackets inserted by the Care Standards Act 2000, s 116, Sch 4, para 14(1), (23)(a)(iv). Date in force (in relation to England): 2 July 2001: see SI 2001/2041, art 2(1)(d)(ii). Date in force (in relation to Wales): 1 April 2002: see SI 2002/920, art 3(3)(d); for transitional provisions see arts 2, 3(2), (4), (6)–(10), Schs 1, 2 thereto.

Sub-s (1): in definition "day care" words "(except in Part XA)" in italics repealed, in relation to Wales, by the Children and Families (Wales) Measure 2010, s 72, Sch 1, paras 5, 7(a)(i). Date in force: 1 April 2011: see SI 2010/2582, art 2, Sch 1; for savings see art 4, Schs 2, 3 thereto.

Sub-s (1): definition "district health authority" (omitted) repealed by the Health Authorities Act 1995, ss 2(1), 5(1), Sch 1, para 118(10)(a), Sch 3.

Sub-s (1): definition "dwelling house" inserted by the Family Law Act 1996, s 52, Sch 6, para 5. Date in force: 1 October 1997: see SI 1997/1892, art 3(1)(a).

Sub-s (1): definition "education functions" inserted by SI 2010/1158, art 5(1), Sch 2, Pt 2, para 37(1), (13)(a). Date in force: 5 May 2010: see SI 2010/1158, art 1.

Sub-s (1): definition "enforcement order" inserted by the Children and Adoption Act 2006, s 15(1), Sch 2, paras 7, 11. Date in force: 8 December 2008: see SI 2008/2870, art 2(2)(e).

Sub-s (1): definition "Health Authority" (omitted) repealed by the National Health Service (Consequential Provisions) Act 2006, s 2, Sch 1, paras 124, 125(a). Date in force: 1 March 2007: see the National Health Service (Consequential Provisions) Act 2006, s 8(2).

Sub-s (1): in definition "health service hospital" words from "means a health" to "National Health Service (Wales) Act 2006" in square brackets substituted by the National Health Service

(Consequential Provisions) Act 2006, s 2, Sch 1, paras 124, 125(b). Date in force: 1 March 2007: see the National Health Service (Consequential Provisions) Act 2006, s 8(2).

Sub-s (1): in definition "hospital" words "(except in Schedule 9A)" in square brackets inserted by the Care Standards Act 2000, s 116, Sch 4, para 14(1), (23)(a)(v). Date in force (in relation to England): 2 July 2001: see SI 2001/2041, art 2(1)(d)(ii). Date in force (in relation to Wales): 1 April 2002: see SI 2002/920, art 3(3)(d); for transitional provisions see arts 2, 3(2), (4), (6)–(10), Schs 1, 2 thereto.

Sub-s (1): in definition "hospital" words "(except in Schedule 9A)" in italics repealed, in relation to Wales, by the Children and Families (Wales) Measure 2010, s 72, Sch 1, paras 5, 7(a)(ii). Date in force: 1 April 2011: see SI 2010/2582, art 2, Sch 1; for savings see art 4, Schs 2, 3 thereto.

Sub-s (1): in definition "hospital" words "special hospital within the meaning of that Act" in italics repealed and subsequent words in square brackets substituted, in relation to England and Wales only, by SI 2000/90, arts 2(1), 3(2), Sch 2, para 5. Date in force: 1 April 2000: see SI 2000/90, art 1.

Sub-s (1): definition "income-based jobseeker's allowance" inserted by the Jobseekers Act 1995, s 41(4), Sch 2, para 19(4).

Sub-s (1): definition "income-based jobseeker's allowance" repealed by the Welfare Reform Act 2012, s 147, Sch 14, Pt 1. Date in force: to be appointed: see the Welfare Reform Act 2012, s 150(3).

Sub-s (1): definition "income-related employment and support allowance" inserted, in relation to England and Wales, by the Welfare Reform Act 2007, s 28(1), Sch 3, para 6(1), (5). Date in force: 27 October 2008: see SI 2008/787, art 2(4)(b), (f).

Sub-s (1): definition "income-related employment and support allowance" repealed by the Welfare Reform Act 2012, s 147, Sch 14, Pt 1. Date in force: to be appointed: see the Welfare Reform Act 2012, s 150(3).

Sub-s (1): definition "independent hospital" (as inserted by the Care Standards Act 2000, s 116, Sch 4, para 14(1), (23)(a)(vi)) substituted by SI 2010/813, art 7(1), (3). Date in force: 1 October 2010: see SI 2010/813, art 1.

Sub-s (1): in definitions "independent school", "registered pupil", "school" and "special educational needs" words "the Education Act 1996" in square brackets substituted by the Education Act 1996, s 582(1), Sch 37, para 91.

Sub-s (1): in definition "local authority" words omitted repealed by the Local Government (Wales) Act 1994, ss 22(4), 66(8), Sch 10, para 13, Sch 18.

Sub-s (1): in definition "local authority" words ", in relation to Wales, the council of a county or a county borough" in square brackets inserted by the Local Government (Wales) Act 1994, ss 22(4), 66(8), Sch 10, para 13.

Sub-s (1): definition "local authority foster parent" substituted by SI 2016/413, regs 55, 106(a). Date in force: 6 April 2016: see SI 2016/413, reg 2(1); for transitional provisions and savings see reg 325, Schedule.

Sub-s (1): definition "local education authority" (omitted) repealed by SI 2010/1158, art 5(1), (2), Sch 2, Pt 2, para 37(1), (13)(b), Sch 3, Pt 2. Date in force: 5 May 2010: see SI 2010/1158, art 1.

Sub-s (1): definition "Local Health Board" inserted by SI 2007/961, art 3, Schedule, para 20(1), (3). Date in force: 1 April 2007: see SI 2007/961, art 1(1).

Sub-s (1): definition "mental nursing home" (omitted) repealed by the Care Standards Act 2000, s 117(2), Sch 6. Date in force (in relation to England): 1 April 2002: see SI 2001/4150, art 3(3)(c)(viii); for transitional provisions see SI 2001/4150, arts 3(2), 4(1)–(3), (5) and SI 2002/1493, art 4 (as amended by SI 2002/1493, art 6). Date in force (in relation to Wales): 1 April 2002: see SI 2002/920, art 3(3)(g)(vi); for transitional provisions see arts 2, 3(2), (5)–(10), Sch 1 thereto.

Sub-s (1): definition "nursing home" (omitted) repealed by the Care Standards Act 2000, s 117(2), Sch 6. Date in force (in relation to England): 1 April 2002: see SI 2001/4150, art 3(3)(c)(viii); for transitional provisions see SI 2001/4150, arts 3(2), 4(1)–(3), (5) and SI 2002/1493, art 4 (as amended by SI 2002/1493, art 6). Date in force (in relation to Wales): 1 April 2002: see SI 2002/920, art 3(3)(g)(vi); for transitional provisions see arts 2, 3(2), (5)–(10), Sch 1 thereto.

Sub-s (1): definition "officer of the Service" inserted by the Criminal Justice and Court Services Act 2000, s 74, Sch 7, Pt II, paras 87, 95. Date in force: 1 April 2001: see SI 2001/919, art 2(f)(ii).

Sub-s (1): in definition "parental responsibility agreement" words "sections 4(1) and 4A(2)" in square brackets substituted by the Adoption and Children Act 2002, s 139(1), Sch 3, paras 54, 70(c). Date in force: 30 December 2005: see SI 2005/2213, art 2(o).

Sub-s (1): in definition "parental responsibility agreement" reference to ", 4ZA(4)" in square brackets inserted by the Human Fertilisation and Embryology Act 2008, s 56, Sch 6, Pt 1, para 31. Date in force (for certain purposes): 6 April 2009: see SI 2009/479, art 6(1)(e). Date in force (for remaining purposes): 1 September 2009: see SI 2009/479, art 6(2).

Sub-s (1): definition "private children's home" inserted by the Care Standards Act 2000, s 116, Sch 4, para 14(1), (23)(a)(vii). Date in force (in relation to England): 1 April 2002: see SI 2001/4150, art 3(3)(a); for transitional provisions see SI 2001/4150, arts 3(2), 4(1), (3), (4) and SI 2002/1493, art 4 (as amended by SI 2002/1493, art 6). Date in force (in relation to Wales): 1 April 2002: see SI 2002/920, art 3(3)(d); for transitional provisions see arts 2, 3(2), (4), (6)–(10), Sch 1 thereto.

Sub-s (1): in definition "private children's home" words from "or Part 1" to "Regulation and Inspection of Social Care (Wales) Act 2016" in square brackets inserted by SI 2018/195, regs 8, 12(c). Date in force: 2 April 2018: see SI 2018/195, reg 2(1).

Sub-s (1): definition "Primary Care Trust" (omitted) inserted, in relation to England and Wales only, by SI 2000/90, arts 2(1), 3(1), Sch 1, para 24(1), (10). Date in force: 8 February 2000: see SI 2000/90, art 1.

Sub-s (1): definition "Primary Care Trust" (omitted) repealed by the Health and Social Care Act 2012, s 55(2), Sch 5, paras 47, 56(1), (2)(b). Date in force: 1 April 2013: see SI 2013/160, art 2; for transitional provisions and savings see arts 5–7 thereof.

Sub-s (1): definition "protected child" (omitted) repealed by the Adoption and Children Act 2002, s 139(1), (3), Sch 3, paras 54, 70(d), Sch 5. Date in force: 30 December 2005: see SI 2005/2213, art 2(o).

Sub-s (1): definition "registered children's home" (omitted) repealed by the Care Standards Act 2000, s 117(2), Sch 6. Date in force (in relation to England): 1 April 2002: see SI 2001/4150, art 3(3)(c)(viii); for transitional provisions see SI 2001/4150, arts 3(2), 4(1)–(3), (5) and SI 2002/1493, art 4 (as amended by SI 2002/1493, art 6). Date in force (in relation to Wales): 1 April 2002: see SI 2002/920, art 3(3)(g)(vi); for transitional provisions see arts 2, 3(2), (5)–(10), Schs 1, 3 thereto.

Sub-s (1): in definition "relative" words "by marriage or civil partnership)" in square brackets substituted by the Civil Partnership Act 2004, s 75(1), (4). Date in force: 5 December 2005: see SI 2005/3175, art 2(1), Sch 1.

Sub-s (1): definition "residence order" (omitted) repealed by the Children and Families Act 2014, s 12(4), Sch 2, Pt 1, paras 1, 38(1), (2)(c). Date in force: 22 April 2014: see SI 2014/889, art 4(b), (f).

Sub-s (1): definition "residential care home" (omitted) repealed by the Care Standards Act 2000, s 117(2), Sch 6. Date in force (in relation to England): 1 April 2002: see SI 2001/4150, art 3(3)(c)(viii); for transitional provisions see SI 2001/4150, arts 3(2), 4(1)–(3), (5) and SI 2002/1493, art 4 (as amended by SI 2002/1493, art 6). Date in force (in relation to Wales): 1 April 2002: see SI 2002/920, art 3(3)(g)(vi); for transitional provisions see arts 2, 3(2), (5)–(10), Sch 1 thereto.

Sub-s (1): definition "section 31A plan" inserted by the Adoption and Children Act 2002, s 139(1), Sch 3, paras 54, 70(b). Date in force: 30 December 2005: see SI 2005/2213, art 2(o).

Sub-s (1): definition "special guardian" and "special guardianship order" inserted by the Adoption and Children Act 2002, s 139(1), Sch 3, paras 54, 70(e). Date in force: 30 December 2005: see SI 2005/2213, art 2(o).

Sub-s (1): definition "Special Health Authority" substituted by the Health Authorities Act 1995, ss 2(1), 5(1), Sch 1, para 118(10)(c).

Sub-s (1): in definition "Special Health Authority" words from "section 28 of" to "National Health Service (Wales) Act 2006," in square brackets substituted by the National Health Service (Consequential Provisions) Act 2006, s 2, Sch 1, paras 124, 125(d). Date in force: 1 March 2007: see the National Health Service (Consequential Provisions) Act 2006, s 8(2).

Sub-s (1): definition "Strategic Health Authority" (omitted) inserted by SI 2002/2469, reg 4, Sch 1, Pt 1, para 16(1), (3). Date in force: 1 October 2002: see SI 2002/2469, reg 1.

Sub-s (1): definition "Strategic Health Authority" (omitted) repealed by the Health and Social Care Act 2012, s 55(2), Sch 5, paras 47, 56(1), (2)(c). Date in force: 1 April 2013: see SI 2013/160, art 2; for transitional provisions and savings see arts 5–7 thereof.

Sub-s (1): definition "Welsh family proceedings officer" inserted by the Children Act 2004, s 40, Sch 3, paras 5, 11. Date in force: 1 April 2005: by virtue of SI 2005/700, art 2(2).

Sub-s (3): repealed by the Children and Families Act 2014, s 12(4), Sch 2, Pt 1, paras 1, 38(1), (3). Date in force: 22 April 2014: see SI 2014/889, art 4(b), (f).

Sub-s (4): substituted by SI 2016/413, regs 55, 106(b). Date in force: 6 April 2016: see SI 2016/413, reg 2(1); for transitional provisions and savings see reg 325, Schedule.

Sub-s (5): words from "of that or any other" to "within the meaning of" in square brackets substituted by the Local Government Act 2000, s 107, Sch 5, para 22. Date in force (in relation to England): 26 October 2000: see SI 2000/2849, art 2(f). Date in force (in relation to Wales): 28 July 2001 (unless the National Assembly for Wales by order provides for this amendment to come into force before that date): see the Local Government Act 2000, s 108(4), (6)(b).

Sub-s (5): words omitted repealed by SI 2016/413, regs 55, 106(c). Date in force: 6 April 2016: see SI 2016/413, reg 2(1); for transitional provisions and savings see reg 325, Schedule.

Sub-s (5A): inserted by the Care Standards Act 2000, s 116, Sch 4, para 14(1), (23)(b). Date in force (in relation to England): 2 July 2001: see SI 2001/2041, art 2(1)(d)(ii). Date in force (in relation to Wales): 1 April 2002: see SI 2002/920, art 3(3)(d); for transitional provisions see arts 2, 3(2), (4), (6)–(10), Schs 1, 2 thereto.

Sub-s (5A): repealed, in relation to Wales, by the Children and Families (Wales) Measure 2010, ss 72, 73, Sch 1, paras 5, 7(b), Sch 2. Date in force: 1 April 2011: see SI 2010/2582, arts 2, 4, Schs 1, 2; for savings see art 4, Sch 2 thereto.

Sub-s (5A): para (a) repealed, in relation to Scotland, by the Regulation of Care (Scotland) Act 2001, s 79, Sch 3, paras 15(1), (2)(a). Date in force: 1 April 2002: see the Regulation of Care (Scotland) Act 2001, s 81(2) and SSI 2002/162, arts 1(2), 2(f), (h); for transitional provisions see SSI 2002/162, arts 3, 4(6), (9), (10), 7, 8(c), 12, 13.

Sub-s (5A): in para (b) words omitted repealed by the Childcare Act 2006, s 103, Sch 2, para 17, Sch 3, Pt 2. Date in force: 1 September 2008: see SI 2008/2261, art 2; for transitional provisions and savings see arts 3, 4, Schs 1, 2 thereto.

Sub-s (5B): inserted in relation to England and Wales by SI 2016/413, reg 106(d); a corresponding amendment has been made in relation to Scotland by the Regulation of Care (Scotland) Act 2001, s 79, Sch 3, paras 15(1), (2)(b). Date in force (in relation to Scotland): 1 April 2002: see the Regulation of Care (Scotland) Act 2001, s 81(2) and SSI 2002/162, arts 1(2), 2(f), (h); for transitional provisions see SSI 2002/162, arts 3, 4(6), (9), (10), 7, 8(c), 12, 13. Date in force (in relation to England and Wales): 6 April 2016: see SI 2016/413, reg 2(1).

Sub-s (6): in para (b) words omitted repealed by the Criminal Justice and Immigration Act 2008, ss 6(2), 149, Sch 4, Pt 1, paras 33, 36(a), Sch 28, Pt 1. Date in force: 30 November 2009: see SI 2009/3074, art 2(f), (k), (l), (p)(v), (t)(i), (u)(xi); for transitional provisions and savings see the Criminal Justice and Immigration Act 2008, s 148(2), Sch 27, Pt 1, paras 1(1), 5.

Sub-s (6): para (ba) inserted by the Criminal Justice and Immigration Act 2008, s 6(2), Sch 4, Pt 1, paras 33, 36(b). Date in force: 30 November 2009: see SI 2009/3074, art 2(f), (k), (p)(v), (t)(i); for transitional provisions and savings see the Criminal Justice and Immigration Act 2008, s 148(2), Sch 27, Pt 1, paras 1(1), 5.

Sub-ss (7A), (7B): inserted by the Health and Social Care Act 2012, s 55(2), Sch 5, paras 47, 55(1), (3). Date in force: 1 April 2013: see SI 2013/160, art 2; for transitional provisions and savings see arts 5–7 thereof.

COURTS AND LEGAL SERVICES ACT 1990

(1990, c 41)

[1 November 1990]

PART II
LEGAL SERVICES

Licensed conveyancers

A1.469

53 The Council for Licensed Conveyancers

[(1) The Council for Licensed Conveyancers has the powers necessary to enable it to become designated as an approved regulator in relation to one or more of the reserved legal activities within subsection (1A).

(1A) The reserved legal activities to which this subsection applies are—

(a) the exercise of a right of audience;

(b) the conduct of litigation;

(c) probate activities.

(2) If the Council becomes an approved regulator in relation to one or more of those activities, it may, in that capacity, authorise a person to carry on a relevant activity . . . .

(3) Where the Council authorises [a person] to carry on a relevant activity, it is to do so by issuing a licence to [the person in respect of that activity].]

(4) [If the person granted a licence under this section is a licensed conveyancer, the] licence may be granted as a separate licence or as part of a composite licence comprising the licensed conveyancer's licence issued under Part II of the Administration of Justice Act 1985 and any other licence which the Council may grant to the licensed conveyancer concerned.

[(4A) If the person granted a licence under this section is not a licensed conveyancer, the licence may be granted as a separate licence or as part of a composite licence comprising that and any other licence under this section which the Council may grant to the person.

(4B) A licence under this section granted to a person who is not a licensed conveyancer ceases to have effect if the person becomes a licensed conveyancer.]

(5) . . .

[(6) Where the Council exercises any of its powers in connection with—

(a) an application for designation as an approved regulator in relation to a reserved legal activity within subsection (1A), or

(b) the authorising of a person to carry on a relevant activity,

it is to do so subject to any requirements to which it is subject in accordance with the provisions of the Legal Services Act 2007.]

(7) Schedule 8 makes further provision in connection with the powers given to the Council by this section and the provision made by the Act of 1985 in relation to licensed conveyancers, including amendments of Part II of that Act.

(8) The [Lord Chancellor] may by order make such—

(a) amendments of, or modifications to, the provisions of Part II of the Act of 1985; or

(b) transitional or consequential provision,

as he considers necessary or expedient in connection with the provision made by this section and Schedule 8.

(9) Subject to any provision made by this section, Schedule 8 or any order made by the [Lord Chancellor] under subsection (8), the provisions of Part II of the Act of 1985 shall, with the necessary modifications, apply with respect to [persons who apply for, or hold, an advocacy, litigation or probate licence and]—

- (a) any application for an advocacy, litigation or probate licence;
- (b) any such licence;
- (c) the practice of any [person] which is carried on by virtue of any such licence;
- (d) rules made by the Council under Schedule 8;
- [(da) any case of an individual who describes himself or herself, or holds himself or herself out, as a licensed CLC practitioner without holding a licence in force under this section;]
- (e) . . .
- (f) any other matter dealt with by this section or Schedule 8,

as they apply with respect to [persons who apply for, or hold, a licence under Part 2 of the Act of 1985 and] the corresponding matters dealt with by Part II of that Act.

[(9A) The modifications mentioned in subsection (9) may differ depending on whether the person applying for, or holding, an advocacy, litigation or probate licence is or is not a licensed conveyancer.

(9B) Subsection (9) does not apply to section 34 of the Act of 1985 (modification of existing enactments relating to conveyancing etc).]

[(10) For the purposes of this section—

- (a) "right of audience", "conduct of litigation", "probate activities" and "reserved legal activity" have the same meaning as in the Legal Services Act 2007;
- (b) references to designation as an approved regulator are to designation as an approved regulator—
  - (i) by Part 1 of Schedule 4 to the Legal Services Act 2007, by virtue of an order under paragraph 5 of Schedule 22 to that Act, or
  - (ii) under Part 2 of Schedule 4 to that Act;
- (c) "relevant activity" means an activity which is a reserved legal activity—
  - (i) which is within subsection (1A), and
  - (ii) in relation to which the Council is designated as an approved regulator by Part 1 of Schedule 4 to that Act (by virtue of an order under paragraph 5 of Schedule 22 to that Act) or under Part 2 of that Schedule.]

[(11) In this section—

"advocacy licence" means a licence issued under this section by which the Council authorises the person concerned to exercise a right of audience;

"CLC practitioner services" has the same meaning as in section 32B of the Act of 1985;

"licensed CLC practitioner" means a person, other than a licensed conveyancer, who holds a licence under this section;

"litigation licence" means a licence issued under this section by which the Council authorises the person concerned to carry on activities which constitute the conduct of litigation;

"the practice of a licensed CLC practitioner" means the provision by a person, as the holder of a licence under this section, of CLC practitioner services in accordance with the licence; and

"probate licence" means a licence issued under this section by which the Council authorises the person concerned to carry on activities that constitute probate activities.]

Sub-ss (1), (1A), (2), (3): substituted, for sub-ss (1)–(3) as originally enacted, by the Legal Services Act 2007, s 182, Sch 17, Pt 2, paras 33, 34(1), (2). Date in force: 1 January 2010: see SI 2009/3250, art 2(f)(iii).

Sub-s (2): words omitted repealed by the Deregulation Act 2015, s 87(1), (2). Date in force: 29 June 2015: see SI 2015/1402, art 2(a).

Sub-s (3): words "a person" in square brackets substituted by the Deregulation Act 2015, s 87(1), (3)(a). Date in force: 29 June 2015: see SI 2015/1402, art 2(a).

Sub-s (3): words "the person in respect of that activity" in square brackets substituted by the Deregulation Act 2015, s 87(1), (3)(b). Date in force: 29 June 2015: see SI 2015/1402, art 2(a).

Sub-s (4): words from "If the person" to "licensed conveyancer, the" in square brackets substituted by the Deregulation Act 2015, s 87(1), (4). Date in force: 29 June 2015: see SI 2015/1402, art 2(a).

Sub-ss (4A), (4B): inserted by the Deregulation Act 2015, s 87(1), (5). Date in force: 29 June 2015: see SI 2015/1402, art 2(a).

Sub-s (5): repealed by the Legal Services Act 2007, ss 182, 210, Sch 17, Pt 2, paras 33, 34(1), (3), Sch 23. Date in force: 1 January 2010: see SI 2009/3250, art 2(f)(iii).

Sub-s (6): substituted by the Legal Services Act 2007, s 182, Sch 17, Pt 2, paras 33, 34(1), (4). Date in force: 1 January 2010: see SI 2009/3250, art 2(f)(iii).

Sub-s (8): words "Lord Chancellor" in square brackets substituted by the Legal Services Act 2007, s 182, Sch 17, Pt 2, paras 33, 34(1), (5). Date in force: 31 March 2009: see SI 2009/503, art 2(c)(ii).

Sub-s (9): words "Lord Chancellor" in square brackets substituted by the Legal Services Act 2007, s 182, Sch 17, Pt 2, paras 33, 34(1), (6)(a). Date in force: 31 March 2009: see SI 2009/503, art 2(c)(ii).

Sub-s (9): words from "persons who apply" to "probate licence and" in square brackets inserted by the Deregulation Act 2015, s 87(1), (6)(a). Date in force: 29 June 2015: see SI 2015/1402, art 2(a).

Sub-s (9): in para (c) word "person" in square brackets substituted by the Deregulation Act 2015, s 87(1), (6)(b). Date in force: 29 June 2015: see SI 2015/1402, art 2(a).

Sub-s (9): para (da) inserted by the Deregulation Act 2015, s 87(1), (6)(c). Date in force: 29 June 2015: see SI 2015/1402, art 2(a).

Sub-s (9): para (e) repealed by the Legal Services Act 2007, ss 182, 210, Sch 17, Pt 2, paras 33, 34(1), (6)(b), Sch 23. Date in force: 31 March 2009: see SI 2009/503, art 2(c)(ii).

Sub-s (9): words from "persons who apply" to "of 1985 and" in square brackets inserted by the Deregulation Act 2015, s 87(1), (6)(d). Date in force: 29 June 2015: see SI 2015/1402, art 2(a).

Sub-ss (9A), (9B): inserted by the Deregulation Act 2015, s 87(1), (7). Date in force: 29 June 2015: see SI 2015/1402, art 2(a).

Sub-s (10): inserted by the Legal Services Act 2007, s 182, Sch 17, Pt 2, paras 33, 34(1), (7). Date in force: 1 January 2010: see SI 2009/3250, art 2(f)(iii).

Sub-s (11): inserted by the Deregulation Act 2015, s 87(1), (8). Date in force: 29 June 2015: see SI 2015/1402, art 2(a).

ADOPTION AND CHILDREN ACT 2002

(2002, c 38)

[7th November 2002]

PART 1
ADOPTION

CHAPTER 1

INTRODUCTORY

A1.498

1 Considerations applying to the exercise of powers

(1) [Subsections (2) to (4) apply] whenever a court or adoption agency is coming to a decision relating to the adoption of a child.

(2) The paramount consideration of the court or adoption agency must be the child's welfare, throughout his life.

(3) The court or adoption agency must at all times bear in mind that, in general, any delay in coming to the decision is likely to prejudice the child's welfare.

(4) The court or adoption agency must have regard to the following matters (among others)—

- (a) the child's ascertainable wishes and feelings regarding the decision (considered in the light of the child's age and understanding),
- (b) the child's particular needs,
- (c) the likely effect on the child (throughout his life) of having ceased to be a member of the original family and become an adopted person,
- (d) the child's age, sex, background and any of the child's characteristics which the court or agency considers relevant,
- (e) any harm (within the meaning of the Children Act 1989 (c 41)) which the child has suffered or is at risk of suffering,
- (f) the relationship which the child has with relatives, [with any person who is a prospective adopter with whom the child is placed,] and with any other person in relation to whom the court or agency considers the relationship to be relevant, including—
  - (i) the likelihood of any such relationship continuing and the value to the child of its doing so,
  - (ii) the ability and willingness of any of the child's relatives, or of any such person, to provide the child with a secure environment in which the child can develop, and otherwise to meet the child's needs,
  - (iii) the wishes and feelings of any of the child's relatives, or of any such person, regarding the child.

(5) [In placing a child for adoption, an adoption agency in Wales] must give due consideration to the child's religious persuasion, racial origin and cultural and linguistic background.

(6) [In coming to a decision relating to the adoption of a child, a court or adoption agency] must always consider the whole range of powers available to it in the child's case (whether under this Act or the Children Act 1989); and the court must not make any order under this Act unless it considers that making the order would be better for the child than not doing so.

(7) In this section, "coming to a decision relating to the adoption of a child", in relation to a court, includes—

- (a) coming to a decision in any proceedings where the orders that might be made by the court include an adoption order (or the revocation of such an order), a placement order (or the revocation of such an order) or an order under section 26 [or 51A] (or the revocation or variation of such an order),

(b) coming to a decision about granting leave in respect of any action (other than the initiation of proceedings in any court) which may be taken by an adoption agency or individual under this Act,

but does not include coming to a decision about granting leave in any other circumstances.

(8) For the purposes of this section—

(a) references to relationships are not confined to legal relationships,

(b) references to a relative, in relation to a child, include the child's mother and father.

[(9) In this section "adoption agency in Wales" means an adoption agency that is—

(a) a local authority in Wales, or

(b) a registered adoption society whose principal office is in Wales.]

Sub-s (1): words "Subsections (2) to (4) apply" in square brackets substituted by the Children and Families Act 2014, s 3(1), (3)(a). Date in force: 25 July 2014: see SI 2014/889, art 6(b).

Sub-s (4): in para (f) words from "with any person" to "child is placed," in square brackets inserted by the Children and Social Work Act 2017, s 9. Date in force: 31 October 2017: see SI 2017/918, reg 2(b).

Sub-s (5): words "In placing a child for adoption, an adoption agency in Wales" in square brackets substituted by the Children and Families Act 2014, s 3(1), (2). Date in force: 25 July 2014: see SI 2014/889, art 6(b).

Sub-s (6): words "In coming to a decision relating to the adoption of a child, a court or adoption agency" in square brackets substituted by the Children and Families Act 2014, s 3(1), (3)(b). Date in force: 25 July 2014: see SI 2014/889, art 6(b).

Sub-s (7): in para (a) words "or 51A" in square brackets inserted by the Children and Families Act 2014, s 9(2). Date in force: 22 April 2014: see SI 2014/889, art 4(a).

Sub-s (9): inserted by the Children and Families Act 2014, s 3(1), (3)(c). Date in force: 25 July 2014: see SI 2014/889, art 6(b).

See further, the application of this section, with modifications, in relation to an external adoption order effected within the period of six months of the making of the adoption, and in respect of adoptions under the 1993 Hague Convention on Protection of Children and Co-operation in respect of Intercountry Adoption: the Adoptions with a Foreign Element Regulations 2005, SI 2005/392, regs 11(1)(a), 52, 55.

See further, in relation to the application of this section, with modifications, to the arrangements by which a parental order may be obtained under the Human Fertilisation and Embryology Act 2008, s 54: the Human Fertilisation and Embryology (Parental Orders) Regulations 2010, SI 2010/985, reg 2, Sch 1.

CHAPTER 3

Placement for Adoption and Adoption Orders

Placement and adoption: general

A1.508

53 Modification of 1989 Act [and 2014 Act] in relation to adoption

(1) Where—

(a) a local authority are authorised to place a child for adoption, or

(b) a child who has been placed for adoption by a local authority is less than six weeks old,

regulations may provide for the following provisions . . . to apply with modifications, or not to apply, in relation to the child.

[(2) The provisions are—

(a) section 22(4)(b), (c) and (d) and (5)(b) of the 1989 Act (duty to ascertain wishes and feelings of certain persons);

(b) sections 6(4)(b) and 78(3)(a) of the 2014 Act (duty to ascertain wishes and feelings of certain persons);

(c) paragraphs 15 and 21 of Schedule 2 to the 1989 Act (promoting contact with parents and parents' obligations to contribute towards maintenance);

(d) section 95 of and paragraph 1 of Schedule 1 to the 2014 Act (promoting contact with parents and parents' obligations to contribute towards maintenance).]

(3) Where a registered adoption society is authorised to place a child for adoption or a child who has been placed for adoption by a registered adoption society is less than six weeks old, regulations may provide—

(a) for section 61 of [the 1989 Act] to have effect in relation to the child whether or not he is accommodated by or on behalf of the society,

(b) for subsections (2)(b) to (d) and (3)(b) of that section (duty to ascertain wishes and feelings of certain persons) to apply with modifications, or not to apply, in relation to the child.

(4) Where a child's home is with persons who have given notice of intention to adopt, no contribution is payable (whether under a contribution order or otherwise) under Part 3 of Schedule 2 to [the 1989 Act (contributions towards maintenance of children looked after by local authorities) or under Schedule 1 to the 2014 Act (contributions towards maintenance of looked after children)] in respect of the period referred to in subsection (5).

(5) That period begins when the notice of intention to adopt is given and ends if—

(a) the period of four months beginning with the giving of the notice expires without the prospective adopters applying for an adoption order, or

(b) an application for such an order is withdrawn or refused.

(6) In this section, "notice of intention to adopt" includes notice of intention to apply for a Scottish or Northern Irish adoption order.

Section heading: words "and 2014 Act" in square brackets inserted by SI 2016/413, regs 188, 197(e). Date in force: 6 April 2016: see SI 2016/413, reg 2(1); for transitional provisions and savings see reg 325, Schedule.

Sub-s (1): words omitted repealed by SI 2016/413, regs 188, 197(a). Date in force: 6 April 2016: see SI 2016/413, reg 2(1); for transitional provisions and savings see reg 325, Schedule.

Sub-s (2): substituted by SI 2016/413, regs 188, 197(b). Date in force: 6 April 2016: see SI 2016/413, reg 2(1); for transitional provisions and savings see reg 325, Schedule.

Sub-s (3): in para (a) words "the 1989 Act" in square brackets substituted by SI 2016/413, regs 188, 197(c). Date in force: 6 April 2016: see SI 2016/413, reg 2(1); for transitional provisions and savings see reg 325, Schedule.

Sub-s (4): words from "the 1989 Act" to "looked after children)" in square brackets substituted by SI 2016/413, regs 188, 197(d). Date in force: 6 April 2016: see SI 2016/413, reg 2(1); for transitional provisions and savings see reg 325, Schedule.

See further, the application of this section, with modifications, in relation to an external adoption order effected within the period of six months of the making of the adoption, and in respect of adoptions under the 1993 Hague Convention on Protection of Children and Co-operation in respect of Intercountry Adoption: the Adoptions with a Foreign Element Regulations 2005, SI 2005/392, regs 11(1)(q), 52, 55.

A1.537

SCHEDULE 6
GLOSSARY

Section 147

In this Act, the expressions listed in the left-hand column below have the meaning given by, or are to be interpreted in accordance with, the provisions of this Act or (where stated) of the 1989 Act [or the 2014 Act] listed in the right-hand column.

Expression	*Provision*
the 1989 Act	section 2(5)
[the 2014 Act	section 2(5)]
Adopted Children Register	section 77
Adoption and Children Act Register	section 125
adoption (in relation to Chapter 4 of Part 1)	section 66
adoption agency	section 2(1)
adoption agency placing a child for adoption	section 18(5)
Adoption Contact Register	section 80
adoption order	section 46(1)
Adoption Service	section 2(1)
adoption society	section 2(5)
adoption support agency	section 8
adoption support services	section 2(6)
appointed day (in relation to Chapter 4 of Part 1)	section 66(2)
appropriate Minister	section 144
Assembly	section 144
body	section 144
by virtue of	section 144
care order	section 105(1) of the 1989 Act
child	sections 49(5) and 144
[child arrangements order	section 8(1) of the 1989 Act]
child assessment order	section 43(2) of the 1989 Act
child in the care of a local authority	section 105(1) of the 1989 Act
[child looked after by a local authority (in relation to a local authority in England)	section 22 of the 1989 Act
child looked after by a local authority (in relation to a local authority in Wales)	section 74 of the 2014 Act]
child placed for adoption by an adoption agency	section 18(5)
child to be adopted, adopted child	section 49(5)
consent (in relation to making adoption orders or placing for adoption)	section 52
the Convention	section 144
Convention adoption	section 66(1)(c)
Convention adoption order	section 144
Convention country	section 144
couple	section 144(4)
court	section 144
disposition (in relation to Chapter 4 of Part 1)	section 73
enactment	section 144
fee	section 144
guardian	section 144

Expression	*Provision*
information	section 144
interim care order	section 38 of the 1989 Act
local authority	section 144
[local authority foster parent	section 105(1) of the 1989 Act]
Northern Irish adoption agency	section 144
Northern Irish adoption order	section 144
notice	section 144
notice of intention to adopt	section 44(2)
overseas adoption	section 87
parental responsibility	section 3 of the 1989 Act
partner, in relation to a parent of a child	section 144(7)
placement order	section 21
placing, or placed, for adoption	sections 18(5) and 19(4)
prohibited steps order	section 8(1) of the 1989 Act
records (in relation to Chapter 5 of Part 1)	section 82
registered adoption society	section 2(2)
registers of live-births (in relation to Chapter 5 of Part 1)	section 82
registration authority (in Part 1)	section 144
regulations	section 144
relative	section 144, read with section 1(8)
. . .	. . .
rules	section 144
Scottish adoption agency	section 144(3)
Scottish adoption order	section 144
specific issue order	section 8(1) of the 1989 Act
subordinate legislation	section 144
supervision order	section 31(11) of the 1989 Act
unitary authority	section 144
voluntary organisation	section 2(5)

Words "or the 2014 Act" in square brackets inserted by SI 2016/413, regs 188, 198(a). Date in force: 6 April 2016: see SI 2016/413, reg 2(1); for transitional provisions and savings see reg 325, Schedule.

Entry "the 2014 Act" inserted by SI 2016/413, regs 188, 198(b). Date in force: 6 April 2016: see SI 2016/413, reg 2(1); for transitional provisions and savings see reg 325, Schedule.

Entry "child arrangements order" inserted by the Children and Families Act 2014, s 12(4), Sch 2, Pt 2, paras 59, 65(1), (2). Date in force: 22 April 2014: see SI 2014/889, art 4(b), (f).

Entries "child looked after by a local authority (in relation to a local authority in England)" and "child looked after by a local authority (in relation to a local authority in Wales)" substituted, for definition "child looked after by a local authority" as originally enacted, by SI 2016/413, regs 188, 198(c). Date in force: 6 April 2016: see SI 2016/413, reg 2(1); for transitional provisions and savings see reg 325, Schedule.

Entry "local authority foster parent" substituted by SI 2016/413, regs 188, 198(d). Date in force: 6 April 2016: see SI 2016/413, reg 2(1); for transitional provisions and savings see reg 325, Schedule.

In entry relating to "local authority foster parent" reference to "23(3)" in italics repealed and subsequent reference in square brackets substituted by the Children and Young Persons Act 2008, s 8(2), Sch 1, para 14. Date in force (in relation to England): 1 April 2011: see SI 2010/2981, art 4(a). Date in force (in relation to Wales): to be appointed: see the Children and Young Persons Act 2008, s 44(3), (4), (5)(a).

Entry "residence order" (omitted) repealed by the Children and Families Act 2014, s 12(4), Sch 2, Pt 2, paras 59, 65(1), (3). Date in force: 22 April 2014: see SI 2014/889, art 4(b), (f).

GENDER RECOGNITION ACT 2004

(2004, CHAPTER 7)

[1st July 2004]

Supplementary

A1.581

25 Interpretation

[(1)] In this Act—

"the acquired gender" is to be construed in accordance with section 1(2),

"approved country or territory" has the meaning given by section 2(4),

"the appointed day" means the day appointed by order under section 26,

. . .

"enactment" includes an enactment contained in an Act of the Scottish Parliament or in any Northern Ireland legislation,

"full gender recognition certificate" and "interim gender recognition certificate" mean the certificates issued as such under section 4[, *5 or 5A*] [4C, 4E, 4F, 5, 5A or 5D] and "gender recognition certificate" means either of those sorts of certificate,

"gender dysphoria" means the disorder variously referred to as gender dysphoria, gender identity disorder and transsexualism,

"Gender Recognition Panel" (and "Panel") is to be construed in accordance with Schedule 1,

["protected civil partnership" means a civil partnership under the law of England and Wales;

"protected marriage" means—

(a) a marriage under the law of England and Wales, or

(b) a marriage under the law of a country or territory outside the United Kingdom,]

["protected Scottish civil partnership" means a civil partnership registered in Scotland,]

["protected Scottish marriage" means a marriage solemnised in Scotland,]

["registered psychologist" means a person registered in the part of the register maintained under [*the Health and Social Work Professions Order 2001*] [the Health Professions Order 2001] which relates to practitioner psychologists,]

["statutory declaration of consent" has the meaning given by section 3(6B)(a),]

"subordinate legislation" means an Order in Council, an order, rules, regulations, a scheme, a warrant, bye-laws or any other instrument made under an enactment, and

"UK birth register entry" has the meaning given by section 10(2).

[(2) A civil partnership which was registered outside the United Kingdom under an Order in Council made under Chapter 1 of Part 5 of the Civil Partnership Act 2004 is to be treated for the purposes of this Act as having been registered in Scotland if—

(a) the parties to the civil partnership elected Scotland as the relevant part of the United Kingdom under the Order, and

(b) details of the civil partnership have been sent to the Registrar General for Scotland.

(3) A marriage which was registered outside the United Kingdom under the Foreign Marriage Act 1892 (other than a marriage registered by virtue of section 18 of that Act) is to be treated for the purposes of this Act as having been solemnised in Scotland if details of the marriage have been sent to the Registrar General for Scotland.

(4) A marriage which was solemnised outside the United Kingdom and registered under an Order in Council made under the Registration of Births, Deaths and Marriages (Special Provisions) Act 1957 is to be treated for the purposes of this Act as having been solemnised in Scotland if details of the marriage have been sent to the Registrar General for Scotland.

(5) A consular marriage in relation to which the relevant part of the United Kingdom is Scotland is to be treated for the purposes of this Act as having been solemnised in Scotland.

(6) In subsection (5)—

"consular marriage" means a marriage solemnised in accordance with Part 1 of Schedule 6 to the Marriage (Same Sex Couples) Act 2013 and any Order in Council made under it,

"relevant part of the United Kingdom", in relation to such a marriage, means the part of the United Kingdom determined in accordance with paragraph 1(2)(b) of that Part of that Schedule for the purposes of the marriage.]

Sub-s (1): numbered as such by the Marriage and Civil Partnership (Scotland) Act 2014, s 29, Sch 2, Pt 1, paras 1, 2(a). Date in force: 16 December 2014: see SSI 2014/287, art 3, Schedule.

Sub-s (1): definition "chartered psychologist" (omitted) repealed by SI 2009/1182, art 4(2), Sch 5, Pt 1, para 8(b). Date in force: 1 July 2009: see SI 2009/1357, art 2(1)(d).

Sub-s (1): in definition ""full gender recognition certificate" and "interim gender recognition certificate"" words ", 5 or 5A" in square brackets substituted by the Civil Partnership Act 2004, s 250(1), (7). Date in force: 5 December 2005: see SI 2005/3175, art 3, Sch 2.

Sub-s (1): in definitions ""full gender recognition certificate" and "interim gender recognition certificate"" words "5 or 5A" in italics repealed and subsequent words in square brackets substituted by the Marriage and Civil Partnership (Scotland) Act 2014, s 29, Sch 2, Pt 1, paras 1, 2(b). Date in force: 16 December 2014: see SSI 2014/287, art 3, Schedule.

Sub-s (1): definitions "protected civil partnership" and "protected marriage" inserted by the Marriage (Same Sex Couples) Act 2013, s 12, Sch 5, Pt 1, paras 1, 14(a). Date in force: to be appointed: see the Marriage (Same Sex Couples) Act 2013, s 21(3).

Sub-s (1): definition "protected Scottish civil partnership" inserted by the Marriage and Civil Partnership (Scotland) Act 2014, s 29, Sch 2, Pt 1, paras 1, 2(c). Date in force: 16 December 2014: see SSI 2014/287, art 3, Schedule.

Sub-s (1): definition "protected Scottish marriage" inserted by the Marriage and Civil Partnership (Scotland) Act 2014, s 29, Sch 2, Pt 1, paras 1, 2(c). Date in force: 16 December 2014: see SSI 2014/287, art 3, Schedule.

Sub-s (1): definition "registered psychologist" inserted by SI 2009/1182, art 4(2), Sch 5, Pt 1, para 8(b). Date in force: 1 July 2009: see SI 2009/1357, art 2(1)(d).

Sub-s (1): in definition "registered psychologist" words "the Health and Social Work Professions Order 2001" in square brackets substituted by the Health and Social Care Act 2012, s 213(8)(d). Date in force: 1 August 2012: see SI 2012/1319, art 2(1), (4).

Sub-s (1): in definition "registered psychologist" words "the Health and Social Work Professions Order 2001" in italics repealed and subsequent words in square brackets substituted by the Children and Social Work Act 2017, s 62, Sch 5, Pt 2, para 48(d). Date in force: to be appointed: see the Children and Social Work Act 2017, s 70(2).

Sub-s (1): definition "statutory declaration of consent" inserted by the Marriage (Same Sex Couples) Act 2013, s 12, Sch 5, Pt 1, paras 1, 14(b). Date in force: to be appointed: see the Marriage (Same Sex Couples) Act 2013, s 21(3).

Sub-ss (2)–(6): inserted by the Marriage and Civil Partnership (Scotland) Act 2014, s 29, Sch 2, Pt 1, paras 1, 2(d). Date in force: 16 December 2014: see SSI 2014/287, art 3, Schedule.

MENTAL CAPACITY ACT 2005

(2005, CHAPTER 9)

[7th April 2005]

PART 1
PERSONS WHO LACK CAPACITY

Lasting powers of attorney

A1.621

13 Revocation of lasting powers of attorney etc

(1) This section applies if—

(a) P has executed an instrument with a view to creating a lasting power of attorney, or

(b) a lasting power of attorney is registered as having been conferred by P,

and in this section references to revoking the power include revoking the instrument.

(2) P may, at any time when he has capacity to do so, revoke the power.

(3) P's bankruptcy[, or the making of a debt relief order (under Part 7A of the Insolvency Act 1986) in respect of P,] revokes the power so far as it relates to P's property and affairs.

(4) But where P is bankrupt merely because an interim bankruptcy restrictions order has effect in respect of him [or where P is subject to an interim debt relief restrictions order (under Schedule 4ZB of the Insolvency Act 1986)], the power is suspended, so far as it relates to P's property and affairs, for so long as the order has effect.

(5) The occurrence in relation to a donee of an event mentioned in subsection (6)—

(a) terminates his appointment, and

(b) except in the cases given in subsection (7), revokes the power.

(6) The events are—

(a) the disclaimer of the appointment by the donee in accordance with such requirements as may be prescribed for the purposes of this section in regulations made by the Lord Chancellor,

(b) subject to subsections (8) and (9), the death or bankruptcy of the donee [or the making of a debt relief order (under Part 7A of the Insolvency Act 1986) in respect of the donee] or, if the donee is a trust corporation, its winding-up or dissolution,

(c) subject to subsection (11), the dissolution or annulment of a marriage or civil partnership between the donor and the donee,

(d) the lack of capacity of the donee.

(7) The cases are—

(a) the donee is replaced under the terms of the instrument,

(b) he is one of two or more persons appointed to act as donees jointly and severally in respect of any matter and, after the event, there is at least one remaining donee.

(8) The bankruptcy of a donee [or the making of a debt relief order (under Part 7A of the Insolvency Act 1986) in respect of a donee] does not terminate his appointment, or revoke the power, in so far as his authority relates to P's personal welfare.

(9) Where the donee is bankrupt merely because an interim bankruptcy restrictions order has effect in respect of him, [or where the donee is subject to an interim debt relief restrictions order (under Schedule 4ZB of the Insolvency Act 1986),] his appointment and the power are suspended, so far as they relate to P's property and affairs, for so long as the order has effect.

(10) Where the donee is one of two or more appointed to act jointly and severally under the power in respect of any matter, the reference in subsection (9) to the suspension of the power is to its suspension in so far as it relates to that donee.

(11) The dissolution or annulment of a marriage or civil partnership does not terminate the appointment of a donee, or revoke the power, if the instrument provided that it was not to do so.

Sub-s (3): words from ", or the making" to "respect of P," in square brackets inserted by SI 2012/2404, art 3(2), Sch 2, para 53(1), (3)(a). Date in force: 1 October 2012: see SI 2012/2404, art 1; for transitional provisions see art 5 thereof.

Sub-s (4): words from "or where P" to "Insolvency Act 1986)" in square brackets inserted by SI 2012/2404, art 3(2), Sch 2, para 53(1), (3)(b). Date in force: 1 October 2012: see SI 2012/2404, art 1; for transitional provisions see art 6 thereof.

Sub-s (6): words from "or the making" to "of the donee" in square brackets inserted by SI 2012/2404, art 3(2), Sch 2, para 53(1), (3)(c). Date in force: 1 October 2012: see SI 2012/2404, art 1; for transitional provisions see art 5 thereof.

Sub-s (8): words from "or the making" to "of a donee" in square brackets inserted by SI 2012/2404, art 3(2), Sch 2, para 53(1), (3)(d). Date in force: 1 October 2012: see SI 2012/2404, art 1; for transitional provisions see art 5 thereof.

Sub-s (9): words from "or where the" to "Insolvency Act 1986)," in square brackets inserted by SI 2012/2404, art 3(2), Sch 2, para 53(1), (3)(e). Date in force: 1 October 2012: see SI 2012/2404, art 1; for transitional provisions see art 6 thereof.

MARRIAGE (SAME SEX COUPLES) ACT 2013

2013 Chapter 30

[17th July 2013]

PART 1
MARRIAGE OF SAME SEX COUPLES IN ENGLAND AND WALES

Other provisions relating to marriages of same sex couples

A1.699

9 Conversion of civil partnership into marriage

(1) The parties to an England and Wales civil partnership may convert their civil partnership into a marriage under a procedure established by regulations made by the Secretary of State.

(2) The parties to a civil partnership within subsection (3) may convert their civil partnership into a marriage under a procedure established by regulations made by the Secretary of State.

(3) A civil partnership is within this subsection if—

- (a) it was formed outside the United Kingdom under an Order in Council made under Chapter 1 of Part 5 of the Civil Partnership Act 2004 (registration at British consulates etc or by armed forces personnel), and
- (b) the part of the United Kingdom that was relevant for the purposes of section 210(2)(b) or (as the case may be) section 211(2)(b) of that Act was England and Wales.

(4) Regulations under this section may in particular make—

(a) provision about the making by the parties to a civil partnership of an application to convert their civil partnership into a marriage;

(b) provision about the information to be provided in support of an application to convert;

(c) provision about the making of declarations in support of an application to convert;

(d) provision for persons who have made an application to convert to appear before any person or attend at any place;

(e) provision conferring functions in connection with applications to convert on relevant officials, relevant armed forces personnel, the Secretary of State, or any other persons;

(f) provision for fees, of such amounts as are specified in or determined in accordance with the regulations, to be payable in respect of—

(i) the making of an application to convert;

(ii) the exercise of any function conferred by virtue of paragraph (e).

(5) Functions conferred by virtue of paragraph (e) of subsection (4) may include functions relating to—

(a) the recording of information on the conversion of civil partnerships;

(b) the issuing of certified copies of any information recorded;

[(ba) the carrying out, on request, of searches of any information recorded and the provision, on request, of records of any information recorded (otherwise than in the form of certified copies);]

(c) the conducting of services or ceremonies (other than religious services or ceremonies) following the conversion of a civil partnership.

[(5A) Subsection (5B) applies where regulations under this section provide for a fee to be payable to a superintendent registrar or registrar.

(5B) The regulations may provide for such part of the fee as may be specified in or determined in accordance with the regulations to be payable by the superintendent registrar or registrar to the Registrar General in such circumstances as may be set out in the regulations.

(5C) The regulations may provide for the reduction, waiver or refund of part or all of a fee whether by conferring a discretion or otherwise.]

(6) Where a civil partnership is converted into a marriage under this section—

(a) the civil partnership ends on the conversion, and

(b) the resulting marriage is to be treated as having subsisted since the date the civil partnership was formed.

(7) In this section—

"England and Wales civil partnership" means a civil partnership which is formed by two people registering as civil partners of each other in England or Wales (see Part 2 of the Civil Partnership Act 2004);

"relevant armed forces personnel" means—

(a) a member of Her Majesty's forces;

(b) a civilian subject to service discipline (within the meaning of the Armed Forces Act 2006);

and for this purpose "Her Majesty's forces" has the same meaning as in the Armed Forces Act 2006;

"relevant official" means—

(a) the Registrar General;

(b) a superintendent registrar;

(c) a registrar;

(d) a consular officer in the service of Her Majesty's government in the United Kingdom;

(e) a person authorised by the Secretary of State in respect of the solemnization of marriages or formation of civil partnerships in a country or territory in which Her Majesty's government in the United Kingdom has for the time being no consular representative.

Sub-s (5): para (ba) inserted by the Deregulation Act 2015, s 99(1), (3). Date in force: 26 May 2015: see the Deregulation Act 2015, s 115(3)(k).

Sub-ss (5A)–(5C): inserted by the Immigration Act 2016, s 89(1), (2)(a), Sch 15, Pt 1, para 5. Date in force: 12 July 2016: see SI 2016/603, reg 3(r), (w).

PART II – FINANCE ACTS ETC.

Note.

For the earlier statutes, since repealed, relating to estate duty, see Appendix I to the Twenty-fifth edition of this work; the provisions of the Finance Acts 1975 et seq, consolidated in the Inheritance Tax/Capital Transfer Tax Act 1984, are to be found in Appendix 1 to the Twenty-sixth edition of this work.

For Tables of Rates of Inheritance Tax and Capital Transfer Tax, see Appendix IV.

For Inheritance Tax and Capital Transfer Tax (Delivery of Accounts) Regulations, see Appendix II.

INHERITANCE TAX ACT 1984

(1984, c 51)

[31 July 1984]

PART I
GENERAL

Rates

A1.727

7 Rates

(1) [Subject to subsections (2), (4) and (5) below] [and to [section 8D and] Schedule 1A] the tax charged on the value transferred by a chargeable transfer made by any transferor shall be charged at the following rate or rates, that is to say—

(a) if the transfer is the first chargeable transfer made by that transferor in the period of [seven years] ending with the date of the transfer, at the rate or rates applicable to that value under the . . . Table in Schedule 1 to this Act;

(b) in any other case, at the rate or rates applicable under that Table to such part of the aggregate of—

(i) that value, and

(ii) the values transferred by previous chargeable transfers made by him in that period,

as is the highest part of that aggregate and is equal to that value.

[(2) Except as provided by subsection (4) below, the tax charged on the value transferred by a chargeable transfer made before the death of the transferor shall be charged at one half of the rate or rates referred to in subsection (1) above.]

(3) In [the Table] in Schedule 1 to this Act any rate shown in the third column is that applicable to such portion of the value concerned as exceeds the lower limit shown in

the first column but does not exceed the upper limit (if any) shown in the second column.

[(4) Subject to subsection (5) below, subsection (2) above does not apply in the case of a chargeable transfer made at any time within the period of seven years ending with the death of the transferor but, in the case of a chargeable transfer made within that period but more than three years before the death, the tax charged on the value transferred shall be charged at the following percentage of the rate or rates referred to in subsection (1) above—

(a) where the transfer is made more than three but not more than four years before the death, 80 per cent;

(b) where the transfer is made more than four but not more than five years before the death, 60 per cent;

(c) where the transfer is made more than five but not more than six years before the death, 40 per cent; and

(d) where the transfer is made more than six but not more than seven years before the death, 20 per cent.

(5) If, in the case of a chargeable transfer made before the death of the transferor, the tax which would fall to be charged in accordance with subsection (4) above is less than the tax which would have been chargeable (in accordance with subsection (2) above) if the transferor had not died within the period of seven years beginning with the date of the transfer, subsection (4) above shall not apply in the case of that transfer.]

Sub-s (1): words "Subject to subsections (2), (4) and (5) below" in square brackets inserted by the Finance Act 1986, s 101(1), (3), Sch 19, Pt I, para 2, with respect to transfers of value made, and other events occurring, on or after 18 March 1986.

Sub-s (1): words in square brackets beginning with the words "and to" inserted by the Finance Act 2012, s 209, Sch 33, paras 2, 3. Date in force: this amendment has effect in cases where D's death occurs on or after 6 April 2012: see the Finance Act 2012, s 209, Sch 33, para 10(1).

Sub-s (1): words "section 8D and" in square brackets inserted by the Finance (No 2) Act 2015, s 9(1), (2). Date in force: this amendment came into force on 18 November 2015 (date of Royal Assent of the Finance (No 2) Act 2015) in the absence of any specific commencement provision.

Sub-s (1): in para (a) words "seven years" in square brackets substituted by the Finance Act 1986, s 101(1), (3), Sch 19, Pt I, para 2, with respect to transfers of value made, and other events occurring, on or after 18 March 1986.

Sub-s (1): in para (a) word omitted repealed by the Finance Act 1986, ss 101(1), (3), 114(6), Sch 19, Pt I, para 2, Sch 23, Pt X, with respect to transfers of value made, and other events occurring, on or after 18 March 1986.

Sub-s (2): substituted by the Finance Act 1986, s 101(1), (3), Sch 19, Part I, para 2, with respect to transfers of value made, and other events occurring, on or after 18 March 1986.

Sub-s (3): words in square brackets substituted by the Finance Act 1986, s 101(1), (3), Sch 19, Part I, para 2, with respect to transfers of value made, and other events occurring, on or after 18 March 1986.

Sub-ss (4), (5): inserted by the Finance Act 1986, s 101(1), (3), Sch 19, Part I, para 2, with respect to transfers of value made, and other events occurring, on or after 18 March 1986.

PART IX
MISCELLANEOUS AND SUPPLEMENTARY

Miscellaneous

* * * * *

A1.742

267 Persons treated as domiciled in United Kingdom

(1) A person not domiciled in the United Kingdom at any time (in this section referred to as "the relevant time") shall be treated for the purposes of this Act as domiciled in the United Kingdom (and not elsewhere) at the relevant time if—

(a) he was domiciled in the United Kingdom within the three years immediately preceding the relevant time, or

[(aa) he is a formerly domiciled resident for the tax year in which the relevant time falls ("the relevant tax year"), or]

[(b) he was resident in the United Kingdom—

(i) for at least fifteen of the twenty tax years immediately preceding the relevant tax year, and

(ii) for at least one of the four tax years ending with the relevant tax year].

(2) Subsection (1) above shall not apply for the purposes of section 6(2) or (3) or 48(4) above and shall not affect the interpretation of any such provision as is mentioned in section 158(6) above.

(3) Paragraph (a) of subsection (1) above shall not apply in relation to a person who (apart from this section) has not been domiciled in the United Kingdom at any time since 9th December 1974, and paragraph (b) of that subsection shall not apply in relation to a person who has not been resident there at any time since that date; and that subsection shall be disregarded—

(a) in determining whether settled property which became comprised in the settlement on or before that date is excluded property,

(b) in determining the settlor's domicile for the purposes of section 65(8) above in relation to settled property which became comprised in the settlement on or before that date, and

(c) in determining for the purposes of section 65(8) above whether the condition in section 82(3) above is satisfied in relation to such settled property.

(4) For the purposes of this section the question whether a person was resident in the United Kingdom [for any tax year] shall be determined as for the purposes of income tax, . . .

[(5) In determining for the purposes of this section whether a person is, or at any time was, domiciled in the United Kingdom, sections 267ZA and 267ZB are to be ignored.]

Sub-s (1): in para (a) word omitted repealed by the Finance (No 2) Act 2017, s 30(1)(a). Date in force: this repeal has effect in relation to times after 5 April 2017: see the Finance (No 2) Act 2017, s 30(9); for effect and transitional provisions see s 30(10)–(17).

Sub-s (1): para (aa) inserted by the Finance (No 2) Act 2017, s 30(1)(b). Date in force: this amendment has effect in relation to times after 5 April 2017: see the Finance (No 2) Act 2017, s 30(9); for effect and transitional provisions see s 30(10)–(17).

Sub-s (1): para (b) substituted by the Finance (No 2) Act 2017, s 30(1)(c). Date in force: this amendment has effect in relation to times after 5 April 2017: see the Finance (No 2) Act 2017, s 30(9); for effect and transitional provisions see s 30(10)–(17).

Sub-s (3): repealed by the Finance (No 2) Act 2017, s 30(2). Date in force: this repeal has effect in relation to times after 5 April 2017: see the Finance (No 2) Act 2017, s 30(9); for effect and transitional provisions see s 30(10)–(17).

Sub-s (4): words "for any tax year" in square brackets substituted by the Finance (No 2) Act 2017, s 30(3). Date in force: this amendment has effect in relation to times after 5 April 2017: see the Finance (No 2) Act 2017, s 30(9); for effect and transitional provisions see s 30(10)–(17).

Sub-s (4): words omitted repealed, in relation to the year 1993–1994 and subsequent years of assessment, by the Finance Act 1993, s 208(3), (5), Sch 23, Part V.

Sub-s (5): inserted by the Finance Act 2013, s 177(1), (2). Date in force: this amendment came into force on 17 July 2013 (date of Royal Assent of the Finance Act 2013) in the absence of any specific commencement provision.

Appendix II

RULES, ORDERS AND REGULATIONS

Contents

Part 1 – Non-Contentious Business

Part II – Contentious Business

PART I – NON-CONTENTIOUS BUSINESS

THE NON-CONTENTIOUS PROBATE RULES 1987

SI 1987/2024

Note.

Shown as amended by the Non-Contentious Probate (Amendment) Rules 1991 (SI 1991/1876), Non-Contentious Probate (Amendment) Rules 1998 (SI 1998/1903), Non-Contentious Probate (Amendment) Rules 1999 (SI 1999/1015), Non-Contentious Probate (Amendment) Rules 2003 (SI 2003/185), Non-Contentious Probate (Amendment) Rules 2004 (SI 2004/2985), Civil Partnership Act 2004 (Amendments to Subordinate Legislation) Order 2005 (SI 2005/2114), Adoption and Children Act (Consequential Amendments) Order 2005 (SI 2005/3504), Mental Capacity Act 2005 (Transitional and Consequential Provisions) Order 2007 (SI 2007/1898), Constitutional Reform Act 2005 (Commencement No 11) Order 2009 (SI 2009/1604), Non-Contentious Probate (Amendment) Rules 2009 (SI 2009/1893), Legal Services Act 2007 (Consequential Amendments) Order 2009 (SI 2009/3348), Child Arrangements Order (Consequential Amendments to Subordinate Legislation) Order 2014 (SI 2014/852), Non-Contentious Probate (Amendment) Rules 2016 (SI 2016/972) and Non-Contentious Probate (Amendment) Rules 2017 (SI 2017/1034). New/inserted text is inside square brackets.

ARRANGEMENT OF RULES

4A. Alternative procedure for grants through solicitors or probate practitioners
5. Personal applications
5A. Alternative procedure for personal applications
5B. Personal applications using statement of truth
6. Duty of [district judge or] registrar on receiving application for grant
7. Grants by registrars
8. Oath in support of grant
9. Grant in additional name.
10. Marking of wills
11. Engrossments for purposes of record
12. Evidence as to due execution of will
13. Execution of will of blind or illiterate testator
14. Evidence as to terms, condition and date of execution of will
15. Attempted revocation of will
16. Affidavit as to due execution, terms, etc, of will
17. Wills proved otherwise than under section 9 of the Wills Act 1837
18. Wills of persons on military service and seamen
19. Evidence of foreign law
20. Order of priority for grant where deceased left a will
21. Grants to attesting witnesses, etc
22. Order of priority for grant in case of intestacy
23. Order of priority for grant in pre-1926 cases
24. Right of assignee to a grant
25. Joinder of administrator
26. Additional personal representatives
27. Grants where two or more persons entitled in same degree
28. Exceptions to rules as to priority
29. Grants in respect of settled land
30. Grants where deceased died domiciled outside England and Wales
31. Grants to attorneys
32. Grants on behalf of minors
33. Grants where a minor is a co-executor
34. Renunciation of the right of a minor to a grant
35. Grants in case of mental incapacity
36. Grants to trust corporations and other corporate bodies
37. Renunciation of probate and administration
38. Notice to Crown of intended application for grant
39. Resealing under Colonial Probates Acts 1892 and 1927
40. Application for leave to sue on guarantee
41. Amendment and revocation of grant
42. Certificate of delivery of Inland Revenue affidavit
43. Standing searches
44. Caveats
45. Probate actions
46. Citations
47. Citation to accept or refuse or to take a grant
48. Citation to propound a will
49. Address for service
50. Application for order to attend for examination or for subpoena to bring in a will
51. Grants to part of an estate under section 113 of the Act
52. Grants of administration under discretionary powers of court, and grants ad colligenda bona
53. Applications for leave to swear to death
54. Grants in respect of nuncupative wills and copies of wills
55. Application for rectification of a will

The President of the Family Division, in exercise of the powers conferred upon him by section 127 of the Senior Courts Act 1981, and section 2(5) of the Colonial Probates Act 1892, and with the concurrence of the Lord Chancellor, hereby makes the following Rules:

A2.40

1 Citation and commencement.—
These Rules may be cited as the Non-Contentious Probate Rules 1987, and shall come into force on 1st January 1988.

A2.41

2 Interpretation
(1) In these Rules, unless the context otherwise requires—

"the Act" means the [Senior Courts Act 1981];

"authorised officer" means any officer of a registry who is for the time being authorised by the President to administer any oath or to take any affidavit required for any purpose connected with his duties;

"the Crown" includes the Crown in right of the Duchy of Lancaster and the Duke of Cornwall for the time being;

["district judge" means a district judge of the Principal Registry;]

"grant" means a grant of probate or administration and includes, where the context so admits, the resealing of such a grant under the Colonial Probates Acts 1892 and 1927;

"gross value" in relation to any estate means the value of the estate without deduction for debts, incumbrances, funeral expenses or inheritance tax (or other capital tax payable out of the estate);

["judge" means a judge of the High Court;]

"oath" means the oath required by rule 8 to be sworn by every applicant for a grant;

"personal applicant" means a person other than a trust corporation who seeks to obtain a grant without employing a solicitor [or probate practitioner], and "personal application" has a corresponding meaning;

["probate practitioner" means a person who, for the purposes of the Legal Services Act 2007, is an authorised person in relation to an activity which constitutes a probate activity (within the meaning of that Act);]

["registrar" means the district probate registrar of the district probate registry—

- (i) to which an application for a grant is made or is proposed to be made,
- (ii) in rules 26, 40, 41 and 61(2), from which the grant issued, and
- (iii) in rules 46, 47 and 48, from which the citation has issued or is proposed to be issued;]

"registry" means the Principal Registry or a district probate registry;

["the senior district judge" means the Senior District Judge of the Family Division or, in his absence, the senior of the district judges in attendance at the Principal Registry;]

< . . . >

< . . . >

"the Treasury Solicitor" means the solicitor for the affairs of Her Majesty's Treasury and includes the solicitor for the affairs of the Duchy of Lancaster and the solicitor of the Duchy of Cornwall;

"trust corporation" means a corporation within the meaning of section 128 of the Act as extended by section 3 of the Law of Property (Amendment) Act 1926.

(2) A form referred to by number means the form so numbered in the First Schedule; and such forms shall be used wherever applicable, with such variation as a [district judge or] registrar may in any particular case direct or approve.

Para (1): in definition "the Act" words "Senior Courts Act 1981" in square brackets substituted by the Constitutional Reform Act 2005, s 59(5), Sch 11, Pt 1, para 1(2). Date in force: 1 October 2009: see SI 2009/1604, art 2(d).

Para (1): definition "district judge" inserted by SI 1991/1876, r 6(a).

Para (1): definition "judge" inserted by SI 1991/1876, r 6(b).

Para (1): in definition "personal applicant" words "or probate practitioner" in square brackets inserted by SI 1998/1903, r 3(a). Date in force: 14 September 1998: see SI 1998/1903, r 1(1).

Para (1): definition "probate practitioner" (as inserted by SI 1998/1903, r 3(b)) substituted by SI 2009/3348, art 7. Date in force: 1 January 2010 (being the day on which the Legal Services Act 2007, s 13 came into force): see SI 2009/3348, art 2(1) and SI 2009/3250, art 2(b)(i).

Para (1): definition "registrar" substituted by SI 1991/1876, r 6(c).

Para (1): definition "the senior district judge" substituted, for definition "the Senior Registrar" as originally enacted, by SI 1991/1876, r 6(d).

Para (1): definition "statutory guardian" omitted revoked by SI 1991/1876, r 2.

Para (1): definition "testamentary guardian" omitted revoked by SI 1991/1876, r 2.

Para (2): words in square brackets substituted by SI 1991/1876, r 7(1).

A2.42

[3 Application of other rules—

(1) Subject to the provisions of these rules and to any enactment, the rules of the Supreme Court 1965 as they were in force immediately before 26th April 1999 shall apply, with any necessary modifications to non-contentious probate matters, and any reference in these rules to those rules shall be construed accordingly.

(2) Nothing in Order 3 of the Rules of the Supreme Court shall prevent time from running in the Long Vacation.]

Substituted by SI 1999/1015, r 2 from 26 April 1999: see SI 1999/1015, r 1.

A2.43

4 Applications for grants through solicitors [or probate practitioners].—
(1) A person applying for a grant through a solicitor [or probate practitioner] may apply at any registry or sub-registry.
[(1A) A person applying for a grant through a solicitor or probate practitioner may also apply for a grant at any registry under rule 4A if invited to do so by that registry.]
(2) Every solicitor [or probate practitioner] through whom an application for a grant is made shall give the address of his place of business within England and Wales.

Provision heading: words 'or probate practitioners' in square brackets inserted by SI 1998/1903, r 4(a) from 14 September 1998: see SI 1998/1903, r 1(1).

Para (1): words 'or probate practitioner' in square brackets inserted by SI 1998/1903, r 4(b) from 14 September 1998: see SI 1998/1903, r 1(1).

Para (1A): inserted by SI 2017/1034, r 2(1). Date in force: 20 November 2017: see SI 2017/1034, r 1(1).

Para (2): words 'or probate practitioner' in square brackets inserted by SI 1998/1903, r 4(b) from 14 September 1998: see SI 1998/1903, r 1(1).

A2.43A

[4A Alternative procedure for applications through solicitors or probate practitioners]
[(1) An application under this rule must be made by completing and sending an online application form in accordance with instructions given by the registry.
(2) Where an application is made under this rule, rule 8 does not apply, and—

- (a) the application must be verified by a statement of truth in the online application form;
- (b) rule 10(1)(a) applies as if for "signatures of the applicant and the person before whom the oath is sworn" there were substituted "signature of the applicant or of the solicitor or probate practitioner through whom the application is made";
- (c) rule 27(1) applies as if at the end there were inserted "or, where the application is made under rule 4A, the solicitor or probate practitioner through whom the application is made shall confirm in accordance with instructions given by the registry that such notice has been given";
- (d) rule 36 applies as if—
  - (i) in paragraph (1), for "such officer shall depose in the oath" there were substituted "the statement of truth must include a statement";
  - (ii) in paragraph (2)(b), for "it shall be deposed in the oath" there were substituted "the statement of truth must include a statement";
  - (iii) in paragraph (4)(c), for "nominee or attorney shall depose in the oath" there were substituted "statement of truth must include a statement".

(3) Where original documents are required by instructions given by the registry to be sent in support of the application, they must be sent separately to the registry in accordance with such instructions.]

Inserted by SI 2017/1034, r 2(2). Date in force: 20 November 2017: see SI 2017/1034, r 1(1).

A2.44

5 Personal applications.—
(1) A personal applicant may apply for a grant at any registry or sub-registry.

(2) Save as provided for by rule 39 a personal applicant may not apply through an agent, whether paid or unpaid, and may not be attended by any person acting or appearing to act as his adviser.

(3) No personal application shall be proceeded with if—

(a) it becomes necessary to bring the matter before the court by action or summons, [unless a judge, district judge or registrar so permits];

(b) an application has already been made by a solicitor [or probate practitioner] on behalf of the applicant and has not been withdrawn; or

(c) the [district judge or] registrar so directs.

(4) After a will has been deposited in a registry by a personal applicant, it may not be delivered to the applicant or to any other person unless in special circumstances the [district judge or] registrar so directs.

(5) A personal applicant shall produce a certificate of the death of the deceased or such other evidence of the death as the [district judge or] registrar may approve.

(6) A personal applicant shall supply all information necessary to enable the papers leading to the grant to be prepared in the registry.

(7) Unless the [district judge or] registrar otherwise directs, every oath or affidavit required on a personal application shall be sworn or executed by all the deponents before an authorised officer.

(8) No legal advice shall be given to a personal applicant by an officer of a registry and every such officer shall be responsible only for embodying in proper form the applicant's instructions for the grant.

[(9) In any case where an application is made under rule 5A (alternative procedure for personal applications), this rule applies with the exceptions and modifications provided by that rule.]

[(10) In any case where an application is made under rule 5B (personal applications using statement of truth), this rule applies with the exceptions and modifications provided by that rule.]

Para (3): in sub-para (a) words ', unless a judge, district judge or registrar so permits' in square brackets inserted by SI 1998/1903, r 5 from 14 September 1998: see SI 1998/1903, r 1(1).

Para (3): in sub-para (b) words 'or probate practitioner' in square brackets inserted by SI 1998/1903, r 6 from 14 September 1998: see SI 1998/1903, r 1(1).

Para (3): in sub-para (c) words 'district judge or' in square brackets inserted by SI 1991/1876, r 7(1).

Para (4): words 'district judge or' in square brackets inserted by SI 1991/1876, r 7(1).

Para (5): words 'district judge or' in square brackets inserted by SI 1991/1876, r 7(1).

Para (7): words 'district judge or' in square brackets inserted by SI 1991/1876, r 7(1).

Para (9): inserted by SI 2016/972, r 2(1). Date in force: 1 November 2016: see SI 2016/972, r 1(1).

Para (10): inserted by SI 2017/1034, r 3(1). Date in force: 20 November 2017: see SI 2017/1034, r 1(1).

A2.44A

[5A Alternative procedure for personal applications]

[(1) A personal applicant may apply for a grant at any registry under this rule if invited to do so by that registry.

(2) An application under this rule must be made by completing and sending an online application form in accordance with instructions given by the registry.

(3) Where an application is made under this rule, rule 5 applies with the following exceptions and modifications—

(a) paragraphs (1), (7) and (8) do not apply;

(b) paragraph (5) applies as if for the words "the district judge or registrar may approve" there were substituted "required by instructions given by the registry"; and

(c) paragraph (6) applies as if for the words after "information" there were substituted "required by instructions given by the registry".

(4) Where an application is made under this rule, rule 8 does not apply, and—

(a) the application must be verified by a statement of truth by the applicant in the online application form;

(b) rule 10(1)(a) applies as if for "signatures of the applicant and the person before whom the oath is sworn" there were substituted "signature of the applicant";

(c) rule 27(1) applies as if at the end there were inserted "or, where the application is made under rule 5A, the applicant shall confirm in accordance with instructions given by the registry that such notice has been given".

(5) Where original documents are required by instructions given by the registry to be sent in support of the application, they must be sent separately to the registry in accordance with such instructions.]

Inserted by SI 2016/972, r 2(2). Date in force: 1 November 2016: see SI 2016/972, r 1(1).

A2.44B

[5B Personal applications using statement of truth]

[(1) A personal applicant may apply for a grant at any registry under this rule if invited to do so by that registry.

(2) An application under this rule must be made by completing and sending an application form in accordance with instructions given by the registry.

(3) Where an application is made under this rule, rule 5 applies with the following exceptions and modifications—

(a) paragraphs (1), (7) and (8) do not apply;

(b) paragraph (5) applies as if for the words "the district judge or registrar may approve" there were substituted "required by instructions given by the registry"; and

(c) paragraph (6) applies as if for the words after "information" there were substituted "required by instructions given by the registry".

(4) Where an application is made under this rule, rule 8 does not apply, and—

(a) the application must be verified by a statement of truth by the applicant in the application form;

(b) rule 9 applies as if for "shall depose to" there were substituted "state in the application";

(c) rule 10(1)(a) applies as if for "signatures of the applicant and the person before whom the oath is sworn" there were substituted "signature of the applicant";

(d) rule 27(1) applies as if at the end there were inserted "or, where the application is made under rule 5B, the applicant shall confirm in accordance with instructions given by the registry that such notice has been given".]

Inserted by SI 2017/1034, r 3(2). Date in force: 20 November 2017: see SI 2017/1034, r 1(1).

A2.45

6 Duty of [district judge or] registrar on receiving application for grant.—

(1) A [district judge or] registrar shall not allow any grant to issue until all inquiries which he may see fit to make have been answered to his satisfaction.

(2) Except with the leave of a [district judge or] registrar, no grant of probate or of administration with the will annexed shall issue within seven days of the death of the deceased and no grant of administration shall issue within fourteen days thereof.

Provision heading: words in square brackets inserted by SI 1991/1876, r 7(1).

Paras (1), (2): words in square brackets inserted by SI 1991/1876, r 7(1).

A2.46

7 Grants by registrars.—

(1) No grant shall be made by a . . . registrar—

- (a) in any case in which there is contention, until the contention is disposed of; or
- (b) in any case in which it appears to him that a grant ought not to be made without the directions of a judge or a [district judge].

(2) In any case in which paragraph (1)(b) applies, the . . . registrar shall send a statement of the matter in question to the Principal Registry for directions.

(3) A [district judge] may either confirm that the matter be referred to a judge and give directions accordingly or may direct the . . . registrar to proceed with the matter in accordance with such instructions as are deemed necessary, which may include a direction to take no further action in relation to the matter.

Paras (1), (3): words omitted revoked, and words in square brackets substituted, by SI 1991/1876, r 7(2), (3).

Para (2): words omitted revoked by SI 1991/1876, r 7(2).

A2.47

8 Oath in support of grant.—

(1) Every application for a grant other than one to which rule 39 applies shall be supported by an oath by the applicant in the form applicable to the circumstances of the case, and by such other papers as the [district judge or] registrar may require.

(2) Unless otherwise directed by a [district judge or] registrar, the oath shall state where the deceased died domiciled.

(3) Where the deceased died on or after 1st January 1926, the oath shall state whether or not, to the best of the applicant's knowledge, information and belief, there was land vested in the deceased which was settled previously to his death and not by his will and which remained settled land notwithstanding his death.

(4) On an application for a grant of administration the oath shall state in what manner all persons having a prior right to a grant have been cleared off and whether any minority or life interest arises under the will or intestacy.

Paras (1), (2): words in square brackets inserted by SI 1991/1876, r 7(1).

A2.48

9 Grant in additional name.—

Where it is sought to describe the deceased in a grant by some name in addition to his true name, the applicant shall depose to the true name of the deceased and shall specify some part of the estate which was held in the other name, or give any other reason for the inclusion of the other name in the grant.

A2.49

10 Marking of wills.—

Subject to paragraph (2) below, every will in respect of which an application for a grant is made—

(a) shall be marked by the signatures of the applicant and the person before whom the oath is sworn; and

(b) shall be exhibited to any affidavit which may be required under these Rules as to the validity, terms, condition or date of execution of the will.

(2) The [district judge or] registrar may allow a facsimile copy of a will to be marked or exhibited in lieu of the original document.

Para (2): words in square brackets inserted by SI 1991/1876, r 7(1).

A2.50

11 Engrossment for purposes of record.—

(1) Where the [district judge or] registrar considers that in any particular case a facsimile copy of the original will would not be satisfactory for purposes of record, he may require an engrossment suitable for facsimile reproduction to be lodged.

(2) Where a will—

(a) contains alterations which are not to be admitted to proof; or

(b) has been ordered to be rectified by virtue of section 20(1) of the Administration of Justice Act 1982,

there shall be lodged an engrossment of the will in the form in which it is to be proved.

(3) Any engrossment lodged under this rule shall reproduce the punctuation, spacing and division into paragraphs of the will and shall follow continuously from page to page on both sides of the paper.

Para (1): words in square brackets inserted by SI 1991/1876, r 7(1).

A2.51

12 Evidence as to due execution of will.—

(1) Subject to paragraphs (2) and (3) below, where a will contains no attestation clause or the attestation clause is insufficient, or where it appears to the [district judge or] registrar that there is doubt about the due execution of the will, he shall before admitting it to proof require an affidavit as to due execution from one or more of the attesting witnesses or, if no attesting witness is conveniently available, from any other person who was present when the will was executed; and if the [district judge or] registrar, after considering the evidence, is satisfied that the will was not duly executed, he shall refuse probate and mark the will accordingly.

(2) If no affidavit can be obtained in accordance with paragraph (1) above, the [district judge or] registrar may accept evidence on affidavit from any person he may think fit to show that the signature on the will is in the handwriting of the deceased, or of any other matter which may raise a presumption in favour of due execution of the will, and may if he thinks fit require that notice of the application be given to any person who may be prejudiced by the will.

(3) A [district judge or] registrar may accept a will for proof without evidence as aforesaid if he is satisfied that the distribution of the estate is not thereby affected.

Para (3): words in square brackets inserted by SI 1991/1876, r 7(1).

A2.52

13 Execution of will of blind or illiterate testator.—

Before admitting to proof a will which appears to have been signed by a blind or illiterate testator or by another person by direction of the testator, or which for any other reason raises doubt as to the testator having had knowledge of the contents of the will at the time of its execution, the [district judge or] registrar shall satisfy himself that the testator had such knowledge.

Words in square brackets inserted by SI 1991/1876, r 7(1).

A2.53

14 Evidence as to terms, condition and date of execution of will.—

(1) Subject to paragraph (2) below, where there appears in a will any obliteration, interlineation, or other alteration which is not authenticated in the manner prescribed by section 21 of the Wills Act 1837, or by the re-execution of the will or by the execution of a codicil, the [district judge or] registrar shall require evidence to show whether the alteration was present at the time the will was executed and shall give directions as to the form in which the will is to be proved.

(2) The provisions of paragraph (1) above shall not apply to any alteration which appears to the [district judge or] registrar to be of no practical importance.

(3) If a will contains any reference to another document in such terms as to suggest that it ought to be incorporated in the will, the [district judge or] registrar shall require the document to be produced and may call for such evidence in regard to the incorporation of the document as he may think fit.

(4) Where there is a doubt as to the date on which a will was executed, the [district judge or] registrar may require such evidence as he thinks necessary to establish the date.

Paras (1), (4): words in square brackets inserted by SI 1991/1876, r 7(1).

A2.54

15 Attempted revocation of will.—

Any appearance of attempted revocation of a will by burning, tearing, or otherwise destroying and every other circumstance leading to a presumption of revocation by the testator, shall be accounted for to the [district judge's or] registrar's satisfaction.

Words in square brackets inserted by SI 1991/1876, r 7(5).

A2.55

16 Affidavit as to due execution, terms, etc, of will.—

A [district judge or] registrar may require an affidavit from any person he may think fit for the purpose of satisfying himself as to any of the matters referred to in rules 13, 14 and 15, and in any such affidavit sworn by an attesting witness or other person present at the time of the execution of a will the deponent shall depose to the manner in which the will was executed.

Words in square brackets inserted by SI 1991/1876, r 7(1).

A2.56

17 Wills proved otherwise than under section 9 of the Wills Act 1837.—

(1) Rules 12 to 15 shall apply only to a will that is to be established by reference to section 9 of the Wills Act 1837 (signing and attestation of wills).

(2) A will that is to be established otherwise than as described in paragraph (1) of this rule may be so established upon the [district judge or] registrar being satisfied as to its terms and validity, and includes (without prejudice to the generality of the foregoing)—

- (a) any will to which rule 18 applies; and
- (b) any will which, by virtue of the Wills Act 1963, is to be treated as properly executed if executed according to the internal law of the territory or state referred to in section 1 of that Act.

Para (2): words in square brackets inserted by SI 1991/1876, r 7(1).

A2.57

18 Wills of persons on military service and seamen.—

Where the deceased died domiciled in England and Wales and it appears to the [district judge or] registrar that there is prima facie evidence that a will is one to which section 11 of the Wills Act 1837 applies, the will may be admitted to proof if the registrar is satisfied that it was signed by the testator or, if unsigned, that it is in the testator's handwriting.

Words in square brackets inserted by SI 1991/1876, r 7(1).

A2.58

19 Evidence of foreign law.—

Where evidence as to the law of any country or territory outside England and Wales is required on any application for a grant, the [district judge or] registrar may accept—

(a) an affidavit from any person whom, having regard to the particulars of his knowledge or experience given in the affidavit, he regards as suitably qualified to give expert evidence of the law in question; or

(b) a certificate by, or an act before, a notary practising in the country or territory concerned.

Words in square brackets inserted by SI 1991/1876, r 7(1).

A2.59

20 Order of priority for grant where deceased left a will.—

Where the deceased died on or after 1 January 1926 the person or persons entitled to a grant in respect of a will shall be determined in accordance with the following order of priority, namely—

(a) the executor (but subject to rule 36(4)(d) below);

(b) any residuary legatee or devisee holding in trust for any other person;

(c) any other residuary legatee or devisee (including one for life) or where the residue is not wholly disposed of by the will, any person entitled to share in the undisposed of residue (including the Treasury Solicitor when claiming bona vacantia on behalf of the Crown), provided that—

 (i) unless a [district judge or] registrar otherwise directs, a residuary legatee or devisee whose legacy or devise is vested in interest shall be preferred to one entitled on the happening of a contingency, and

 (ii) where the residue is not in terms wholly disposed of, the [district judge or] registrar may, if he is satisfied that the testator has nevertheless disposed of the whole or substantially the whole of the known estate, allow a grant to be made to any legatee or devisee entitled to, or to share in, the estate so disposed of, without regard to the persons entitled to share in any residue not disposed of by the will;

(d) the personal representative of any residuary legatee or devisee (but not one for life, or one holding in trust for any other person), or of any person entitled to share in any residue not disposed of by the will;

(e) any other legatee or devisee (including one for life or one holding in trust for any other person) or any creditor of the deceased, provided that, unless a [district judge or] registrar otherwise directs, a legatee or devisee whose legacy or devise is vested in interest shall be preferred to one entitled on the happening of a contingency;

(f) the personal representative of any other legatee or devisee (but not one for life or one holding in trust for any other person) or of any creditor of the deceased.

Paras (c), (e): words in square brackets inserted by SI 1991/1876, r 7(1).

A2.60

21 Grants to attesting witnesses, etc.

Where a gift to any person fails by reason of section 15 of the Wills Act 1837, such person shall not have any right to a grant as a beneficiary named in the will, without prejudice to his right to a grant in any other capacity.

A2.61

22 Order of priority for grant in case of intestacy.—

(1) Where the deceased died on or after 1st January 1926, wholly intestate, the person or persons having a beneficial interest in the estate shall be entitled to a grant of administration in the following classes in order of priority, namely—

(a) the surviving [spouse or civil partner];

(b) the children of the deceased and the issue of any deceased child who died before the deceased;

(c) the father and mother of the deceased;

(d) brothers and sisters of the whole blood and the issue of any deceased brother or sister of the whole blood who died before the deceased;

(e) brothers and sisters of the half blood and the issue of any deceased brother or sister of the half blood who died before the deceased;

(f) grandparents;

(g) uncles and aunts of the whole blood and the issue of any deceased uncle or aunt of the whole blood who died before the deceased;

(h) uncles and aunts of the half blood and the issue of any deceased uncle or aunt of the half blood who died before the deceased.

(2) In default of any person having a beneficial interest in the estate, the Treasury Solicitor shall be entitled to a grant if he claims bona vacantia on behalf of the Crown.

(3) If all persons entitled to a grant under the foregoing provisions of this rule have been cleared off, a grant may be made to a creditor of the deceased or to any person who, notwithstanding that he has no immediate beneficial interest in the estate, may have a beneficial interest in the event of an accretion thereto.

(4) Subject to paragraph (5) of rule 27, the personal representative of a person in any of the classes mentioned in paragraph (1) of this rule or the personal representative of a creditor of the deceased shall have the same right to a grant as the person whom he represents provided that the persons mentioned in sub-paragraphs (b) to (h) of paragraph (1) above shall be preferred to the personal representative of a spouse [or civil partner] who has died without taking a beneficial interest in the whole estate of the deceased as ascertained at the time of the application for the grant.

Para (1): in sub-para (a) words 'spouse or civil partner' in square brackets substituted by SI 2005/2114, art 2(6), Sch 6, para 2(1), (2) from 5 December 2005: see SI 2005/2114, art 1.

Para (4): words 'or a civil partner' in square brackets inserted by SI 2005/2114, art 2(6), Sch 6, para 2(1), (3) from 5 December 2005: see SI 2005/2114, art 1.

A2.62

23 Order of priority for grant in pre-1926 cases.—

Where the deceased died before 1 January 1926, the person or persons entitled to a grant shall, subject to the provisions of any enactment, be determined in accordance with the principles and rules under which the court would have acted at the date of death.

A2.63

24 Right of assignee to a grant.—

(1) Where all the persons entitled to the estate of the deceased (whether under a will or on intestacy) have assigned their whole interest in the estate to one or more persons, the assignee or assignees shall replace, in the order of priority for a grant of administration, the assignor or, if there are two or more assignors, the assignor with the highest priority.

(2) Where there are two or more assignees, administration may be granted with the consent of the others to any one or more (not exceeding four) of them.

(3) In any case where administration is applied for by an assignee the original instrument of assignment shall be produced and a copy of the same lodged in the registry.

A2.64

25 Joinder of administrator.—

(1) A person entitled in priority to a grant of administration may, without leave, apply for a grant with a person entitled in a lower degree, provided that there is no other person entitled in a higher degree to the person to be joined, unless every other such person has renounced.

(2) Subject to paragraph (3) below, an application for leave to join with a person entitled in priority to a grant of administration a person having no right or no immediate right thereto shall be made to a [district judge or] registrar, and shall be supported by an affidavit by the person entitled in priority, the consent of the person proposed to be joined as administrator and such other evidence as the [district judge or] registrar may direct.

(3) Unless a [district judge or] registrar otherwise directs, there may without any such application be joined with a person entitled in priority to administration—

- (a) any person who is nominated under paragraph (3) of rule 32 or paragraph (3) of rule 35;
- (b) a trust corporation.

Paras (2), (3): words in square brackets inserted by SI 1991/1876, r 7(1).

A2.65

26 Additional personal representatives.—

(1) An application under section 114(4) of the Act to add a personal representative shall be made to a [district judge or] registrar and shall be supported by an affidavit by the applicant, the consent of the person proposed to be added as personal representative and such other evidence as the [district judge or] registrar may require.

(2) On any such application the [district judge or] registrar may direct that a note shall be made on the original grant of the addition of a further personal representative, or he may impound or revoke the grant or make such other order as the circumstances of the case may require.

Words in square brackets inserted by SI 1991/1876, r 7(1).

A2.66

27 Grants where two or more persons entitled in same degree.—

(1) Subject to paragraphs (1A), (2) and (3) below, where, on an application for probate, power to apply for a like grant is to be reserved to such other of the executors as have not renounced probate, notice of the application shall be given to the executor or executors to whom power is to be reserved; and unless the [district judge or] registrar otherwise directs, the oath shall state that such notice has been given.

(1A) Where power is to be reserved to executors who are . . . partners in a firm, . . . notice need not be given to them under paragraph (1) above if probate is applied for by another partner in that firm.

(2) Where power is to be reserved to partners of a firm, notice for the purposes of paragraph (1) above may be given to the partners by sending it to the firm at its principal or last known place of business.

(3) A [district judge or] registrar may dispense with the giving of notice under paragraph (1) above if he is satisfied that the giving of such a notice is impracticable or would result in unreasonable delay or expense.

(4) A grant of administration may be made to any person entitled thereto without notice to other persons entitled in the same degree.

(5) Unless a [district judge or] registrar otherwise directs, administration shall be granted to a person of full age entitled thereto in preference to a guardian of a minor, and to a living person entitled thereto in preference to the personal representative of a deceased person.

(6) A dispute between persons entitled to a grant in the same degree shall be brought by summons before a [district judge or] registrar.

(7) The issue of a summons under this rule in a registry shall be noted forthwith in the index of pending grant applications.

(8) If the issue of a summons under this rule is known to the [district judge or] registrar, he shall not allow any grant to be sealed until such summons is finally disposed of.

Paras (1), (1A): substituted for original para (1) by SI 1991/1876, r 8(1).

Para (1A): words omitted revoked by SI 1998/1903, r 7(1) from 14 September 1998: see SI 1998/1903, r 1(1).

Paras (3), (5), (6), (8): words in square brackets inserted by SI 1991/1876, r 7(1).

Para (7): substituted by SI 1998/1903, r 7(2) from 14 September 1998: see SI 1998/1903, r 1(1).

A2.67

28 Exceptions to rules as to priority.—

(1) Any person to whom a grant may or is required to be made under any enactment shall not be prevented from obtaining such a grant notwithstanding the operation of rules 20, 22, 25 or 27.

(2) Where the deceased died domiciled outside England and Wales rules 20, 22, 25 or 27 shall not apply except in a case to which paragraph (3) of rule 30 applies.

A2.68

[29 Grants in respect of settled land.—

(1) In this rule 'settled land' means land vested in the deceased which was settled prior to his death and not by his will and which remained settled land notwithstanding his death.

(2) The person or persons entitled to a grant of administration limited to settled land shall be determined in accordance with the following order of priority:

(i) the special executors in regard to settled land constituted by section 22 of the Administration of Estates Act 1925;

(ii) the trustees of the settlement at the time of the application for the grant; and

(iii) the personal representatives of the deceased.

(3) Where there is settled land and a grant is made in respect of the free estate only, the grant shall expressly exclude the settled land.]

Substituted by SI 1991/1876, r 9.

A2.69

30 Grants where deceased died domiciled outside England and Wales.—

(1) Subject to paragraph (3) below, where the deceased died domiciled outside England and Wales, [a district judge or registrar may order that a grant, limited in such way as the district judge or registrar may direct,] do issue to any of the following persons—

(a) to the person entrusted with the administration of the estate by the court having jurisdiction at the place where the deceased died domiciled; or

(b) where there is no person so entrusted, to the person beneficially entitled to the estate by the law of the place where the deceased died domiciled or, if there is more than one person so entitled, to such of them as the [district judge or] registrar may direct; or

(c) if in the opinion of the [district judge or] registrar the circumstances so require, to such person as the [district judge or] registrar may direct.

(2) A grant made under paragraph (1)(a) or (b) above may be issued jointly with such person as the [district judge or] registrar may direct if the grant is required to be made to not less than two administrators.

(3) Without any order made under paragraph (1) above—

(a) probate of any will which is admissible to proof may be granted—

(i) if the will is in the English or Welsh language, to the executor named therein; or

(ii) if the will describes the duties of a named person in terms sufficient to constitute him executor according to the tenor of the will, to that person; and

(b) where the whole or substantially the whole of the estate in England and Wales consists of immovable property, a grant in respect of the whole estate may be made in accordance with the law which would have been applicable if the deceased had died domiciled in England and Wales.

Para (1): first words in square brackets substituted and other words in square brackets inserted by SI 1991/1876, rr 7(1), 10.

Para (2): words in square brackets inserted by SI 1991/1876, r 7(1).

A2.70

31 Grants to attorneys.—

(1) Subject to paragraphs (2) and (3) below, the lawfully constituted attorney of a person entitled to a grant may apply for administration for the use and benefit of the donor, and such grant shall be limited until further representation be granted, or in such other way as the [district judge or] registrar may direct.

(2) Where the donor referred to in paragraph (1) above is an executor, notice of the application shall be given to any other executor unless such notice is dispensed with by the [district judge or] registrar.

[(3) Where the donor referred to in paragraph (1) above lacks capacity within the meaning of the Mental Capacity Act 2005 (c 9) and the attorney is acting under an enduring power of attorney or lasting power of attorney, the application shall be made in accordance with rule 35.]

Paras (1), (2): words in square brackets inserted by SI 1991/1876, r 7(1).

Para (3): substituted by SI 2007/1898, art 6, Sch 1, para 13(1), (2) from 1 October 2007: see SI 2007/1898, art 1.

A2.71

32 Grants on behalf of minors

(1) Where a person to whom a grant would otherwise be made is a minor, administration for his use and benefit, limited until he attains the age of eighteen years, shall, unless otherwise directed, and subject to paragraph (2) of this rule, be granted to

- [(a) a parent of the minor who has, or is deemed to have, parental responsibility for him in accordance with—
  - [(i) section 2(1), 2(1A), 2(2), 2(2A), 4 or 4ZA of the Children Act 1989,]
  - (ii) paragraph 4 or 6 of Schedule 14 to that Act, or
  - (iii) an adoption order within the meaning of section 12(1) of the Adoption Act 1976 [or section 46(1) of the Adoption and Children Act 2002], or
- [(aa) a person who has, or is deemed to have, parental responsibility for the minor by virtue of section 12(2) of the Children Act 1989(a) where the court has made a [child arrangements order under section 8 of that Act which names that person as a person with whom the minor is to live]; or]
- [(ab) a step-parent of the minor who has parental responsibility for him in accordance with section 4A of the Children Act 1989; or]
- (b) a guardian of the minor who is appointed, or deemed to have been appointed, in accordance with section 5 of the Children Act 1989 or in accordance with paragraph 12, 13 or 14 of Schedule 14 to that Act]; [or]
- [(ba) a special guardian of the minor who is appointed in accordance with section 14A of the Children Act 1989; or
- (bb) an adoption agency which has parental responsibility for the minor by virtue of section 25(2) of the Adoption and Children Act 2002; or]
- [(c) a local authority which has, or is deemed to have, parental responsibility for the minor by virtue of section 33(3) of the Children Act 1989 where the court has made a care order under section 31(1)(a) of that Act in respect of the minor and that local authority is designated in that order;]

provided that where the minor is sole executor and has no interest in the residuary estate of the deceased, administration for the use and benefit of the minor limited as aforesaid, shall, unless a [district judge or] registrar otherwise directs, be granted to the person entitled to the residuary estate.

[(2) A district judge or registrar may by order appoint a person to obtain administration for the use and benefit of the minor, limited as aforesaid, in default of, or jointly with, or to the exclusion of, any person mentioned in paragraph (1) of this rule; and the person intended shall file an affidavit in support of his application to be appointed.]

(3) Where there is only one person competent and willing to take a grant under the foregoing provisions of this rule, such person may, unless a [district judge or] registrar otherwise directs, nominate any fit and proper person to act jointly with him in taking the grant.

Para (1): sub-paras (a), (b) substituted by SI 1991/1876, r 3.

Para (1): sub-para (a)(i) substituted by SI 2009/1893, rr 2, 3. Date in force: 1 September 2009: see SI 2009/1893, r 1.

Para (1): in sub-para (a)(iii) words "or section 46(1) of the Adoption and Children Act 2002" in square brackets inserted by SI 2005/3504, art 4(a). Date in force: 30 December 2005: see SI 2005/3504, art 1.

Para (1): sub-para (aa) inserted by SI 1998/1903, r 8(1). Date in force: 14 September 1998: see SI 1998/1903, r 1(1).

Para (1): in sub-para (aa) words from "child arrangements order" to "is to live" in square brackets substituted by SI 2014/852, art 3. Date in force: 22 April 2014: see SI 2014/852, art 1.

Para (1): sub-para (ab) inserted by SI 2005/3504, art 4(b). Date in force: 30 December 2005: see SI 2005/3504, art 1.

Para (1): in sub-para (b) word "or" in square brackets inserted by SI 1998/1903, r 8(2). Date in force: 14 September 1998: see SI 1998/1903, r 1(1).

Para (1): sub-paras (ba), (bb) inserted by SI 2005/3504, art 4(c). Date in force: 30 December 2005: see SI 2005/3504, art 1.

Para (1): sub-para (c) inserted by SI 1998/1903, r 8(3). Date in force: 14 September 1998: see SI 1998/1903, r 1(1).

Para (1): words "district judge or" in square brackets inserted by SI 1991/1876, r 7(1).

Para (2): substituted by SI 1991/1876, r 4.

Para (3): words in square brackets inserted by SI 1991/1876, r 7(1).

A2.72

33 Grants where a minor is a co-executor.—

(1) Where a minor is appointed executor jointly with one or more other executors, probate may be granted to the executor or executors not under disability with power reserved to the minor executor, and the minor executor shall be entitled to apply for probate on attaining the age of eighteen years.

(2) Administration for the use and benefit of a minor executor until he attains the age of eighteen years may be granted under rule 32 if, and only if, the executors who are not under disability renounce or, on being cited to accept or refuse a grant, fail to make an effective application therefor.

A2.73

34 Renunciation of the right of a minor to a grant.—

(1) The right of a minor executor to probate on attaining the age of eighteen years may not be renounced by any person on his behalf.

(2) The right of a minor to administration may be renounced only by a person [appointed] under paragraph (2) of rule 32, and authorised by the [district judge or] registrar to renounce on behalf of the minor.

Para (2): first word in square brackets substituted and second words in square brackets inserted by SI 1991/1876, rr 5, 7(1).

A2.74

35 Grants in case of [lack of mental capacity].—

(1) Unless a [district judge or] registrar otherwise directs, no grant shall be made under this rule unless all persons entitled in the same degree as the [person who lacks capacity within the meaning of the Mental Capacity Act 2005] referred to in paragraph (2) below have been cleared off.

(2) Where a [district judge or] registrar is satisfied that a person entitled to a grant [lacks capacity within the meaning of the Mental Capacity Act 2005 to manage] his affairs, administration for his use and benefit, limited until further representation be granted or in such other way as the [district judge or] registrar may direct, may be granted in the following order of priority—

(a) to the person authorised by the Court of Protection to apply for a grant;

(b) where there is no person so authorised, to the lawful attorney of the [person who lacks capacity within the meaning of the Mental Capacity Act 2005] acting under a registered enduring power of attorney [or lasting power of attorney];

(c) where there is no such attorney entitled to act, or if the attorney shall renounce administration for the use and benefit of the [person who lacks capacity within the meaning of the Mental Capacity Act 2005], to the person entitled to the residuary estate of the deceased.

(3) Where a grant is required to be made to not less than two administrators, and there is only one person competent and willing to take a grant under the foregoing provisions of this rule, administration may, unless a [district judge or] registrar otherwise directs, be granted to such person jointly with any other person nominated by him.

(4) Notwithstanding the foregoing provisions of this rule, administration for the use and benefit of the [person who lacks capacity within the meaning of the Mental Capacity Act 2005] may be granted to such [other person] as the [district judge or] registrar may by order direct.

(5) [Unless the applicant is the person authorised in paragraph (2)(a) above,] notice of an intended application under this rule shall be given to the Court of Protection.

Provision heading: words 'lack of mental capacity' in square brackets substituted by SI 2007/1898, art 6, Sch 1, para 13(1), (3) from 1 October 2007: see SI 2007/1898, art 1.

Para (1): words 'district judge or' in square brackets inserted by SI 1991/1876, r 7(1).

Para (1): words 'person who lacks capacity within the meaning of the Mental Capacity Act 2005' in square brackets substituted by SI 2007/1898, art 6, Sch 1, para 13(1), (4) from 1 October 2007: see SI 2007/1898, art 1.

Para (2): words 'district judge or' in square brackets in both places they occur inserted by SI 1991/1876, r 7(1).

Para (2): words 'lacks capacity within the meaning of the Mental Capacity Act 2005 to manage' in square brackets substituted by SI 2007/1898, art 6, Sch 1, para 13(1), (5)(a) from 1 October 2007: see SI 2007/1898, art 1.

Para (2): in sub-paras (b), (c) words 'person who lacks capacity within the meaning of the Mental Capacity Act 2005' in square brackets substituted by virtue of SI 2007/1898, art 6, Sch 1, para 13(1), (5)(b) from 1 October 2007: see SI 2007/1898, art 1.

Para (2): in sub-para (b) words 'or lasting power of attorney' in square brackets inserted by SI 2007/1898, art 6, Sch 1, para 13(1), (5)(c) from 1 October 2007: see SI 2007/1898, art 1.

Para (3): words 'district judge or' in square brackets inserted by SI 1991/1876, r 7(1).

Para (4): words 'person who lacks capacity within the meaning of the Mental Capacity Act 2005' in square brackets substituted by SI 2007/1898, art 6, Sch 1, para 13(1), (6) from 1 October 2007: see SI 2007/1898, art 1.

Para (4): words 'other person' in square brackets substituted by SI 1998/1903, r 9(1) from 14 September 1998: see SI 1998/1903, r 1(1).

Para (4): words 'district judge or' in square brackets inserted by SI 1991/1876, r 7(1).

Para (5): words from 'Unless' to 'paragraph (2)(a) above,' in square brackets inserted by SI 1998/1903, r 9(2) from 14 September 1998: see SI 1998/1903, r 1(1).

A2.75

36 Grants to trust corporations and other corporate bodies.—

(1) An application for a grant to a trust corporation shall be made through one of its officers, and such officer shall depose in the oath that the corporation is a trust corporation as defined by these Rules and that it has power to accept a grant.

(2)

(a) Where the trust corporation is the holder of an official position, any officer whose name is included on a list filed with the [senior district judge] of persons authorised to make affidavits and sign documents on behalf of the office holder may act as the officer through whom the holder of that official position applies for the grant.

(b) In all other cases a certified copy of the resolution of the trust corporation authorising the officer to make the application shall be lodged, or it shall be deposed in the oath that such certified copy has been filed with the [senior district judge], that the officer is therein identified by the position he holds, and that such resolution is still in force.

(3) A trust corporation may apply for administration otherwise than as a beneficiary or the attorney of some person, and on any such application there shall be lodged the consents of all persons entitled to a grant and of all persons interested in the residuary estate of the deceased save that the [district judge or] registrar may dispense with any such consents as aforesaid on such terms, if any, as he may think fit.

(4)

(a) Subject to sub-paragraph (d) below, where a corporate body would, if an individual, be entitled to a grant but is not a trust corporation as defined by these Rules, administration for its use and benefit, limited until further representation be granted, may be made to its nominee or to its lawfully constituted attorney.

(b) A copy of the resolution appointing the nominee or the power of attorney (whichever is appropriate) shall be lodged, and such resolution or power of attorney shall be sealed by the corporate body, or be otherwise authenticated to the district judge's or registrar's satisfaction.

(c) The nominee or attorney shall depose in the oath that the corporate body is not a trust corporation as defined by these Rules.

(d) The provisions of paragraph (4)(a) above shall not apply where a corporate body is appointed executor jointly with an individual unless the right of the individual has been cleared off.

Para (2): words in square brackets substituted by SI 1991/1876, r 7(4).

Paras (3), (4): words in square brackets inserted by SI 1991/1876, r 7(1), (5).

A2.76

37 Renunciation of probate and administration.—

(1) Renunciation of probate by an executor shall not operate as renunciation of any right which he may have to a grant of administration in some other capacity unless he expressly renounces such right.

(2) Unless a [district judge or] registrar otherwise directs, no person who has renounced administration in one capacity may obtain a grant thereof in some other capacity.

[(2A) Renunciation of probate or administration by members of a partnership—

(a) may be effected, or

(b) subject to paragraph (3) below, may be retracted by any two of them with the authority of the others and any such renunciation or retraction shall recite such authority.]

(3) A renunciation of probate or administration may be retracted at any time with the leave of a [district judge or] registrar; provided that only in exceptional circumstances may leave be given to an executor to retract a renunciation of probate after a grant has been made to some other person entitled in a lower degree.

(4) A direction or order giving leave under this rule may be made either by the registrar of a district probate registry where the renunciation is filed or by [a district judge].

Paras (2), (3): words in square brackets inserted by SI 1991/1876, r 7(1).

Para (2A): inserted by SI 1998/1903, r 10 from 14 September 1998: see SI 1998/1903, r 1(1).

Para (4): words in square brackets substituted by SI 1991/1876, r 7(3).

A2.77

38 Notice to Crown of intended application for grant.—

In any case in which it appears that the Crown is or may be beneficially interested in the estate of a deceased person, notice of intended application for a grant shall be given by the applicant to the Treasury Solicitor, and the [district judge or] registrar may direct that no grant shall issue within 28 days after the notice has been given.

Words in square brackets inserted by SI 1991/1876, r 7(1).

A2.78

39 Resealing under Colonial Probates Acts 1892 and 1927.—

(1) An application under the Colonial Probates Acts 1892 and 1927 for the resealing of probate or administration granted by the court of a country to which those Acts apply may be made by the person to whom the grant was made or by any person authorised in writing to apply on his behalf.

(2) On any such application an Inland Revenue affidavit or account shall be lodged.

(3) Except by leave of a [district judge or] registrar, no grant shall be resealed unless it was made to such a person as is mentioned in sub-paragraph (a) or (b) of paragraph (1) of rule 30 or to a person to whom a grant could be made under sub-paragraph (a) of paragraph (3) of that rule.

(4) No limited or temporary grant shall be resealed except by leave of a [district judge or] registrar.

(5) Every grant lodged for resealing shall include a copy of any will to which the grant relates or shall be accompanied by a copy thereof certified as correct by or under the authority of the court by which the grant was made, and where the copy of the grant required to be deposited under subsection (1) of section 2 of the Colonial Probates Act 1892 does not include a copy of the will, a copy thereof shall be deposited in the registry before the grant is resealed.

(6) The [district judge or] registrar shall send notice of the resealing to the court which made the grant.

(7) Where notice is received in the Principal Registry of the resealing of a grant issued in England and Wales, notice of any amendment or revocation of the grant shall be sent to the court by which it was resealed.

Paras (3), (4), (6): words in square brackets inserted by SI 1991/1876, r 7(1).

A2.79

40 Application for leave to sue on guarantee.—

An application for leave under section 120(3) of the Act or under section 11(5) of the Administration of Estates Act 1971 to sue a surety on a guarantee given for the purposes of either of those sections shall, unless the [district judge or] registrar otherwise directs under rule 61, be made by summons to a [district judge or] registrar and notice of the application shall be served on the administrator, the surety and any co-surety.

Words in square brackets inserted by SI 1991/1876, r 7(1).

A2.80

41 Amendment and revocation of grant.—

(1) Subject to paragraph (2) below, if a [district judge or] registrar is satisfied that a grant should be amended or revoked he may make an order accordingly.

(2) Except on the application or with the consent of the person to whom the grant was made, the power conferred in paragraph (1) above shall be exercised only in exceptional circumstances.

Para (1): words in square brackets inserted by SI 1991/1876, r 7(1).

A2.81

42 Certificate of delivery of Inland Revenue affidavit.—

Where the deceased died before 13th March 1975 the certificate of delivery of an Inland Revenue affidavit required by section 30 of the Customs and Inland Revenue Act 1881 to be borne by every grant shall be in Form 1.

A2.82

43 Standing searches.—

[(1) Any person who wishes to be notified of the issue of a grant may enter a standing search for the grant by lodging at, or sending by post to any registry or sub-registry, a notice in Form 2.]

(2) A person who has entered a standing search will be sent an office copy of any grant which corresponds with the particulars given on the completed Form 2 and which—

- (a) issued not more than twelve months before the entry of the standing search; or
- (b) issues within a period of six months after the entry of the standing search.

(3)

- (a) Where an applicant wishes to extend the said period of six months, he or his solicitor [or probate practitioner] may lodge at, or send by post to, the registry or sub-registry at which the standing search was entered written application for extension.
- (b) An application for extension as aforesaid must be lodged, or received by post, within the last month of the said period of six months, and the standing search shall thereupon be effective for an additional period of six months from the date on which it was due to expire.
- (c) A standing search which has been extended as above may be further extended by the filing of a further application for extension subject to the same conditions as set out in sub-paragraph (b) above.

Para (1): substituted by SI 1991/1876, r 11(1).

Para (3): in sub-para (a) words 'or probate practitioner' in square brackets inserted by SI 1998/1903, r 6 from 14 September 1998: see SI 1998/1903, r 1(1).

Para (3): in sub-para (a) words from 'the registry' to 'search was entered' in square brackets substituted by SI 1991/1876, r 11(2).

A2.83

44 Caveats.—

(1) Any person who wishes to show cause against the sealing of a grant may enter a caveat in any registry or sub-registry, and the [district judge or] registrar shall not allow any grant to be sealed (other than a grant ad colligenda bona or a grant under

section 117 of the Act) if he has knowledge of an effective caveat; provided that no caveat shall prevent the sealing of a grant on the day on which the caveat is entered.

(2) Any person wishing to enter a caveat (in these Rules called 'the caveator'), or a solicitor [or probate practitioner] on his behalf, may effect entry of a caveat—

- (a) by completing Form 3 in the appropriate book at any registry or sub-registry; or
- (b) by sending by post at his own risk a notice in Form 3 to any registry or sub-registry and the proper officer shall provide an acknowledgment of the entry of the caveat.

(3)

- (a) Except as otherwise provided by this rule or by rules 45 or 46, a caveat shall be effective for a period of six months from the date of entry thereof, and where a caveator wishes to extend the said period of six months, he or his solicitor [or probate practitioner] may lodge at, or send by post to, the registry or sub-registry at which the caveat was entered a written application for extension.
- (b) An application for extension as aforesaid must be lodged, or received by post, within the last month of the said period of six months, and the caveat shall thereupon (save as otherwise provided by this rule) be effective for an additional period of six months from the date on which it was due to expire.
- (c) A caveat which has been extended as above may be further extended by the filing of a further application for extension subject to the same conditions as set out in sub-paragraph (b) above.

[(4) An index of caveats entered in any registry or sub-registry shall be maintained and upon receipt of an application for a grant, the registry or sub-registry at which the application is made shall cause a search of the index to be made and the appropriate district judge or registrar shall be notified of the entry of a caveat against the sealing of a grant for which the application has been made.]

(5) Any person claiming to have an interest in the estate may cause to be issued from the [nominated registry] a warning in Form 4 against the caveat, and the person warning shall state his interest in the estate of the deceased and shall require the caveator to give particulars of any contrary interest in the estate; and the warning or a copy thereof shall be served on the caveator forthwith.

(6) A caveator who has no interest contrary to that of the person warning, but who wishes to show cause against the sealing of a grant to that person, may within eight days of service of the warning upon him (inclusive of the day of such service), or at any time thereafter if no affidavit has been filed under paragraph (12) below, issue and serve a summons for directions.

(7) On the hearing of any summons for directions under paragraph (6) above the [district judge or] registrar may give a direction for the caveat to cease to have effect.

(8) Any caveat in force when a summons for directions is issued shall remain in force until the summons has been disposed of unless a direction has been given under paragraph (7) above or until it is withdrawn under paragraph (11) below.

(9) The issue of a summons under this rule shall be notified forthwith to the [nominated registry].

(10) A caveator having an interest contrary to that of the person warning may within eight days of service of the warning upon him (inclusive of the day of such service) or at any time thereafter if no affidavit has been filed under paragraph (12) below, enter an appearance in the [nominated registry] by filing Form 5; and he shall serve forthwith on the person warning a copy of Form 5 sealed with the seal of the court.

(11) A caveator who has not entered an appearance to a warning may at any time withdraw his caveat by giving notice at the registry or sub-registry at which it was

entered, and the caveat shall thereupon cease to have effect; and, where the caveat has been so withdrawn, the caveator shall forthwith give notice of withdrawal to the person warning.

(12) If no appearance has been entered by the caveator or no summons has been issued by him under paragraph (6) of this rule, the person warning may at any time after eight days after service of the warning upon the caveator (inclusive of the day of such service) file an affidavit in the [nominated registry] as to such service and the caveat shall thereupon cease to have effect provided that there is no pending summons under paragraph (6) of this rule.

(13) Unless a [district judge or, where application to discontinue a caveat is made by consent, a registrar] by order made on summons otherwise directs, any caveat in respect of which an appearance to a warning has been entered shall remain in force until the commencement of a probate action.

(14) Except with the leave of a [district judge] no further caveat may be entered by or on behalf of any caveator whose caveat is either in force or has ceased to have effect under paragraphs (7) or (12) of this rule or under rule 45(4) or rule 46(3).

[(15) In this rule, 'nominated registry' means the registry nominated for the purpose of this rule by the senior district judge or in the absence of any such nomination the Leeds District Probate Registry.]

Para (1): words 'district judge or' in square brackets inserted by SI 1991/1876, r 7(1).

Para (2): words 'or probate practitioner' in square brackets inserted by SI 1998/1903, r 6 from 14 September 1998: see SI 1998/1903, r 1(1).

Para (3): in sub-para (a) words 'or probate practitioner' in square brackets inserted by SI 1998/1903, r 6 from 14 September 1998: see SI 1998/1903, r 1(1).

Para (4): substituted by SI 1998/1903, r 11(1) from 14 September 1998: see SI 1998/1903, r 1(1).

Para (5): words 'nominated registry' in square brackets substituted by SI 1998/1903, r 11(2) from 14 September 1998: see SI 1998/1903, r 1(1).

Para (7): words 'district judge or' in square brackets inserted by SI 1991/1876, r 7(1).

Para (8): words in square brackets inserted by SI 1991/1876, r 12(1).

Para (9): words 'nominated registry' in square brackets substituted by SI 1998/1903, r 11(2) from 14 September 1998: see SI 1998/1903, r 1(1).

Para (10): words 'nominated registry' in square brackets substituted by SI 1998/1903, r 11(2) from 14 September 1998: see SI 1998/1903, r 1(1).

Para (10): words omitted revoked by SI 1991/1876, r 12(2).

Para (12): words 'nominated registry' in square brackets substituted by SI 1998/1903, r 11(2) from 14 September 1998: see SI 1998/1903, r 1(1).

Para (13): words in square brackets substituted by SI 1991/1876, rr 7(3), 12(3).

Para (14): words in square brackets substituted by SI 1991/1876, r 7(3).

Para (15): inserted by SI 1998/1903, r 11(3) from 14 September 1998: see SI 1998/1903, r 1(1).

A2.84

45 Probate actions.—

(1) Upon being advised by the court concerned of the commencement of a probate action the [senior district judge] shall give notice of the action to every caveator other than the plaintiff in the action in respect of each caveat that is in force.

(2) In respect of any caveat entered subsequent to the commencement of a probate action the [senior district judge] shall give notice to that caveator of the existence of the action.

(3) Unless a [district judge] by order made on summons otherwise directs, the commencement of a probate action shall operate to prevent the sealing of a grant

(other than a grant under section 117 of the Act) until application for a grant is made by the person shown to be entitled thereto by the decision of the court in such action.
(4) Upon such application for a grant, any caveat entered by the plaintiff in the action, and any caveat in respect of which notice of the action has been given, shall cease to have effect.

Paras (1), (2): words in square brackets substituted by SI 1991/1876, r 7(4).

Para (3): words in square brackets substituted by SI 1991/1876, r 7(3).

A2.85

46 Citations.—

(1) Any citation may issue from the Principal Registry or a district probate registry and shall be settled by a [district judge or] registrar before being issued.
(2) Every averment in a citation, and such other information as the registrar may require, shall be verified by an affidavit sworn by the person issuing the citation (in these Rules called the 'citor'), provided that the [district judge or] registrar may in special circumstances accept an affidavit sworn by the citor's solicitor [or probate practitioner].
(3) The citor shall enter a caveat before issuing a citation and, unless a [district judge] by order made on summons otherwise directs, any caveat in force at the commencement of the citation proceedings shall, unless withdrawn pursuant to paragraph (11) of rule 44, remain in force until application for a grant is made by the person shown to be entitled thereto by the decision of the court in such proceedings, and upon such application any caveat entered by a party who had notice of the proceedings shall cease to have effect.
(4) Every citation shall be served personally on the person cited unless the [district judge or] registrar, on cause shown by affidavit, directs some other mode of service, which may include notice by advertisement.
(5) Every will referred to in a citation shall be lodged in a registry before the citation is issued, except where the will is not in the citor's possession and the [district judge or] registrar is satisfied that it is impracticable to require it to be lodged.
(6) A person who has been cited to appear may, within eight days of service of the citation upon him (inclusive of the day of such service), or at any time thereafter if no application has been made by the citor under paragraph (5) of rule 47 or paragraph (2) of rule 48, enter an appearance in the registry from which the citation issued by filing Form 5 and shall forthwith thereafter serve on the citor a copy of Form 5 sealed with the seal of the registry.

Para (1): words 'district judge or' in square brackets inserted by SI 1991/1876, r 7(1).

Para (2): words 'district judge or' in square brackets inserted by SI 1991/1876, r 7(1).

Para (2): words 'or probate practitioner' in square brackets inserted by SI 1998/1903, r 6 from 14 September 1998: see SI 1998/1903, r 1(1).

Para (3): words in square brackets substituted by SI 1991/1876, r 7(3).

Para (4): words 'district judge or' in square brackets inserted by SI 1991/1876, r 7(1).

Para (5): words 'district judge or' in square brackets inserted by SI 1991/1876, r 7(1).

A2.86

47 Citation to accept or refuse or to take a grant.—

(1) A citation to accept or refuse a grant may be issued at the instance of any person who would himself be entitled to a grant in the event of the person cited renouncing his right thereto.
(2) Where power to make a grant to an executor has been reserved, a citation calling on him to accept or refuse a grant may be issued at the instance of the executors who

have proved the will or the survivor of them or of the executors of the last survivor of deceased executors who have proved.

(3) A citation calling on an executor who has intermeddled in the estate of the deceased to show cause why he should not be ordered to take a grant may be issued at the instance of any person interested in the estate at any time after the expiration of six months from the death of the deceased, provided that no citation to take a grant shall issue while proceedings as to the validity of the will are pending.

(4) A person cited who is willing to accept or take a grant may, after entering an appearance, apply ex parte by affidavit to a [district judge or] registrar for an order for a grant to himself.

(5) If the time limited for appearance has expired and the person cited has not entered an appearance, the citor may—

- (a) in the case of a citation under paragraph (1) of this rule, apply to a [district judge or] registrar for an order for a grant to himself;
- (b) in the case of a citation under paragraph (2) of this rule, apply to a [district judge or] registrar for an order that a note be made on the grant that the executor in respect of whom power was reserved has been duly cited and has not appeared and that all his rights in respect of the executorship have wholly ceased; or
- (c) in the case of a citation under paragraph (3) of this rule, apply to a [district judge or] registrar by summons (which shall be served on the person cited) for an order requiring such person to take a grant within a specified time or for a grant to himself or to some other person specified in the summons.

(6) An application under the last foregoing paragraph shall be supported by an affidavit showing that the citation was duly served.

(7) If the person cited has entered an appearance but has not applied for a grant under paragraph (4) of this rule, or has failed to prosecute his application with reasonable diligence, the citor may—

- (a) in the case of a citation under paragraph (1) of this rule, apply by summons to a [district judge or] registrar for an order for a grant to himself;
- (b) in the case of a citation under paragraph (2) of this rule, apply by summons to a [district judge or] registrar for an order striking out the appearance and for the endorsement on the grant of such a note as is mentioned in sub-paragraph (b) of paragraph (5) of this rule; or
- (c) in the case of a citation under paragraph (3) of this rule, apply by summons to a [district judge or] registrar for an order requiring the person cited to take a grant within a specified time or for a grant to himself or to some other person specified in the summons;

and the summons shall be served on the person cited.

Paras (4), (5), (7): words in square brackets inserted by SI 1991/1876, r 7(1).

A2.87

48 Citation to propound a will.—

(1) A citation to propound a will shall be directed to the executors named in the will and to all persons interested thereunder, and may be issued at the instance of any citor having an interest contrary to that of the executors or such other persons.

(2) If the time limited for appearance has expired, the citor may—

- (a) in the case where no person has entered an appearance, apply to a [district judge or] registrar for an order for a grant as if the will were invalid and such application shall be supported by an affidavit showing that the citation was duly served; or

(b) in the case where no person who has entered an appearance proceeds with reasonable diligence to propound the will, apply to a [district judge or] registrar by summons, which shall be served on every person cited who has entered an appearance, for such an order as is mentioned in paragraph (a) above.

Para (2): words in square brackets inserted by SI 1991/1876, r 7(1).

A2.88

49 Address for service.—

All caveats, citations, warnings and appearances shall contain an address for service in England and Wales.

A2.89

50 Application for order to attend for examination or for subpoena to bring in a will.—

(1) An application under section 122 of the Act for an order requiring a person to attend for examination may, unless a probate action has been commenced, be made to a [district judge or] registrar by summons which shall be served on every such person as aforesaid.

(2) An application under section 123 of the Act for the issue by a [district judge or] registrar of a subpoena to bring in a will shall be supported by an affidavit setting out the grounds of the application, and if any person served with the subpoena denies that the will is in his possession or control he may file an affidavit to that effect in the registry from which the subpoena issued.

Words in square brackets inserted by SI 1991/1876, r 7(1).

A2.90

51 Grants to part of an estate under section 113 of the Act.—

An application for an order for a grant under section 113 of the Act to part of an estate may be made to a [district judge or] registrar, and shall be supported by an affidavit setting out the grounds of the application, and—

(a) stating whether the estate of the deceased is known to be insolvent; and

(b) showing how any person entitled to a grant in respect of the whole estate in priority to the applicant has been cleared off.

Words in square brackets inserted by SI 1991/1876, r 7(1).

A2.91

52 Grants of administration under discretionary powers of court, and grants ad colligenda bona.—

An application for an order for—

(a) a grant of administration under section 116 of the Act; or

(b) a grant of administration ad colligenda bona,

may be made to a [district judge or] registrar and shall be supported by an affidavit setting out the grounds of the application.

Words in square brackets inserted by SI 1991/1876, r 7(1).

A2.92

53 Applications for leave to swear to death.—
An application for leave to swear to the death of a person in whose estate a grant is sought may be made to a [district judge or] registrar, and shall be supported by an affidavit setting out the grounds of the application and containing particulars of any policies of insurance effected on the life of the presumed deceased together with such further evidence as the [district judge or] registrar may require.

Words in square brackets inserted by SI 1991/1876, r 7(1).

A2.93

54 Grants in respect of nuncupative wills and copies of wills.—
(1) Subject to paragraph (2) below, an application for an order admitting to proof a nuncupative will, or a will contained in a copy or reconstruction thereof where the original is not available, shall be made to a [district judge or] registrar.
(2) In any case where a will is not available owing to its being retained in the custody of a foreign court or official, a duly authenticated copy of the will may be admitted to proof without the order referred to in paragraph (1) above.
(3) An application under paragraph (1) above shall be supported by an affidavit setting out the grounds of the application, and by such evidence on affidavit as the applicant can adduce as to—

- (a) the will's existence after the death of the testator or, where there is no such evidence, the facts on which the applicant relies to rebut the presumption that the will has been revoked by destruction;
- (b) in respect of a nuncupative will, the contents of that will; and
- (c) in respect of a reconstruction of a will, the accuracy of that reconstruction.

(4) The [district judge or] registrar may require additional evidence in the circumstances of a particular case as to due execution of the will or as to the accuracy of the copy will, and may direct that notice be given to persons who would be prejudiced by the application.

Paras (1), (4): words in square brackets inserted by SI 1991/1876, r 7(1).

A2.94

55 Application for rectification of a will.—
(1) An application for an order that a will be rectified by virtue of section 20(1) of the Administration of Justice Act 1982 may be made to a [district judge or] registrar, unless a probate action has been commenced.
(2) The application shall be supported by an affidavit, setting out the grounds of the application, together with such evidence as can be adduced as to the testator's intentions and as to whichever of the following matters as are in issue:—

- (a) in what respects the testator's intentions were not understood; or
- (b) the nature of any alleged clerical error.

(3) Unless otherwise directed, notice of the application shall be given to every person having an interest under the will whose interest might be prejudiced[, or such other person who might be prejudiced], by the rectification applied for and any comments in writing by any such person shall be exhibited to the affidavit in support of the application.
(4) If the [district judge or] registrar is satisfied that, subject to any direction to the contrary, notice has been given to every person mentioned in paragraph (3) above, and that the application is unopposed, he may order that the will be rectified accordingly.

Paras (1), (4): words in square brackets inserted by SI 1991/1876, r 7(1).

Para (3): words ', or such other person who might be prejudiced,' in square brackets inserted by SI 1998/1903, r 12 from 14 September 1998: see SI 1998/1903, r 1(1).

A2.95

56 Notice of election by surviving spouse [or civil partner] to redeem life interest.—
(1) Where a surviving spouse [or civil partner] who is the sole or sole surviving personal representative of the deceased is entitled to a life interest in part of the residuary estate and elects under section 47A of the Administration of Estates Act 1925 to have the life interest redeemed, he may give written notice of the election to the [senior district judge] in pursuance of subsection (7) of that section by filing a notice in Form 6 in the Principal Registry or in the district probate registry from which the grant issued.
(2) Where the grant issued from a district probate registry, the notice shall be filed in duplicate.
(3) A notice filed under this rule shall be noted on the grant and the record and shall be open to inspection.

Provision heading: words 'or civil partner' in square brackets inserted by SI 2005/2114, art 2(6), Sch 6, para 2(1), (4) from 5 December 2005: see SI 2005/2114, art 1.

Para (1): words 'or civil partner' in square brackets inserted by SI 2005/2114, art 2(6), Sch 6, para 2(1), (4) from 5 December 2005: see SI 2005/2114, art 1.

Para (1): words 'senior district judge' in square brackets substituted by SI 1991/1876, r 7(4).

A2.96

[57 Index of grant applications—
(1) The senior district judge shall maintain an index of every pending application for a grant made in any registry or sub-registry.
(2) Every registry or sub-registry in which an application is made shall cause the index to be searched and shall record the result of the search.]

Substituted by SI 1998/1903, r 13 from 14 September 1998: see SI 1998/1903, r 1(1).

A2.97

58 Inspection of copies of original wills and other documents.—
An original will or other document referred to in section 124 of the Act shall not be open to inspection if, in the opinion of a [district judge or] registrar, such inspection would be undesirable or otherwise inappropriate.

Words in square brackets inserted by SI 1991/1876, r 7(1).

A2.98

59 Issue of copies of original wills and other documents.—
Where copies are required of original wills or other documents deposited under section 124 of the Act, such copies may be facsimile copies sealed with the seal of the court and issued either as office copies or certified under the hand of a [district judge or] registrar to be true copies.

Words in square brackets inserted by SI 1991/1876, r 7(1).

A2.99

60 Taxation of costs.—
[(1) Order 62 of the Rules of the Supreme Court 1965 shall not apply to costs in non-contentious probate matters, and Parts 43, 44 (except rules 44.9 to 44.12), 47 and

48 of the Civil Procedure Rules 1998 ('the 1998 Rules') shall apply to costs in those matters, with the modifications contained in paragraphs (3) to (7) of this rule.

(2) Where detailed assessment of a bill of costs is ordered, it shall be referred—

- (a) where the order was made by a district judge, to a district judge, a costs judge or an authorised court officer within rule 43.2(1)(d)(iii) or (iv) of the 1998 Rules;
- (b) where the order was made by a registrar, to that registrar or, where this is not possible, in accordance with sub-paragraph (a) above.

(3) Every reference in Parts 43, 44, 47 and 48 of the 1998 Rules to a district judge shall be construed as referring only to a district judge of the Principal Registry.

(4) The definition of 'costs officer' in rule 43.2(1)(c) of the 1998 Rules shall have effect as if it included a paragraph reading–

'(iv) a district probate registrar.'

(5) The definition of 'authorised court officer' in rule 43.2(1)(d) of the 1998 Rules shall have effect as if paragraphs (i) and (ii) were omitted.

(6) Rule 44.3(2) of the 1998 Rules (costs follow the event) shall not apply.

(7) Rule 47.4(2) of the 1998 Rules shall apply as if after the words 'Supreme Court Costs Office' there were inserted ', the Principal Registry of the Family Division or such district probate registry as the court may specify'.

(8) Except in the case of an appeal against a decision of an authorised court officer (to which rules 47.20 to 47.23 of the 1998 Rules apply), an appeal against a decision in assessment proceedings relating to costs in non-contentious probate matters shall be dealt with in accordance with the following paragraphs of this rule.

(9) An appeal within paragraph (8) above against a decision made by a district judge, a costs judge (as defined by rule 43.2(1)(b) of the 1998 Rules) or a registrar, shall lie to a judge of the High Court.

(10) Part 52 of the 1998 Rules applies to every appeal within paragraph (8) above, and any reference in Part 52 to a judge or a district judge shall be taken to include a district judge of the Principal Registry of the Family Division.

(11) The 1998 Rules shall apply to an appeal to which Part 52 or rules 47.20 to 47.23 of those Rules apply in accordance with paragraph (8) above in the same way as they apply to any other appeal within Part 52 or rules 47.20 to 47.23 of those Rules as the case may be; accordingly the Rules of the Supreme Court 1965 and the County Court Rules 1981 shall not apply to any such appeal.]

Substituted by SI 1991/1876, r 13.

Substituted by SI 2003/185, rr 4, 5 from: 24 February 2003: see SI 2003/185, r 1; for transitional provisions see r 3 thereof.

A2.100

61 Power to require application to be made by summons.—

(1) Subject to rule 7(2), a [district judge or] a registrar may require any application to be made by summons to a [district judge or] registrar in chambers or a judge in chambers or open court.

(2) An application for an inventory and account shall be made by summons to a [district judge or] registrar.

(3) A summons for hearing by a [district judge or] registrar shall be issued out of the registry in which it is to be heard.

(4) A summons to be heard by a judge shall be issued out of the Principal Registry.

Paras (1)–(3): words in square brackets inserted by SI 1991/1876, rr 7(1), 14.

A2.101

62 Transfer of applications.—
A registrar to whom any application is made under these Rules may order the transfer of the application to another [district judge or] registrar having jurisdiction.

Words in square brackets inserted by SI 1991/1876, r 7(1).

A2.102

62A Exercise of a registrar's jurisdiction by another registrar.—
A registrar may hear and dispose of an application under these Rules on behalf of any other registrar by whom the application would otherwise have been heard, if that other registrar so requests or an application in that behalf is made by a party making an application under these Rules; and where the circumstances require it, the registrar shall, without the need for any such request or application, hear and dispose of the application.]

Inserted by SI 1998/1903, r 14 from 14 September 1998: see SI 1998/1903, r 1(1).

A2.103

63 Power to make orders for costs.—
On any application dealt with by him on summons, the . . . registrar shall have full power to determine by whom and to what extent the costs are to be paid.

Words omitted revoked by SI 1991/1876, r 7(2).

A2.104

64 Exercise of powers of judge during Long Vacation.—
All powers exercisable under these Rules by a judge in chambers may be exercised during the Long Vacation by a [district judge].

Words in square brackets substituted by SI 1991/1876, r 7(3).

A2.105

65 Appeals from [district judges or] registrars.—
(1) An appeal against a decision or requirement of a [district judge or] registrar shall be made by summons to a judge.
(2) If, in the case of an appeal under the last foregoing paragraph, any person besides the appellant appeared or was represented before the [district judge or] registrar from whose decision or requirement the appeal is brought, the summons shall be issued within seven days thereof for hearing on the first available day and shall be served on every such person as aforesaid.
[(3) This rule does not apply to an appeal against a decision in proceedings for the assessment of costs.]

Para (1): words 'district judge or' in square brackets inserted by SI 1991/1876, r 7(1), (6).

Para (2): words 'district judge or' in square brackets inserted by SI 1991/1876, r 7(1), (6).

Para (3): inserted by SI 2003/185, r 6 from 24 February 2003: see SI 2003/185, r 1; for transitional provisions see r 3 thereof.

A2.106

66 Service of summons.—
(1) A judge [or district judge] or, where the application is to be made to a district probate registrar, that registrar, may direct that a summons for the service of which no

other provision is made by these Rules shall be served on such person or persons as the [judge, district judge or] registrar] [may direct].

(2) Where by these Rules or by any direction given under the last foregoing paragraph a summons is required to be served on any person, it shall be served not less than two clear days before the day appointed for the hearing, unless a judge or [district judge or] registrar at or before the hearing dispenses with service on such terms, if any, as he may think fit.

Para (1): words 'district judge' in square brackets substituted by SI 1991/1876, r 7(3).

Para (1): words 'judge, district judge or registrar' in square brackets substituted by SI 1998/1903, r 15 from 14 September 1998: see SI 1998/1903, r 1(1).

Para (1): words 'may direct' in square brackets substituted by SI 1991/1876, r 7(7).

Para (2): words 'district judge or' in square brackets inserted by SI 1991/1876, r 7(1).

A2.107

67 Notices, etc.—

Unless a [district judge or] registrar otherwise directs or these Rules otherwise provide, any notice or other document required to be given to or served on any person may be given or served in the manner prescribed by Order 65, rule 5 of the Rules of the Supreme Court 1965.

Words in square brackets inserted by SI 1991/1876, r 7(1).

A2.108

68 Application to pending proceedings.—

Subject in any particular case to any direction given by a judge or [district judge or] registrar, these Rules shall apply to any proceedings which are pending on the date on which they come into force as well as to any proceedings commenced on or after that date.

Words in square brackets inserted by SI 1991/1876, r 7(1).

A2.109

69 Revocation of previous rules.—

(1) Subject to paragraph (2) below, the rules set out in the Second Schedule are hereby revoked.

(2) The rules set out in the Second Schedule shall continue to apply to such extent as may be necessary for giving effect to a direction under rule 68.

SCHEDULE 1

FORMS

Rule 2(2)

FORM 1

CERTIFICATE OF DELIVERY OF INLAND REVENUE AFFIDAVIT

A2.110

Rule 42

And it is hereby certified that an Inland Revenue affidavit has been delivered wherein it is shown that the gross value of the said estate in the United Kingdom (exclusive of what the said deceased may have been possessed of or entitled to as a trustee and not beneficially) amounts to £. and that the net value of the estate amounts to £.

And it is further certified that it appears by a receipt signed by an Inland Revenue officer on the said affidavit that £. on account of estate duty and interest on such duty has been paid.

FORM 2

STANDING SEARCH

Rule 43(1)

In the High Court of Justice Family Division

[The Principal or . . . . District Probate Registry]

I/We apply for the entry of a standing search so that there shall be sent to me/us an office copy of every grant of representation in England and Wales in the estate of—

Full name of deceased: . . . .

Full address: . . . .

Alternative or alias names: . . . .

Exact date of death: . . . .

which either has issued not more than 12 months before the entry of this application or issues within 6 months thereafter.

Signed . . . .

Name in block letters. . . . .

Full address . . . .

Reference No. (if any) . . . .

Words in square brackets substituted by SI 1991/1876, r 11(3).

FORM 3

CAVEAT

Rule 44(2)

In the High Court of Justice Family Division

The Principal [*or*. . . . . District Probate] Registry.

Let no grant be sealed in the estate of (*full name and address*) deceased, who died on the . . . . day of . . . . 19/20. . . . . without notice to (*name of party by whom or on whose behalf the caveat is entered*).

Dated this . . . . day of . . . . 20. . . . .

(*Signed*) (*to be signed by the caveator's solicitor or probate practitioner or by the caveator if acting in person*)

whose address for service is: . . . .

Solicitor[/probate practitoner] for the said . . . . (*If the caveator is acting in person, substitute 'In person'.*)

Words 'or probate practitioner' in square brackets inserted by SI 1998/1903, r 16(a) from 14 September 1998: see SI 1998/1903, r 1(1).

Words '/probate practitioner' in square brackets inserted by SI 1998/1903, r 16(b) from 14 September 1998: see SI 1998/1903, r 1(1).

FORM 4

WARNING TO CAVEATOR

Rule 44(5)

In the High Court of Justice Family Division

[(The nominated registry as defined by rule 44(15))]

To . . . . of . . . . a party who has entered a caveat in the estate of . . . . deceased.

You have eight days (starting with the day on which this warning was served on you):

(i) to enter an appearance either in person or by your solicitor [or probate practitioner], at the [(name and address of the nominated registry)] setting out what interest you have in the estate of the above-named . . . . of . . . . deceased contrary to that of the party at whose instance this warning is issued; or

(ii) if you have no contrary interest but wish to show cause against the sealing of a grant to such party, to issue and serve a summons for [directions by a district judge of the Principal Registry or a registrar of] a district probate registry.

If you fail to do either of these, the court may proceed to issue a grant of probate or administration in the said estate notwithstanding your caveat.

Dated this . . . . . . day of . . . . 20. . . . .

Issued at the instance of . . . .

(*Here set out the name and interest (including the date of the will, if any, under which the interest arises) of the party warning, the name of his solicitor* [*or probate practitioner*] *and the address for service. If the party warning is acting in person, this must be stated.*) . . . . Registrar

Words '(The nominated registry as defined by rule 44(15))' in square brackets substituted by SI 1998/1903, r 17(b) from 14 September 1998: see SI 1998/1903, r 1(1).

Words 'or probate practitioner' in square brackets in both places they occur inserted by SI 1998/1903, r 17(a) from 14 September 1998: see SI 1998/1903, r 1(1).

Words '(name and address of the nominated registry)' in square brackets substituted by SI 1998/1903, r 17(c) from 14 September 1998: see SI 1998/1903, r 1(1).

Words from 'directions by' to 'a registrar of' in square brackets substituted by SI 1991/1876, r 7(8).

FORM 5

APPEARANCE TO WARNING OR CITATION

Rules 44(10), 46(6)

In the High Court of Justice Family Division

The Principal (*or* District Probate) Registry

Caveat No . . . . . . dated the . . . . . . day of . . . . 20 . . . .

(Citation dated the . . . . . . day of . . . . 20. . . . .)

Full name and address of deceased: . . . .

Full name and address of person warning (*or* citor): . . . .

(*Here set out the interest of the person warning, or citor, as shown in warning or citation.*)

Full name and address of caveator (or person cited). . . . .

(*Here set out the interest of the caveator or person cited, stating the date of the will (if any) under which such interest arises.*)

Enter an appearance for the above-named caveator [or person cited] in this matter.

Dated this . . . . day of . . . . 20. . . . .

(*Signed*) . . . .

whose address for service is: . . . .

Solicitor[/Probate practitioner] (*or* 'In person') . . . .

Words '/probate practitioner' in square brackets inserted by SI 1998/1903, r 18 from 14 September 1998: see SI 1998/1903, r 1(1).

FORM 6

NOTICE OF ELECTION TO REDEEM LIFE INTEREST

Rule 56

In the High Court of Justice Family Division

The Principal (*or*. . . . . District Probate) Registry

In the estate of . . . . deceased.

Whereas . . . . of . . . . died on the . . . . . . day of . . . . 20. . . . .

wholly/partially intestate leaving his/her lawful wife/husband[/civil partner] and . . . . lawful issue of the said deceased;

And whereas Probate/Letters of Administration of the estate of the said were granted to me, the said . . . . [and to . . . . of . . . .] at the Probate Registry on the . . . . . . day of . . . . 20. . . . .;

And whereas (the said . . . . has ceased to be a personal representative because . . . .) and I am (now) the sole personal representative;

Now I, the said . . . . hereby give notice in accordance with section 47A of the Administration of Estates Act 1925 that I elect to redeem the life interest to which I am entitled in the estate of the late . . . . by retaining £ . . . . its capital value, and £ . . . . the costs of the transaction.

Dated this . . . . . . day of . . . . 20. . . . .

(Signed) . . . .

To the [senior district judge] of the Family Division.

Words '/civil partner' in square brackets inserted by SI 2005/2114, art 2(6), Sch 6, para 2(1), (5) from 5 December 2005: see SI 2005/2114, art 1.

Words 'senior district judge' in square brackets substituted by SI 1991/1876, r 7(4).

SCHEDULE 2

REVOCATIONS

A2.111

Rules revoked	References
The Non-Contentious Probate Rules 1954	SI 1954/796
The Non-Contentious Probate (Amendment) Rules 1961	SI 1961/72
The Non-Contentious Probate (Amendment) Rules 1962	SI 1962/2653
The Non-Contentious Probate (Amendment) Rules 1967	SI 1967/748
The Non-Contentious Probate (Amendment) Rules 1968	SI 1968/1675
The Non-Contentious Probate (Amendment) Rules 1969	SI 1969/1689
The Non-Contentious Probate (Amendment) Rules 1971	SI 1971/1977
The Non-Contentious Probate (Amendment) Rules 1974	SI 1974/597
The Non-Contentious Probate (Amendment) Rules 1976	SI 1976/1362

The Non-Contentious Probate (Amendment) Rules 1982	SI 1982/446
The Non-Contentious Probate (Amendment) Rules 1983	SI 1983/623
The Non-Contentious Probate (Amendment) Rules 1985	SI 1985/1232

THE PARENTAL RESPONSIBILITY AGREEMENT REGULATIONS 1991

Note.

These regulations are amended and the Schedule substituted by the Parental Responsibility Agreement (Amendment) Regulations 2005, SI 2005/2808, SI 2009/2026 and the Crime and Courts Act 2013 (Family Court: Consequential Provision) (No.2) Order 2014 SI 2014/879 with effect from 22 April 2014.

INHERITANCE TAX (DELIVERY OF ACCOUNTS) (EXCEPTED ESTATES) REGULATIONS 2004

A2.119

2 Interpretation

In these Regulations—

"the Board" means the [Commissioners for Her Majesty's Revenue and Customs];

"the 1984 Act" means the Inheritance Tax Act 1984;

"an excepted estate" has the meaning given in regulation 4;

["IHT threshold" has the meaning given in regulation 5A;]

'IHT threshold' means the lower limit shown in the Table in Schedule 1 of the 1984 Act applicable to—

(a) *chargeable transfers made in the year before that in which a person's death occurred if—*

(i) *that person died on or after 6th April and before 6th August, and*

(ii) *an application for a grant of representation or, in Scotland, an application for confirmation, is made before 6th August in that year; or*

(b) *chargeable transfers made in the year in which a person's death occurred in any other case,*

and for this purpose 'year' means a period of twelve months ending with 5th April;

'the prescribed period' in relation to any person is the period beginning with that person's death and ending—

(a) *in England, Wales and Northern Ireland, 35 days after the making of the first grant of representation in respect of that person (not being a grant limited in duration, in respect of property or to any special purpose); or*

(b) *in Scotland, 60 days after the date on which confirmation to that person's estate was first issued;*

['section 131 rights' means the rights of issue under section 131(2) of the Civil Partnership Act 2004;]

'spouse[, civil partner] and charity transfer' has the meaning given in regulation 5;

'value' means value for the purpose of tax.

In definition 'the Board' words 'Commissioners for Her Majesty's Revenue and Customs' in square brackets substituted by SI 2006/2141, regs 2, 3 from 1 September 2006: see SI 2006/2141, reg 1(2).

Definition "IHT threshold" substituted by SI 2011/214, reg 2. Date in force: 1 March 2011 (with effect in relation to deaths occurring on or after 6 April 2010): see SI 2011/214, reg 1(2), (3).

Definition 'section 131 rights' inserted by SI 2005/3230, reg 15(1), (2)(b) from 5 December 2005: see SI 2005/3230, reg 1.

In definition 'spouse, civil partner and charity transfer' words ', civil partner' in square brackets inserted by SI 2005/3230, reg 15(1), (2)(a) from 5 December 2005: see SI 2005/3230, reg 1.

LASTING POWERS OF ATTORNEY, ENDURING POWERS OF ATTORNEY AND PUBLIC GUARDIAN REGULATIONS 2007

SI 2007/1253

PART 1
PRELIMINARY

A2.145

2 Interpretation

(1) In these Regulations—

"the Act" means the Mental Capacity Act 2005;

"court" means the Court of Protection;

"LPA certificate", in relation to an instrument made with a view to creating a lasting power of attorney, means the certificate which is required to be included in the instrument by virtue of paragraph 2(1)(e) of Schedule 1 to the Act;

"[person to notify]", in relation to an instrument made with a view to creating a lasting power of attorney, means a person who[, under Schedule 1, paragraph 2(1)(c)(i) of the Act,] is named in the instrument as being a person to be notified of any application for the registration of the instrument;

"prescribed information", in relation to any instrument intended to create a lasting power of attorney, means the information contained in the form used for the instrument which appears under the heading ["Section 8—Your legal rights and responsibilities"].

Para (1): in definition "person to notify" words "person to notify" in square brackets substituted by SI 2015/899, regs 2, 4(a)(i). Date in force: 1 July 2015: see SI 2015/899, reg 1(2); for transitional provisions see regs 17–19.

Para (1): in definition "person to notify" words ", under Schedule 1, paragraph 2(1)(c)(i) of the Act," in square brackets inserted by SI 2015/899, regs 2, 4(a)(ii). Date in force: 1 July 2015: see SI 2015/899, reg 1(2); for transitional provisions see regs 17–19.

Para (1): in definition "prescribed information" words ""Section 8—Your legal rights and responsibilities"" in square brackets substituted by SI 2015/899, regs 2, 4(b). Date in force: 1 July 2015: see SI 2015/899, reg 1(2); for transitional provisions see regs 17–19.

PART 2
LASTING POWERS OF ATTORNEY

Instruments intended to create a lasting power of attorney

A2.148

6 Maximum number of [people to notify]

The maximum number of [people to notify] that the donor of a lasting power of attorney may specify in the instrument intended to create the power is 5.

Provision heading: words "people to notify" in square brackets substituted by SI 2015/899, regs 2, 5. Date in force: 1 July 2015: see SI 2015/899, reg 1(2); for transitional provisions see regs 17–19.

Words "person to notify" in square brackets substituted by SI 2015/899, regs 2, 5. Date in force: 1 July 2015: see SI 2015/899, reg 1(2); for transitional provisions see regs 17–19.

A2.149

7 . . .

. . .

Revoked by SI 2015/899, regs 2, 6. Date in force: 1 July 2015: see SI 2015/899, reg 1(2); for transitional provisions see regs 17–19.

A2.150

8 Persons who may provide an LPA certificate

(1) Subject to paragraph (3), the following persons may give an LPA certificate—

(a) a person chosen by the donor as being someone who has known him personally for the period of at least two years which ends immediately before the date on which that person signs the LPA certificate;

(b) a person chosen by the donor who, on account of his professional skills and expertise, reasonably considers that he is competent to make the judgments necessary to certify the matters set out in paragraph (2)(1)(e) of Schedule 1 to the Act.

(2) The following are examples of persons within paragraph (1)(b)—

(a) a registered health care professional;

(b) a barrister, solicitor or advocate called or admitted in any part of the United Kingdom;

(c) a registered social worker; or

(d) an independent mental capacity advocate.

(3) A person is disqualified from giving an LPA certificate in respect of any instrument intended to create a lasting power of attorney if that person is—

(a) a family member of the donor;

(b) a donee of that power;

(c) a donee of—

(i) any other lasting power of attorney, or

(ii) an enduring power of attorney,

which has been executed by the donor (whether or not it has been revoked);

(d) a family member of a donee within sub-paragraph (b);

(e) a director or employee of a trust corporation acting as a donee within sub-paragraph (b);

(f) a business partner or employee of—

(i) the donor, or

(ii) a donee within sub-paragraph (b);

(g) an owner, director, manager or employee of any care home in which the donor is living when the instrument is executed; or

(h) a family member of a person within sub-paragraph (g).

(4) In this regulation—

["care home" means—

(a) a care home in England within the meaning given by section 3 of the Care Standards Act 2000, and

(b) a place in Wales at which a care home service, within the meaning of Part 1 of the Regulation and Inspection of Social Care (Wales) Act 2016, is provided wholly or mainly to persons aged 18 or over;]

"registered health care professional" means a person who is a member of a profession regulated by a body mentioned in section 25(3) of the National Health Service Reform and Health Care Professions Act 2002; and

"registered social worker" means a person registered as a social worker in a register maintained by—

[(a) the Health and Care Professions Council;]

(b) [Social Care Wales];

(c) the Scottish Social Services Council; or

(d) the Northern Ireland Social Care Council.

Para (4): definition "care home" substituted by SI 2018/48, reg 2, Sch 1, para 18. Date in force: 2 April 2018: see SI 2018/48, reg 1(2).

Para (4): in definition "registered social worker" para (a) substituted by SI 2012/1479, art 11, Schedule, Pt 2, para 81. Date in force: 1 August 2012: see SI 2012/1479, art 1(2).

Para (4): in definition "registered social worker" in para (b) words "Social Care Wales" in square brackets substituted by SI 2017/52, reg 2, Sch 1, para 15(1), (2). Date in force: 3 April 2017: see SI 2017/52, reg 1(2).

A2.151

9 Execution of instrument

(1) An instrument intended to create a lasting power of attorney must be executed in accordance with this regulation.

(2) The donor must read (or have read to him) all the prescribed information.

(3) As soon as reasonably practicable after the steps required by paragraph (2) have been taken, the donor must—

(a) complete the provisions of [Sections 1 to 7] of the instrument that apply to him (or direct another person to do so); and

[(b) subject to paragraph (7), in the presence of a witness—

(i) sign Section 9 of the instrument if the instrument is intended to create a lasting power of attorney for property and financial affairs (Form LP1F); or

(ii) sign Sections 5 and 9 of the instrument if the instrument is intended to create a lasting power of attorney for health and welfare (Form LP1H)].

(4) As soon as reasonably practicable after the steps required by paragraph (3) have been taken—

(a) the person giving an LPA certificate . . .

(b) . . .

must complete the LPA certificate at [Section 10] of the instrument and sign it.

(5) As soon as reasonably practicable after the steps required by paragraph (4) have been taken—

(a) the donee, or

(b) if more than one, each of the donees,

must read (or have read to him) all the prescribed information.

(6) As soon as reasonably practicable after the steps required by paragraph (5) have been taken, the donee or, if more than one, each of them—

(a) must complete the provisions of [Section 11] of the instrument that apply to him (or direct another person to do so); and

(b) subject to paragraph (7), must sign [Section 11] of the instrument in the presence of a witness.

(7) If the instrument is to be signed by any person at the direction of the donor, or at the direction of any donee, the signature must be done in the presence of two witnesses.

(8) For the purposes of this regulation—

(a) the donor may not witness any signature required for the power;

(b) a donee may not witness any signature required for the power apart from that of another donee.

(9) A person witnessing a signature must—

(a) sign the instrument; and

(b) give his full name and address.

(10) Any reference in this regulation to a person signing an instrument (however expressed) includes his signing it by means of a mark made on the instrument at the appropriate place.

Para (3): in sub-para (a) words "Sections 1 to 7" in square brackets substituted by SI 2015/899, regs 2, 7(a). Date in force: 1 July 2015: see SI 2015/899, reg 1(2); for transitional provisions see regs 17–19.

Para (3): sub-para (b) substituted by SI 2015/899, regs 2, 7(b). Date in force: 1 July 2015: see SI 2015/899, reg 1(2); for transitional provisions see regs 17–19.

Para (4): in sub-para (a) word omitted revoked by SI 2015/899, regs 2, 7(c). Date in force: 1 July 2015: see SI 2015/899, reg 1(2); for transitional provisions see regs 17–19.

Para (4): sub-para (b) revoked by SI 2015/899, regs 2, 7(d). Date in force: 1 July 2015: see SI 2015/899, reg 1(2); for transitional provisions see regs 17–19.

Para (4): words "Section 10" in square brackets substituted by SI 2015/899, regs 2, 7(e). Date in force: 1 July 2015: see SI 2015/899, reg 1(2); for transitional provisions see regs 17–19.

Para (6): in sub-paras (a), (b) words "Section 11" in square brackets substituted by SI 2015/899, regs 2, 7(f). Date in force: 1 July 2015: see SI 2015/899, reg 1(2); for transitional provisions see regs 17–19.

Registering the instrument

A2.152

10 Notice to be given by a person about to apply for registration of lasting power of attorney

Schedule 2 to these Regulations sets out the form of notice [(Form LPA3)] which must be given by a donor or donee who is about to make an application for the registration of an instrument intended to create a lasting power of attorney.

Words "(Form LPA3)" in square brackets substituted by SI 2015/899, regs 2, 8. Date in force: 1 July 2015: see SI 2015/899, reg 1(2); for transitional provisions see regs 17–19.

A2.153

11 Application for registration

[(1) An application to the Public Guardian for the registration of an instrument intended to create a lasting power of attorney that is in Form LP1F or LP1H must be made by completion of Sections 12 and 13, the relevant parts of Section 14 and Section 15 of that Form.

(2) An application to the Public Guardian for the registration of an instrument intended to create a lasting power of attorney that is in a pre-July 2015 form must be made by using Form LP2 set out in Schedule 3 to these Regulations.

(3) An application to the Public Guardian for the registration of an instrument intended to create a lasting power of attorney where the application is a repeat application ("a reduced fee repeat application") may only be made if—

- (a) the initial application for the registration of a lasting power of attorney is made on or after 1st October 2011;
- (b) the initial application was returned to the applicant as invalid;
- (c) the reduced fee repeat application is submitted for registration within three months of the date on which the initial application was returned to the applicant as invalid; and
- (d) the reduced fee for such applications applies.

(4) Where the initial application for the registration of the lasting power of attorney was made in accordance with paragraph (1) using Form LP1F or LP1H, a reduced fee repeat application must also be made by the completion of Form LP1F or LP1H as appropriate, including completion of the repeat application option in Section 14 of that Form.

(5) Where the initial application for the registration of the lasting power of attorney was made in accordance with paragraph (2) using a pre-July 2015 form, a reduced fee repeat application must be made by the completion of Form LP1F or LP1H as appropriate, including completion of the repeat application option in Section 14 of that Form.

(6) Where the instrument to be registered which is sent with the application is neither—

- (a) the original instrument intended to create the power; nor
- (b) a certified copy of it,

the Public Guardian must not register the instrument unless the court directs the Public Guardian to do so.

(7) In this regulation—

- (a) "pre-July 2015 form" means a valid instrument intended to create a lasting power of attorney that is not in Form LP1F or LP1H but that complies with these Regulations as they were in force immediately before 1st July 2015; and
- (b) "certified copy" means a photographic or other facsimile copy which is certified as an accurate copy by—
  - (i) the donor; or
  - (ii) a solicitor or notary.]

Substituted by SI 2015/899, regs 2, 9. Date in force: 1 July 2015: see SI 2015/899, reg 1(2); for transitional provisions see regs 17–19.

PART II — CONTENTIOUS BUSINESS

CPR PART 57 — [PROBATE, INHERITANCE AND PRESUMPTION OF DEATH]

SI 1987/2024s

Inserted by SI 2001/1388, r 14, Schedule. Date in force: 15 October 2001 (except in relation to proceedings where a claim form is issued before that date): see SI 2001/1388, rr 1(b), 19.

Words "Probate, Inheritance and Presumption of Death" in square brackets substituted by SI 2014/2044, r 10(a). Date in force: 1 October 2014: see SI 2014/2044, r 2.

A2.166

57.1 Scope of this Part and definitions

[(1) This Part contains rules about—

(a) probate claims;

(b) claims for the rectification of wills; . . .

(c) claims and applications to—

(i) substitute another person for a personal representative; or

(ii) remove a personal representative;

(d) claims under the Inheritance (Provision for Family and Dependants) Act 1975][; and

(e) proceedings under the Presumption of Death Act 2013].

(2) In this Part:

(a) "probate claim" means a claim for—

(i) the grant of probate of the will, or letters of administration of the estate, of a deceased person;

(ii) the revocation of such a grant; or

(iii) a decree pronouncing for or against the validity of an alleged will;

not being a claim which is non-contentious (or common form) probate business;

(Section 128 of the [Senior Courts Act 1981] defines non-contentious (or common form) probate business.)

(b) "relevant office" means—

(i) in the case of High Court proceedings in a Chancery district registry, that registry;

(ii) in the case of any other High Court proceedings, Chancery Chambers at the Royal Courts of Justice, Strand, London, WC2A 2LL; and

[(iii) in the case of County Court proceedings, the office of the County Court hearing centre in question;]

(c) "testamentary document" means a will, a draft of a will, written instructions for a will made by or at the request of, or under the instructions of, the testator, and any document purporting to be evidence of the contents, or to be a copy, of a will which is alleged to have been lost or destroyed;

(d) "will" includes a codicil.]

Inserted by SI 2001/1388, r 14, Schedule. Date in force: 15 October 2001 (except in relation to proceedings where a claim form is issued before that date): see SI 2001/1388, rr 1(b), 19.

Para (1): in sub-para (b) word omitted revoked by SI 2002/2058, r 23(c)(i). Date in force: 2 December 2002: see SI 2002/2058, r 1(b).

Para (1): sub-para (d) and word "and" immediately preceding it inserted by SI 2002/2058, r 23(c)(ii). Date in force: 2 December 2002: see SI 2002/2058, r 1(b).

Para (1): in sub-para (c)(ii) word omitted revoked by SI 2014/2044, r 10(c)(i). Date in force: 1 October 2014: see SI 2014/2044, r 2.

Para (1): sub-para (e) and word "; and" immediately preceding it inserted by SI 2014/2044, r 10(c)(ii). Date in force: 1 October 2014: see SI 2014/2044, r 2.

Para (2): words "Senior Courts Act 1981" in square brackets substituted by the Constitutional Reform Act 2005, s 59(5), Sch 11, Pt 1, para 1(2). Date in force: 1 October 2009: see SI 2009/1604, art 2(d).

Para (2): sub-para (b)(iii) substituted by virtue of SI 2014/407, r 24(a). Date in force: 22 April 2014: see SI 2014/954, art 2(a) and SI 2014/407, r 2(1); for transitional provisions see SI 2014/954, art 3.

I
PROBATE CLAIMS

A2.167

57.2 General

[(1) This Section contains rules about probate claims.

(2) Probate claims in the High Court are assigned to the Chancery Division.

[(3) Probate claims in the county court must only be [started by sending the claim to, or making the claim at]—

- (a) a [County Court hearing centre] where there is also a Chancery district registry; or
- (b) the [County Court at Central London].].

(4) All probate claims are allocated to the multi-track.

Inserted by SI 2001/1388, r 14, Schedule. Date in force: 15 October 2001 (except in relation to proceedings where a claim form is issued before that date): see SI 2001/1388, rr 1(b), 19.

Para (3): substituted by SI 2003/2113, r 15. Date in force: 6 October 2003: see SI 2003/2113, r 1(c).

Para (3): words "started by sending the claim to, or making the claim at" in square brackets substituted by SI 2014/407, r 24(b)(i). Date in force: 22 April 2014: see SI 2014/954, art 2(a) and SI 2014/407, r 2(1); for transitional provisions see SI 2014/954, art 3.

Para (3): in sub-para (a) words "County Court hearing centre" in square brackets substituted by SI 2014/407, r 24(b)(ii). Date in force: 22 April 2014: see SI 2014/954, art 2(a) and SI 2014/407, r 2(1); for transitional provisions see SI 2014/954, art 3.

Para (3): in sub-para (b) words "County Court at Central London" in square brackets substituted by SI 2014/407, r 24(b)(iii). Date in force: 22 April 2014: see SI 2014/954, art 2(a) and SI 2014/407, r 2(1); for transitional provisions see SI 2014/954, art 3.

A2.174

57.9 Probate counterclaim in other proceedings

[(1) In this rule "probate counterclaim" means a counterclaim in any claim other than a probate claim by which the defendant claims any such remedy as is mentioned in rule 57.1(2)(a).

(2) Subject to the following paragraphs of this rule, this Part shall apply with the necessary modifications to a probate counterclaim as it applies to a probate claim.

(3) A probate counterclaim must contain a statement of the nature of the interest of each of the parties in the estate of the deceased to which the probate counterclaim relates.

(4) Unless an application notice is issued within 7 days after the service of a probate counterclaim for an order under rule 3.1(2)(e) or 3.4 for the probate counterclaim to be dealt with in separate proceedings or to be struck out, and the application is granted, the court [will] order the transfer of the proceedings to either—

(a) the Chancery Division (if it is not already assigned to that Division) and to either the Royal Courts of Justice or a Chancery district registry (if it is not already proceeding in one of those places); or

[(b) if the County Court has jurisdiction, to a County Court hearing centre where there is also a Chancery District Registry or the County Court at Central London].

(5) If an order is made that a probate counterclaim be dealt with in separate proceedings, the order shall order the transfer of the probate counterclaim as required under paragraph (4).

Inserted by SI 2001/1388, r 14, Schedule. Date in force: 15 October 2001 (except in relation to proceedings where a claim form is issued before that date): see SI 2001/1388, rr 1(b), 19.

Para (4): word "will" in square brackets substituted by SI 2014/407, r 24(c)(i). Date in force: 22 April 2014: see SI 2014/954, art 2(a) and SI 2014/407, r 2(1); for transitional provisions see SI 2014/954, art 3.

Para (4): sub-para (b) substituted by SI 2014/407, r 24(c)(ii). Date in force: 22 April 2014: see SI 2014/954, art 2(a) and SI 2014/407, r 2(1); for transitional provisions see SI 2014/954, art 3.

Appendix III

FEES (NON-CONTENTIOUS BUSINESS)

THE NON-CONTENTIOUS PROBATE FEES ORDER 2004

SI 2004/3120

Note.

1. Shown as amended by the Non-Contentious Probate Fees (Amendment) Orders, SI 2007/2174, SI 2011/588, SI 2013/2302, SI 2014/513, SI 2014/590 and SI 2014/876. New/inserted text is inside square brackets.

2. The Government previously announced that it would implement proposals for reforming fees payable for applications for grants of probate. The proposals were contained in the draft Non-Contentious Probate Fees Order 2017 which was due to take effect in May 2017. In addition, the proposed reform of fees would have removed probate fees from the scheme for fees remission set out in Schedule 1A of the current Fees Order.

3. After further consideration, the Government decided not to give effect to the proposals contained in the draft Non-Contentious Probate Fees Order 2017 outlined in Note 2 above.

A3.01

1

(1) This Order may be cited as the Non-Contentious Probate Fees Order 2004 and shall come into force on the 4th January 2005.

(2) In this Order—

- (a) a fee referred to by number means the fee so numbered in Schedule 1 to this Order;
- (b) 'assessed value' means the value of the net real and personal estate (excluding settled land if any) passing under the grant as shown—
  - (i) in the Inland Revenue affidavit (for a death occurring before 13th March 1975), or
  - (ii) in the Inland Revenue account (for a death occurring on or after 13th March 1975), or
  - (iii) in the case in which, in accordance with arrangements made between the President of the Family Division and the Commissioners of the Inland Revenue, or regulations made under section 256(1)(a) of the Inheritance Tax Act 1984 and from time to time in force, no such affidavit or account is required to be delivered, in the oath which is sworn to lead to the grant,

  and in the case of an application to reseal means the value, as shown, passing under the grant upon its being resealed;
- (c) 'authorised place of deposit' means any place in which, by virtue of a direction given under section 124 of the [Senior Courts Act 1981] original wills and other documents under the control of the High Court

(either in the principal registry or in any district registry) are deposited and preserved;

(d) 'grant' means a grant of probate or letters of administration;

(e) 'district registry' includes the probate registry of Wales, any district probate registry and any sub-registry attached to it;

(f) 'the principal registry' means the Principal Registry of the Family Division and any sub-registry attached to it.

Para (2): in sub-para (c) words 'Senior Courts Act 1981' in square brackets substituted by the Constitutional Reform Act 2005, s 59(5), Sch 11, Pt 1, para 1(2). Date in force: 1 October 2009: see SI 2009/1604, art 2(d).

A3.02

2. Fees to be taken

The fees set out in column 2 of Schedule 1 to this Order shall be taken in the principal registry and in each district registry in respect of the items described in column 1 in accordance with and subject to any directions specified in column 1.

A3.03

3. Exclusion of certain death gratuities

In determining the value of any personal estate for the purposes of this Order there shall be excluded the value of a death gratuity payable under section 17(2) of the Judicial Pensions Act 1981 or section 4(3) of the Judicial Pensions and Retirement Act 1993, or payable to the personal representatives of a deceased civil servant by virtue of a scheme made under section 1 of the Superannuation Act 1972.

A3.04

[4. Remission of fees

Schedule 1A applies for the purpose of ascertaining whether a party is entitled to a remission or part remission of a fee prescribed by this Order.]

Substituted by SI 2007/2174, art 3. Date in force: 1 October 2007: see SI 2007/2174, art 1.

A3.05

5

. . .

Revoked by SI 2013/2302, art 3(1), (3). Date in force: 7 October 2013: see SI 2013/2302, art 1; for transitional provisions see art 13 thereof.

A3.06

6.

(1) Where by any convention entered into by Her Majesty with any foreign power it is provided that no fee shall be required to be paid in respect of any proceedings, the fees specified in this Order shall not be taken in respect of those proceedings.

(2) Where any application for a grant is withdrawn before the issue of a grant, a registrar may reduce or remit a fee.

(3) Fee 7 shall not be taken where a search is made for research or similar purposes by permission of the President of the Family Division for a document over 100 years old filed in the principal registry or a district registry or another authorised place of deposit.

A3.07

7. Special exemption – Armed Forces

Where a fee has been paid or fees have been paid for the application of a grant (other than fee 3.2) and at the time of payment of that fee or those fees –

(a) the application for the grant was in respect of an estate exempt from Inheritance Tax by virtue of section 154 of the Inheritance Tax Act 1984 (exemption for members of the armed forces etc); and

(b) was in respect of a death occurring before 20th March 2003;

the Lord Chancellor shall upon receiving a written application refund the difference between any fee or fees paid and fee 3.2.

A3.08

8. Revocation

The Order specified in Schedule 2 in so far as it was made under section 128 of the Finance Act 1990 shall be revoked.

SCHEDULE 1

FEES TO BE TAKEN

A3.09

[Column 1	Column 2
Number and description of fee	**Amount of fee**
1. Application for a grant	
On an application for a grant (or for resealing a grant) other than on an application to which fee 3 applies, where the assessed value of the estate exceeds £5,000	[£155]
2. Personal application fee	
Where the application under fee 1 is made by a personal applicant (not being an application to which fee 3 applies) fee 2 is payable in addition to fee 1, where the assessed value of the estate exceeds £5,000	£60
3. Special applications	
3.1 For a duplicate or second or subsequent grant (including one following a revoked grant) in respect of the same deceased person, other than a grant preceded only by a grant limited to settled land, to trust property, or to part of the estate	£20
3.2 On an application for a grant relating to a death occurring on or after 20th March 2003 and in respect of an estate exempt from inheritance tax by virtue of section 154 of the Inheritance Tax Act 1984 (exemption for members of the armed forces etc)	£10
4. Caveats	
For the entry or the extension of a caveat	£20
5. Search	
On an application for a standing search to be carried out in an estate, for each period of six months including the issue of a copy grant and will, if any (irrespective of the number of pages)	[£10]

[Column 1 Number and description of fee	Column 2 Amount of fee
6. Deposit of wills On depositing a will for safe custody in the principal registry or a district registry	£20
7. Inspection On inspection of any will or other document retained by the registry (in the presence of an officer of the registry)	£20
8. Copy documents On a request for a copy of any document whether or not provided as a certified copy:	
(a) for the first copy	[£10]
(b) for every subsequent copy of the same document if supplied at the same time	[50p]
(c) where copies of any document are made available on a computer disk or in other electronic form, for each such copy	[£10]
(d) where a search of the index is required, in addition to fee 8(a), (b) or (c) as appropriate, for each period of 4 years searched after the first 4 years	£4
9. Oaths Except on a personal application for a grant, for administering an oath,	
9.1 for each deponent to each affidavit	[£11]
9.2 for marking each exhibit	£2
10. Determination of costs For determining costs	The same fees as are payable from time to time for determining costs under the Civil Proceedings Fees Order 2004, (the relevant fees are set out in fee 5 in Schedule 1 to that Order)
11. Settling documents For perusing and settling citations, advertisements, oaths, affidavits, or other documents, for each document settled	£12]

Substituted by SI 2011/588, arts 2, 3, Schedule. Date in force: 4 April 2011: see SI 2011/588, art 1.

Item 1: in column 2 sum "£155" in square brackets substituted by SI 2014/876, art 2(1), (2)(a). Date in force: 22 April 2014: see SI 2014/876, art 1.

Item 5: in column 2 sum "£10" in square brackets substituted by SI 2014/876, art 2(1), (2)(b). Date in force: 22 April 2014: see SI 2014/876, art 1.

Item 8: in para (a) in column 2 sum "£10" in square brackets substituted by SI 2014/876, art 2(1), (2)(c). Date in force: 22 April 2014: see SI 2014/876, art 1.

Item 8: in para (b) in column 2 sum "50p" in square brackets substituted by SI 2014/876, art 2(1), (2)(d). Date in force: 22 April 2014: see SI 2014/876, art 1.

Item 8: in para (c) in column 2 sum "£10" in square brackets substituted by SI 2014/876, art 2(1), (2)(e). Date in force: 22 April 2014: see SI 2014/876, art 1.

Item 9.1: in column 2 sum "£11" in square brackets substituted by SI 2014/876, art 2(1), (2)(f). Date in force: 22 April 2014: see SI 2014/876, art 1.

[SCHEDULE 1A
REMISSIONS AND PART-REMISSIONS]

[Article 4]

A3.10

1 [Interpretation

(1) In this Schedule—

"child" means a person—

(a) whose main residence is with a party and who is aged—

(i) under 16 years; or

(ii) 16 to 19 years; and is—

(aa) not married or in a civil partnership; and

(bb) enrolled or accepted in full-time education that is not advanced education, or approved training; or

(b) in respect of whom a party or their partner pays child support maintenance or periodic payments in accordance with a maintenance agreement,

and "full-time education", "advanced education" and "approved training" have the meaning given by the Child Benefit (General) Regulations 2006;

"child support maintenance" has the meaning given in section 3(6) of the Child Support Act 1991;

"couple" has the meaning given in section 3(5A) of the Tax Credits Act 2002;

"disposable capital" has the meaning given in paragraph 5;

["excluded benefits" means any of the following—

(a) any of the following benefits payable under the Social Security Contributions and Benefits Act 1992 or the corresponding provisions of the Social Security Contributions and Benefits (Northern Ireland) Act 1992—

(i) *attendance allowance under section 64;* any payment of bereavement support payment under section 30 of the Pensions Act 2014;]

(ii) severe disablement allowance;

(iii) carer's allowance;

(iv) disability living allowance;

(v) constant attendance allowance under section 104 as an increase to a disablement pension;

(vi) any payment made out of the social fund;

(vii) housing benefit;

(viii) widowed parents allowance;

(b) any of the following benefit payable under the Tax Credits Act 2002—

(i) any disabled child element or severely disabled child element of the child tax credit;

(ii) any childcare element of the working tax credit;

(c) any direct payment made under the Community Care, Services for Carers and Children's Services (Direct Payments) (England) Regulations 2009, . . . the Carers and Direct Payments Act (Northern Ireland) 2002, . . . [the Social Care (Self-directed Support) (Scotland) Act 2013] [or under regulations made under sections 50 to 53 of the Social Services and Well-being (Wales) Act 2014];

(d) a back to work bonus payable under section 26 of the Jobseekers Act 1995, or article 28 of the Jobseekers (Northern Ireland) Order 1995;
(e) any exceptionally severe disablement allowance paid under the Personal Injuries (Civilians) Scheme 1983;
(f) any payments from the Industrial Injuries Disablement Benefit;
(g) any pension paid under the Naval, Military and Air Forces etc (Disablement and Death) Service Pension Order 2006;
(h) any payment made from the Independent Living Funds;
(i) any payment made from the Bereavement Allowance;
(j) any financial support paid under an agreement for the care of a foster child;
(k) any housing credit element of pension credit;
(l) any armed forces independence payment;
(m) any personal independence payment payable under the Welfare Reform Act 2012;
(n) any payment on account of benefit as defined in the Social Security (Payments on Account of Benefit) Regulations 2013;
(o) any of the following amounts, as defined by the Universal Credit Regulations 2013, that make up an award of universal credit—
    (i) an additional amount to the child element in respect of a disabled child;
    (ii) a housing costs element;
    (iii) a childcare costs element;
    (iv) a carer element;
    (v) a limited capability for work or limited capacity for work and work -related activity element;]

"family help (higher)" has the meaning given in paragraph 15(3) of the Civil Legal Aid (Merits Criteria) Regulations 2013;
"family help (lower)" has the meaning given in paragraph 15(2) of the Civil Legal Aid (Merits Criteria) Regulations 2013;
"gross monthly income" has the meaning given in paragraph 13;
"Independent Living Funds" means the funds listed at regulation 20(2)(b) of the Criminal Legal Aid (Financial Resources) Regulations 2013;
"legal representation" has the meaning given in paragraph 18(2) of the Civil Legal Aid (Merits Criteria) Regulations 2013;
"maintenance agreement" has the meaning given in subsection 9(1) of the Child Support Act 1991;
"partner" means a person with whom the party lives as a couple and includes a person with whom the party is not currently living but from whom the party is not living separate and apart;
"party" means the individual who would, but for this Schedule, be liable to pay a fee under this Order;
"restraint order" means—
(a) an order under section 42(1A) of the Senior Courts Act 1981;
(b) an order under section 33 of the Employment Tribunals Act 1996;
(c) a civil restraint order made under rule 3.11 of the Civil Procedure Rules 1998, or a practice direction made under that rule; or
(d) a civil restraint order under rule 4.8 of the Family Procedure Rules 2010, or the practice direction referred to in that rule.

(2) References to remission of a fee are to be read as including references to a part remission of a fee as appropriate and remit and remitted shall be construed accordingly.

2 Fee remission

If a party satisfies the disposable capital test, the amount of any fee remission is calculated by applying the gross monthly income test.

Disposable capital test

3 Disposable capital test

(1) Subject to paragraph 4, a party satisfies the disposable capital test if—

(a) the fee payable by the party and for which an application for remission is made, falls within a fee band set out in column 1 of Table 1; and

(b) the party's disposable capital is less than the amount in the corresponding row of column 2.

Table 1

Column 1 (fee band)	*Column 2 (disposable capital)*
Up to and including £1,000	£3,000
£1,001 to £1,335	£4,000
£1,336 to £1,665	£5,000
£1,666 to £2,000	£6,000
£2,001 to £2,330	£7,000
£2,331 to £4,000	£8,000
£4,001 to £5,000	£10,000
£5,001 to £6,000	£12,000
£6,001 to £7,000	£14,000
£7,001 or more	£16,000

4

Subject to paragraph 14, if a party or their partner is aged 61 or over, that party satisfies the disposable capital test if that party's disposable capital is less than £16,000.

5 Disposable capital

Subject to paragraph 14, disposable capital is the value of every resource of a capital nature belonging to the party on the date on which the application for remission is made, unless it is treated as income by this Order, or it is disregarded as excluded disposable capital.

6 Disposable capital—non-money resources

The value of a resource of a capital nature that does not consist of money is calculated as the amount which that resource would realise if sold, less—

(a) 10% of the sale value; and

(b) the amount of any borrowing secured against that resource that would be repayable on sale.

7 Disposable capital—resources held outside the United Kingdom

(1) Capital resources in a country outside the United Kingdom count towards disposable capital.

(2) If there is no prohibition in that country against the transfer of a resource into the United Kingdom, the value of that resource is the amount which that resource would realise if sold in that country, in accordance with paragraph 6.

(3) If there is a prohibition in that country against the transfer of a resource into the United Kingdom, the value of that resource is the amount that resource would realise if sold to a buyer in the United Kingdom.

8 Disposable capital—foreign currency resources

Where disposable capital is held in currency other than sterling, the cost of any banking charge or commission that would be payable if that amount were converted into sterling, is deducted from its value.

9 Disposable capital—jointly owned resources

Where any resource of a capital nature is owned jointly or in common, there is a presumption that the resource is owned in equal shares, unless evidence to the contrary is produced.

10 Excluded disposable capital

The following things are excluded disposable capital—

(a) a property which is the main or only dwelling occupied by the party;

(b) the household furniture and effects of the main or only dwelling occupied by the party;

(c) articles of personal clothing;

(d) any vehicle, the sale of which would leave the party, or their partner, without motor transport;

(e) tools and implements of trade, including vehicles used for business purposes;

(f) the capital value of the party's or their partner's business, where the party or their partner is self-employed;

(g) the capital value of any funds or other assets held in trust, where the party or their partner is a beneficiary without entitlement to advances of any trust capital;

(h) a jobseeker's back to work bonus;

(i) a payment made as a result of a determination of unfair dismissal by a court or tribunal, or by way of settlement of a claim for unfair dismissal;

(j) any compensation paid as a result of a determination of medical negligence or in respect of any personal injury by a court, or by way of settlement of a claim for medical negligence or personal injury;

(k) the capital held in any personal or occupational pension scheme;

(l) any cash value payable on surrender of a contract of insurance;

(m) any capital payment made out of the Independent Living Funds;

(n) *any bereavement payment;* any bereavement support payment in respect of the rate set out in regulation 3(2) or (5) of the Bereavement Support Payment Regulations 2017 (rate of bereavement support payment);]

(o) any capital insurance or endowment lump sum payments that have been paid as a result of illness, disability or death;

(p) any student loan or student grant;

(q) any payments under the criminal injuries compensation scheme.

Gross monthly income test

11 Remission of fees—gross monthly income

(1) If a party satisfies the disposable capital test, no fee is payable under this Order if, at the time when the fee would otherwise be payable, the party or their partner has the number of children specified in column 1 of Table 2 and—

(a) if the party is single, their gross monthly income does not exceed the amount set out in the appropriate row of column 2; or

(b) if the party is one of a couple, the gross monthly income of that couple does not exceed the amount set out in the appropriate row of column 3.

Table 2

Column 1 Number of children of party	Column 2 Single	Column 3 Couple
no children	£1,085	£1,245
1 child	£1,330	£1,490
2 children	£1,575	£1,735

(2) If a party or their partner has more than 2 children, the relevant amount of gross monthly income is the appropriate amount specified in Table 2 for 2 children, plus the sum of £245 for each additional child.

(3) For every £10 of gross monthly income received above the appropriate amount in Table 2, including any additional amount added under sub-paragraph (2), the party must pay £5 towards the fee payable, up to the maximum amount of the fee payable.

(4) This paragraph is subject to paragraph 12.

12 Gross monthly income cap

(1) No remission is available if a party or their partner has the number of children specified in column 1 of Table 3 and—

(a) if the party is single, their gross monthly income exceeds the amount set out in the appropriate row of column 2 of Table 3; or

(b) if the party is one of a couple, the gross monthly income of that couple exceeds the amount set out in the appropriate row of column 3 of Table 3.

Table 3

Column 1 Number of children of party	Column 2 Single	Column 3 Couple
no children	£5,085	£5,245
1 child	£5,330	£5,490
2 children	£5,575	£5,735

(2) If a party or their partner has more than 2 children, the relevant amount of gross monthly income is the appropriate amount specified in Table 3 for 2 children, plus the sum of £245 for each additional child.

13 Gross monthly income

(1) Subject to paragraph 14, gross monthly income means the total monthly income, for the month preceding that in which the application for remission is made, from all sources, other than receipt of any of the excluded benefits.

(2) Income from a trade, business or gainful occupation other than an occupation at a wage or salary is calculated as—

(a) the profits which have accrued or will accrue to the party; and

(b) the drawings of the party;

in the month preceding that in which the application for remission is made.

(3) In calculating profits under sub-paragraph (2)(a), all sums necessarily expended to earn those profits are deducted.

General

14 Resources and income treated as the party's resources and income

(1) Subject to sub-paragraph (2), the disposable capital and gross monthly income of a partner of a party is to be treated as disposable capital and gross monthly income of the party.

(2) Where the partner of a party has a contrary interest to the party in the matter to which the fee relates, the disposable capital and gross monthly income of that partner, if any, is not treated as the disposable capital and gross monthly income of the party.

15 Application for remission of a fee

(1) An application for remission of a fee must be made at the time when the fee would otherwise be payable.

(2) Where an application for remission of a fee is made, the party must—

- (a) indicate the fee to which the application relates;
- (b) declare the amount of their disposable capital; and
- (c) provide documentary evidence of their gross monthly income and the number of children relevant for the purposes of paragraphs 11 and 12.

(3) Where an application for remission of a fee is made on or before the date on which a fee is payable, the date for payment of the fee is disapplied.

(4) Where an application for remission is refused, or if part remission of a fee is granted, the amount of the fee which remains unremitted must be paid within the period notified in writing to the party.

16 Remission in exceptional circumstances

A fee specified in this Order may be remitted where the Lord Chancellor is satisfied that there are exceptional circumstances which justify doing so.

17 Refunds

(1) Subject to sub-paragraph (3), where a party pays a fee at a time when that party would have been entitled to a remission if they had provided the documentary evidence required by paragraph 15, the fee, or the amount by which the fee would have been reduced as the case may be, must be refunded if documentary evidence relating to the time when the fee became payable is provided at a later date.

(2) Subject to sub-paragraph (3), where a fee has been paid at a time when the Lord Chancellor, if all the circumstances had been known, would have remitted the fee under paragraph 15, the fee or the amount by which the fee would have been reduced, as the case may be, must be refunded to the party.

(3) No refund shall be made under this paragraph unless the party who paid the fee applies within 3 months of the date on which the fee was paid.

(4) The Lord Chancellor may extend the period of 3 months mentioned in sub-paragraph (3) if the Lord Chancellor considers that there is a good reason for a refund being made after the end of the period of 3 months.

18 Legal Aid

A party is not entitled to a fee remission if, under Part 1 of the Legal Aid, Sentencing and Punishment of Offenders Act 2012, they are in receipt of the following civil legal services—

- (a) Legal representation; or
- (b) Family help (higher); or
- (c) Family help (lower) in respect of applying for a consent order.

19 Vexatious litigants

(1) This paragraph applies where—

- (a) a restraint order is in force against a party; and

(b) that party makes an application for permission to—
  (i) issue proceedings or take a step in proceedings as required by the restraint order;
  (ii) apply for amendment or discharge of the order; or
  (iii) appeal the order.

(2) The fee prescribed by this Order for the application is payable in full.

(3) If the party is granted permission, they are to be refunded the difference between—
  (a) the fee paid; and
  (b) the fee that would have been payable if this Schedule had been applied without reference to this paragraph.

20 Exceptions

No remissions or refunds are available in respect of the fee payable for—
  (a) copy or duplicate documents;
  (b) searches.]

Substituted by SI 2013/2302, art 3(1), (2), Schedule. Date in force: 7 October 2013: see SI 2013/2302, art 1; for transitional provisions see art 13 thereof.

Para 1: in sub-para (1) definition "excluded benefits" substituted by SI 2014/590, art 6(1), (2). Date in force: 6 April 2014: see SI 2014/590, art 1.

Para 1: in sub-para (1) in definition "excluded benefits" in para (c) first words omitted revoked by SI 2016/211, reg 3, Sch 3, Pt 2, para 189(a). Date in force: 6 April 2016: see SI 2016/211, reg 1(2).

Para 1: in sub-para (1) in definition "excluded benefits" para (a)(i) substituted by SI 2017/422, art 23(a). Date in force: 6 April 2017: see SI 2017/422, art 1(2); for provision as to later commencement in specified cases see arts 2, 3.

Para 1: in sub-para (1) in definition "excluded benefits" in para (c) second word omitted revoked by SI 2016/211, reg 3, Sch 3, Pt 2, para 189(b). Date in force: 6 April 2016: see SI 2016/211, reg 1(2).

Para 1: in sub-para (1) in definition "excluded benefits" para (c) words "the Social Care (Self—directed Support) (Scotland) Act 2013" in square brackets substituted by SI 2014/513, art 2, Schedule, para 9. Date in force: 1 April 2014: see SI 2014/513, art 1(2).

Para (1): in sub-para (1) in definition "excluded benefits" in para (c) words from "or under regulations" to "Social Services and Well-being (Wales) Act 2014" in square brackets inserted by SI 2016/211, reg 3, Sch 3, Pt 2, para 189(c). Date in force: 6 April 2016: see SI 2016/211, reg 1(2).

Para 10: sub-para (n) substituted by SI 2017/422, art 23(b). Date in force: 6 April 2017: see SI 2017/422, art 1(2); for provision as to later commencement in specified cases see arts 2, 3.

SCHEDULE 2

ORDER REVOKED

A3.11

Title	*Reference*
The Non-Contentious Probate Fees (Amendment) Order 2000	SI 2000/642

RATES OF INHERITANCE TAX AND CAPITAL TRANSFER TAX

A4.10 For deaths on or after 15 March 1988.

Effective dates	*Taxable threshold*	*Rate of tax*	*Legislation*
15/3/88–5/4/89	£110,000	40%	FA 1988, s 136
6/4/89–5/4/90	£118,000	40%	SI 1989/468
6/4/90–5/4/91	£128,000	40%	SI 1990/680
6/4/91–9/3/92	£140,000	40%	SI 1991/735
10/3/95–5/4/95	£150,000	40%	FA [No2] 1992, s 72
6/4/95–5/4/96	£154,000	40%	SI 1994/3011
6/4/96–5/4/97	£200,000	40%	FA 1996, s 183
6/4/97–5/4/98	£215,000	40%	FA 1997, s 93
6/4/98–5/4/99	£223,000	40%	SI 1998/756
6/4/99–5/4/00	£231,000	40%	SI 1999/596
6/4/00–5/4/01	£234,000	40%	SI 2000/967
6/4/01–5/4/02	£242,000	40%	SI 2001/639
6/4/02–5/4/03	£250,000	40%	FA 2002, s 118
6/4/03–5/4/04	£255,000	40%	SI 2003/841
6/4/04–5/4/05	£263,000	40%	SI 2004/771
6/4/05–5/4/06	£275,000	40%	FA 2005, s 98
6/4/06–5/4/07	£285,000	40%	FA 2005, s 98
6/4/07–5/4/08	£300,000	40%	FA 2005, s 98
6/4/08–5/4/09	£312,000	40%	FA 2006, s 155
6/4/09–5/4/21	£325,000	40%	FA (No2) 2015, s 10 negated the indexation provisions for a further 3 years up to 5 April 2021. FA 2014, Sch 25 negated the indexation provisions for a further 3 years up to 5 April 2018.

Effective dates	*Taxable threshold*	*Rate of tax*	*Legislation*
			FA 2006, s 155, subject to the potential application of IHTA 1984, s 8. FA 2010, s 8 extended the use of the threshold of £325,000 until 5 April 2015 by negating the indexation provisions until that date. FA 2012, s 208 revised the content of s 8(1) of the IHTA 1984 by substituting 'consumer prices index for the month of September in any year' for 'retail prices index for the month of September in any year' with effect from 6 April 2015. Section 8(2) IHTA 1984 was amended to 'consumer prices index' instead of 'retail prices index'. Section 8(3) of the IHTA 1984 was amended to read 'consumer prices index' and means the all items consumer prices index published by the Statistics Board.

Appendix VI

FORMS

Contents

Part II – Forms for use in Probate Claims

Acknowledgments of service

Administrator's account

Affidavits and witness statements

Claim form

Guarantee

Notices

Orders

Statements of case

I. Indorsements of interest and brief details of claim

II. Particulars of claim

III. Defences

IV. Replies and defences to counterclaims

Subpoena

* denotes a form included in this Supplement.

No	*Description*	*Para*
Part I – Forms for use in Non-contentious Probate Matters		
1	General heading of affidavit (and other forms)	**A6.01**
2	General heading of witness statement	**A6.02**
3	Affidavit of execution of a will or codicil	**A6.03**
3A	Will signed in attestation clause or testimonium clause	**A6.04**
3B	Execution by acknowledgment of signature	**A6.05**
3C	Imperfect signature, or will signed by mark, or in foreign characters: knowledge of contents	**A6.06**
3D	Will signed by another person by direction of testator	**A6.07**
3E	Signature of testator appears below those of the witnesses	**A6.08**
4	Affidavit in support of due execution (evidence of execution not available)	**A6.09**
5	Affidavit of handwriting	**A6.10**
6	Affidavit of plight and condition and finding	**A6.11**
7	Affidavit of search for will	**A6.12**
8	Affidavit as to alterations in a will (deponent an attesting witness)	**A6.13**
9	Affidavit verifying alterations in a will (deposed to by the writer of it)	**A6.14**

No	*Description*	*Para*
36	Affidavit to lead revocation of grant by consent	**A6.41**
37	Affidavit of service of citation	**A6.42**
38	Affidavit of service of warning (NCPR SI 1987/2024 rr 44, 67)	**A6.43**
39*	Non-Contentious Probate Rules 1987 Form 5: Appearance to warning or citation NCPR SI 1987/2024 rr 44(10), 46(6)	**A6.44**
40	Appointment of nominee of a county council to take grant	**A6.45**
41*	Non-contentious Probate Rules 1987 Form 4: Caveat... NCPR SI 1987/2024 r 44(2)	**A6.46**
42	Citation to accept or refuse probate (NCPR SI 1987/2024 r 47(1))	**A6.47**
43*	Citation to accept or refuse administration (NCPR SI 1987/2024 r 47(1))	**A6.48**
44*	Citation by creditor against kin (if any) to accept or refuse administration (NCPR SI 1987/2024 r 47(1))	**A6.49**
45*	Citation by creditor against a minor to accept or refuse administration (NCPR SI 1987/2024 r 47(1); RSC Order 80, r 16(2))	**A6.50**
46*	Citation, by executor of executor, against executor to whom power was reserved, to accept or refuse probate (NCPR SI 1987/2024 r 47(2))	**A6.51**
47*	Citation to take probate against an executor who has intermeddled (NCPR SI 1987/2024 r 47(3))	**A6.52**
48*	Citation to propound paper writing (NCPR SI 1987/2024 r 48)	**A6.53**
49	Abstract of citation for advertisement	**A6.54**
50	Consent to proof of will	**A6.55**
51	Consent by assignee to grant to other assignees	**A6.56**
52	Consent to trust corporation applying	**A6.57**
52A*	Disclaimer on intestacy	**A6.57A**
52B*	Disclaimer of interest under a will	**A6.57B**
53	Notice to Leeds District Probate Registry to produce documents	**A6.58**
54	Inventory and account	**A6.59**
55	Notice of motion (RSC Order 8, r 3)	**A6.60**
56	Nomination of a second administrator; minority interest (NCPR SI 1987/2024 r 32(3))	**A6.61**
57	Nomination of a second administrator; lack of mental capacity within the meaning of the Mental Capacity Act 2005 and minority or life interest (NCPR SI 1987/2024 r 35(3))	**A6.62**
58	Form 7: A6.12 Notice of Election to Redeem Life Interest Rule 56	**A6.63**
59	Notice of application for probate to executor to whom power is to be reserved	**A6.64**
60	Oath for probate (general form)	**A6.65**
61	Oath for probate to a trust corporation	**A6.66**
62	Oath for probate to the Public Trustee	**A6.67**

No	*Description*	*Para*
84	Oath for administrators where net value of the estate exceeds £250,000 for death on or after 1 February 2009 and there are issue (husband or widow applying with next person entitled under NCPR SI 1987/2024 r 22)	**A6.89**
85	Oath for administrators – net estate exceeding £250,000 for death on or after 1 February 2009: widow (or husband) and minor child survive: application by spouse and nominated co-administrator	**A6.90**
86	Oath for administrators – net estate exceeding £250,000 for death on or after 1 February 2009: civil partner and minor child survive: application by civil partner who has parental responsibility for minor and nominated co-administrator	**A6.91**
87	Oath for administrator – spouse or civil partner applies alone on assignment by children (net estate exceeding £250,000 for death on or after 1 February 2009)	**A6.92**
88	Oath for administrator (husband's, or widow's, or civil partner's representative applies, whole estate having passed to surviving spouse or civil partner)	**A6.93**
89	Oath for administrator where net estate exceeds in value £250,000 for death on or after 1 February 2009 – issue apply on renunciation of surviving spouse [surviving civil partner]	**A6.94**
90	Oath for administrator where the net estate is under £250,000 for death on or after 1 February 2009 – son or daughter applies on renunciation of surviving spouse [or surviving civil partner]	**A6.95**
91	Oath for administration to child, or other issue having a beneficial interest – spouse [or civil partner] survived but has since died	**A6.96**
92	Oath for administration to child, or other issue having a beneficial interest – spouse [civil partner] survived but has since died without acquiring a beneficial interest	**A6.97**
93	Oath for administration to child (on assignment by surviving spouse [civil partner])	**A6.98**
94	Oath for administration to child or other issue having a beneficial interest – no surviving spouse [civil partner]	**A6.99**
95	Oath for administration to issue having a beneficial interest – no surviving spouse [civil partner] and forfeiture rule precludes a child from acquiring a benefit in the estate (death on or after 1 February 2012)	**A6.100**
96	Oath for administration to a person entitled, jointly with attorney of person equally entitled	**A6.101**
97	Oath for administration to child or children the only issue, save and except others alienated by adoption order made during the lifetime of intestate	**A6.102**
98*	Oath for administration to person entitled, issue being alienated by adoption order made during the lifetime of intestate	**A6.103**

PART I – FORMS FOR USE IN NON-CONTENTIOUS PROBATE MATTERS

Affidavits / witness statement

A6.02

2. General heading of witness statement

In the High Court of Justice

Family Division

The Principal [*or*. . . . . District Probate] Registry [*or* The Probate Registry of Wales]

In the estate of A B deceased

I, C D, of . . . . wish to rely on the following evidence in support of this application for [order for . . . .] [*or as appropriate*]

[facts in support – adapt from precedents below of affidavit and oaths etc.]

I believe that the facts stated in this witness statement are true.

(Signed)

[Print full name] C D. . . . .

(Date)

[**Note.–**

When new rules replace the current Non-Contentious Probate Rules 1987 witness statements will replace affidavits and oaths and regard must be had to Practice Directions which supplement each rule when completing witness statements. Form 2 anticipates this forthcoming change.]

A6.22A

17A. Affidavit to lead order for appointing person to obtain administration for the use and benefit of a person who lacks capacity within the meaning of the Mental Capacity Act 2005

(*Heading as in Form 1:*A6.01)

I, E F, of. . . . . make oath and say that:

1. A B of. . . . . deceased, died on the. . . . . . day of . . . . 20. . . . . . intestate, domiciled in England and Wales, leaving C D her lawful husband, the only person now entitled to her estate.
2. C D by reason of dementia now lacks capacity to manage his property and affairs within the meaning of the Mental Capacity Act 2005.

3. No one has been authorised by the Court of Protection to obtain a grant of representation of the estate of the deceased for the use and benefit of C D.
4. There is no lawful attorney of C D acting under a registered lasting power of attorney [*or* a registered enduring power of attorney].
5. No minority or life interest arises under the intestacy.
6. C D resides at [Moorhouse Residential Home] and is under the care of [Park Medical Practice].
7. I am the [daughter] of the deceased and C D and I am responsible for his needs and finances.
8. The gross value of the estate of the deceased amounts to £.and after deduction of debts and incumbrances the net value of the estate is £.
9. In the circumstances I apply for an order under rule 35(4) of the Non-Contentious Probate Rules 1987 that letters of administration of the estate of the deceased be granted to me for the use and benefit of C D limited until further representation be granted.

Sworn etc

Appearance

A6.44

39. Non-Contentious Probate Rules 1987
Form 5: Appearance to warning or citation
NCPR SI 1987/2024 rr 44(10), 46(6)

In the High Court of Justice

Family Division

The Principal [*or*. . . . . District Probate] Registry

Caveat No. . . . . . dated the. . . . . . day of. . . . . 20. . . . . .

[Citation dated the day of. . . . . 20. . . . . . .]

Full name and address of deceased:. . . . .

Full name and address of person warning [*or* citor]:

[Here set out the interest of the person warning, or citor, as shown in warning or citation.]

Full name and address of caveator [or person cited].

[Here set out the interest of the caveator or person cited, stating the date of the will [if any] under which such interest arises.]

Enter an appearance for the above-named caveator [*or* person cited] in this matter.

Dated the. . . . . . day of. . . . . 20. . . . . . .

[Signed]

whose address for service is:

Solicitor (*or* 'In person').

Caveat

A6.46

41. Non-contentious Probate Rules 1987
Form 4: Caveat...
NCPR SI 1987/2024 r 44(2)

In the High Court of Justice

Family Division

The Principal [*or*. . . . . District Probate] Registry.

Let no grant be sealed in the estate of [*full name and address*] deceased, who died on the. . . . . . day of. . . . . 20. . . . . . without notice to [*name of party by whom or on whose behalf the caveat is entered*].

Dated this. . . . . . day of. . . . . 20. . . . . . .

[Signed] [to be signed by the caveator's probate practitioner or by the caveator if acting in person]

whose address for service is:. . . . .

Probate Practitioner for the. . . . . [*If the caveator is acting in person, substitute 'In person'*.]

Citations

A6.48

43. Citation to accept or refuse administration (NCPR SI 1987/2024 r 47(1))

(*Heading as in Form 1:* **A6.01**)

Elizabeth the Second etc (*as in Form 42:* **A6.47**).

To E B of. . . . .

Take notice that C B and D B have stated in a joint affidavit, sworn the. . . . . . day of. . . . . 20. . . . . . that A B of. . . . . died on the. . . . . . day of. . . . . 20. . . . . . domiciled in England and Wales intestate, leaving you E B his lawful widow and one of the persons entitled to share in his estate and C B and D B his lawful* [*or* natural*] sons and two of the persons entitled to share in the estate of the deceased:

Now this is to command you E B that within eight days after service of this citation on you, inclusive of the day of such service, you do cause an appearance to be entered in the Principal Registry of the Family Division of the High Court of Justice at First Avenue House, 42–49 High Holborn, London WC1V 6NP [*or* in the . . . . District Probate Registry at. . . . .] and accept or refuse letters of administration of all the estate which by law devolves to and vests in the personal representative of the deceased, or show cause why they should not be granted to C B and D B. And take further notice that, in default of your so appearing and accepting and extracting the letters of administration, our court will proceed to grant letters of administration of the estate to C B and D B, your absence notwithstanding.

Dated at. . . . . this. . . . . . day of. . . . . 20. . . . . . .

Extracted by. . . . .

of. . . . . *(Signed)*

Solicitor. District Judge/Registrar.

[*If the deceased died on or after 4 April 1988 the word 'lawful' or 'natural' can be omitted.]

[**Note.**–
This form may be adapted for use in cases where specific persons are cited by a creditor.]
(Form of affidavit to lead citation, *Form 28*: **A6.33**.)

A6.49

44. Citation by creditor against kin (if any) to accept or refuse administration (NCPR SI 1987/2024 r 47(1))

(*Heading as in Form 1:* **A6.01**)

Elizabeth the Second etc *(as in Form 42)*: **A6.47**

To the kin (if any) who are entitled to share and all other persons having or claiming any interest in the estate of A B deceased.

Take notice that C D has stated in an affidavit sworn the. . . . . . day of . . . . 20. . . . . . that AB of. . . . . died on the. . . . . . day of. . . . . 20. . . . . . domiciled in England and Wales intestate, a widower/surviving civil partner without known issue or parent, brother or sister of the whole or half blood or their issue, grandparent, uncle or aunt of the whole or half blood or their issue, or any other person entitled in priority to share in his estate by virtue of any enactment, and that C D is a creditor of the deceased:

Now this is to command you that within one month after service by publication of this citation on you, inclusive of the day of such service, you do cause an appearance to be entered in the Principal Registry of the Family Division of the High Court of Justice at First Avenue House, 42–49 High Holborn, London WC1V 6NP [*or* in the. . . . . District Probate Registry at. . . . .] and accept or refuse letters of administration of all the estate which by law devolves to and vests in the personal representative of the deceased, or show cause why letters of administration of his estate should not be granted to C D. And take further notice that, in default of your so appearing and accepting and extracting letters of administration as aforesaid, our court will proceed to grant letters of administration of the estate of the deceased to C D, your absence notwithstanding.

Dated at. . . . . this. . . . . . day of. . . . . 20. . . . . . .

Extracted by. . . . .

of. . . . . *(Signed)*

Solicitor. District Judge/Registrar.

[Note.–

If the applicant is the nominee of a county council, he should be so described, and the sealed or certified appointment lodged (see *Form 40*: **A6.45**).]

(Form of affidavit to lead citation, *Form 29*: **A6.34**.)

A6.50

45. Citation by creditor against a minor to accept or refuse administration (NCPR SI 1987/2024 r 47(1); RSC Order 80, r 16(2))

(*Heading as in Form 1:* **A6.01**)

Elizabeth the Second etc (*as in Form 42:* **A6.47**):

To G H of. . . . .

Take notice that E F has stated in an affidavit sworn the. . . . . . day of . . . . 20. . . . . . that A B of. . . . . died on the. . . . . . day of. . . . . 20. . . . . . domiciled in England and Wales intestate, a bachelor without issue or parent or any other person entitled in priority to share in his estate by virtue of any enactment, leaving you G H, his lawful* brother of the whole blood and the only person entitled to his estate, that E F is a creditor of the deceased, that you G H are a minor, and that C D is your lawful father [*or* your guardian or the person with whom you reside *or* under whose care you are [*as the case may be*]]:

Now this is to command you G H that within eight days after service of this citation on you, inclusive of the day of such service, you do cause an appearance to be entered in the Principal Registry of the Family Division of the High Court of Justice at First Avenue House, 42–49 High Holborn, London WC1V 6NP [*or* in the . . . . District Probate Registry at. . . . .] and accept or refuse letters of administration of all the estate which by law devolves to and vests in the personal representative of the deceased, or show cause why they should not be granted to E F and another. And take further notice that, in default of your so appearing and accepting and extracting the letters of administration, our said court will proceed to grant letters of administration of the estate to E F and another, your absence notwithstanding.

Dated at. . . . . this. . . . . . day of. . . . . 20. . . . . . .

Extracted by. . . . .

of. . . . . *(Signed)*

Solicitor. District Judge/Registrar.

[*If the deceased died on or after 4 April 1988 the relationship, except in the case of a spouse, need not be lawful and, with that exception, the word 'lawful' may be omitted.]

A6.51

46. Citation, by executor of executor, against executor to whom power was reserved, to accept or refuse probate (NCPR SI 1987/2024 r 47(2))

(*Heading as in Form 1:* **A6.01**)

Elizabeth the Second etc (*as in Form 42:* **A6.47**):

To E F of. . . . .

Take notice that G H has stated in an affidavit sworn the. . . . . . day of . . . . 20. . . . . . that probate of the will of A B of. . . . . deceased, was on the. . . . . . day of. . . . . granted by our High Court of Justice at the Principal Registry of the Family Division [*or* at the. . . . . District Probate Registry] to C D one of the executors named therein, power being reserved of making a like grant to you E F the other executor named therein, that C D died on the. . . . . . day of. . . . . leaving part of the estate of the deceased unadministered and that on the. . . . . . day of . . . . 20. . . . . . probate of the will of C D deceased, was granted by this court at the registry [*or* at the. . . . . District Probate Registry] to G H the sole executor thereof:

Now this is to command you E F that within eight days after service of this citation on you, inclusive of the day of such service, you do cause an appearance to be entered in the Principal Registry of the Family Division of this court at First Avenue House, 42–49 High Holborn, London WC1V 6NP [*or* in the. . . . . District Probate Registry at. . . . .] and accept or refuse probate of the will of A B deceased. And take further notice that, in default of your so appearing and accepting and extracting probate of the will, your rights as such executor will wholly cease, and the representation to the estate of A B deceased will devolve as if you had not been appointed executor.

Dated at. . . . . this. . . . . . day of. . . . . 20. . . . . . .

Extracted by. . . . .

of. . . . . *(Signed)*

Solicitor. District Judge/Registrar.

(Form of affidavit to lead citation, *Form 30*: **A6.35**.)

A6.52

47. Citation to take probate against an executor who has intermeddled (NCPR SI 1987/2024 r 47(3))

(*Heading as in Form 1:* **A6.01**)

Elizabeth the Second etc (*as in Form 42:* **A6.47**):

To E F of. . . . .

Take notice that C D has stated in an affidavit sworn the. . . . . . day of . . . . 20. . . . . . that A B of. . . . . died on the. . . . . . day of. . . . . 20. . . . . . domiciled in England and Wales, having made and duly executed his last will and testament bearing date the. . . . . . day of . . . . 20. . . . . . [now remaining in the Principal Registry of the Family Division of the High Court of Justice *or* in the. . . . . District Probate Registry], that you E F are appointed sole executor in that will, that C D is interested in the estate of the deceased under the will and that you E F have intermeddled in the estate of the deceased:

Now this is to command you E F that within eight days after service of this citation on you, inclusive of the day of such service, you do cause an appearance to be entered in the Principal Registry of the Family Division at First Avenue House, 42–49 High Holborn, London WC1V 6NP [*or* in the. . . . . District Probate

Registry at. . . . .] and show cause why you should not be ordered to take probate of the will.

Dated at. . . . . this. . . . . . day of. . . . . 20. . . . . . .

Extracted by. . . . .

of. . . . . *(Signed)*

Solicitor. District Judge/Registrar.

(Form of affidavit to lead citation, *Form 31*: **A6.36**.)

A6.53

48. Citation to propound paper writing (NCPR SI 1987/2024 r 48)

(Heading as in Form 48: **A6.53***)*

Elizabeth the Second etc (*as in Form 42:* **A6.47**):

To E F of. . . . .

Take notice that C D has stated in an affidavit sworn the. . . . . . day of . . . . 20. . . . . . that A B of. . . . . died on the. . . . . . day of. . . . . 20. . . . . . domiciled in England and Wales a widower leaving C D, his lawful* [*or* natural*] son and the only person entitled to his estate and that the deceased left a certain paper writing dated the. . . . . . day of. . . . . 20. . . . . . purporting to be a will [now remaining in the Principal Registry of the Family Division or in the. . . . . District Probate Registry] whereby he appointed you E F sole executrix and residuary legatee and devisee:

Now this is to command you E F that within eight days after service of this citation on you, inclusive of the day of such service, you do cause an appearance to be entered in the Principal Registry of the Family Division of the High Court of Justice at First Avenue House, 42–49 High Holborn, London WC1V 6NP [*or* in the . . . . District Probate Registry at. . . . .] and propound the paper writing should you think it for your interest so to do, or show cause why letters of administration of all the estate which by law devolves to and vests in the personal representative of the deceased should not be granted to C D. And take further notice that in default of your so appearing and doing as aforesaid our court will proceed to issue a grant of representation of the said estate as if the purported will were invalid, your absence notwithstanding.

Dated at. . . . . this. . . . . . day of. . . . . 20. . . . . . .

Extracted by. . . . .

of. . . . . *(Signed)*

Solicitor. District Judge/Registrar.

[*If the deceased died on or after 4 April 1988 the word 'lawful' or 'natural' can be omitted.]

(Form of affidavit to lead citation, *Form 32*: **A6.37**.)

Disclaimer

A6.57A

52A. Deed of disclaimer of interest under intestacy

(*Heading as in Form 1:* **A6.01** *optional*)

THIS DEED OF DISCLAIMER is made the. . . . . . day of. . . . . 20 . . . .

BY A B of . . . .

WHEREAS

1. C D ('the Intestate') late of. . . . . died on the. . . . . day of. . . . . . 20. . . . . . .
2. A B is the spouse/civil partner of the Intestate and is the sole beneficiary/one of statutory beneficiaries entitled to the estate of the Intestate under section 46, Administration of Estates Act 1925.
3. A B has not taken or accepted any share in the estate.
4. A B desires and intends to disclaim all that is his/her interest in the estate of the Intestate.

NOW THIS DEED WITNESSES that A B hereby disclaims all that is his/her interest in and right to and title over the property comprised in the estate of the Intestate or any part of it

AND A B hereby acknowledges that on the execution of this disclaimer he/she will be treated for the purpose of section 46A, Administration of Estates Act 1925 as having died immediately before the Intestate.

AS WITNESS of which A B has set his/her hand the day and date first written

(Signed)

In the presence of

[Name and address of witness]

A6.57B

52B. Deed of disclaimer of interest under a will

(*Heading as in Form 1:* **A6.01** *optional*)

THIS DEED OF DISCLAIMER is made on the. . . . . . day of. . . . . 20 . . . .

By A B of . . . .

WHEREAS

1. C D ('the Testator') late of. . . . . died on the. . . . . . day of . . . . 20. . . . . . having made a will dated the. . . . . . day of . . . . 20. . . . . . (the Will).
2. A B is the sole beneficiary/one of the beneficiaries named in the Will.
3. A B has not accepted any share in the estate.
4. A B desires and intends to disclaim all his/her interest under the Will or otherwise in the estate of the Testator.

NOW THIS DEED WITNESSES that A B hereby disclaims all that may be his/her interest in and right to and title over the property or any part of it given to him/her under the Will

AND A B hereby acknowledges that on the execution of this disclaimer he/she will be treated for the purposes of section 33A, Wills Act 1837 as having died immediately before the testator.

AS WITNESS of which A B has set his/her hand the day and date first written

(Signed)

In the presence of

[Name and address of witness]

Oaths

A6.103

98. Oath for administration to person entitled, issue being alienated by adoption order made during the lifetime of intestate

(*Death on or after 1 January 1950*)

(*Heading as in Form 1:* **A6.01**)

I, E F, of. . . . . make oath and say that:

1. A B of. . . . . deceased, was born on the. . . . . . day of . . . . 19. . . . . . and died on the. . . . . . day

of. . . . . 20. . . . . . aged. . . . . . years, domiciled in England and Wales intestate a widow[er][surviving civil partner*] without issue entitled to her [his] estate or any other person entitled in priority to share in the estate by virtue of any enactment;

2. By virtue of an adoption order made under the authority of the Adoption Act 1958 [*or as the case may be*] during the lifetime of the deceased, which order is still subsisting, C D, the son [*or* daughter] and only issue of the deceased was duly adopted and the estate of the deceased devolves in all respects as if C D were the lawful child of the adopter [*or* adopters] and not the child of the deceased;
3. *[Clear off any intervening classes.]*
4. No life or minority interest arises under the intestacy.
5. [*add statement as to settled land*];
6. I am the. . . . . and only person entitled to [*or* one of the persons entitled to share in] the estate of the deceased;
7. I will:

   (i) collect, get in and administer [etc – *complete as in Form 83*: **A6.88**].

* Deaths on or after 5 December 2006

[Note.–

The adoption order should not be exhibited to the oath, and the child should be referred to by the name by which he was known prior to the adoption (Registrar's Circular, 2 March 1966).]

A6.136

131. Oath for administration to guardians of a minor as personal representatives of the person entitled

(*Heading as in Form 1:* **A6.01**)

We, C D of. . . . . and R F of. . . . . make oath and say that:

1. A B of. . . . . deceased, was born on the. . . . . . day of . . . . 19. . . . . . and died on the. . . . . . day of. . . . . 20. . . . . . aged. . . . . . years, domiciled in England and Wales intestate, a widower [*or as the case may be*], leaving E B, his son and the only person entitled to his estate, who has since died without having taken upon himself letters of administration of the estate of the intestate;
2. No minority or life interest arises under the intestacy;
3. [*add statement as to settled land*];
4. E B died intestate a bachelor leaving F B his son and only person entitled to his estate;
5. We are the administrators (as guardians and for the use and benefit of F B, who is now a minor) of the estate of E B, letters of administration of his estate having been granted to us at the Principal [*or*. . . . . District Probate] Registry on the. . . . . . day of. . . . . 20. . . . . . ;
6. We will:

   (i) collect, get in and administer according to law the real and personal estate of the deceased, for the use and benefit of F B until he attains the age of eighteen years and until further representation be granted;

(ii) when required to do so by the Court, exhibit in the Court a full inventory of the estate and render an account thereof to the Court; and

(iii) when required to do so by the High Court, deliver up to that Court the grant of letters of administration;

[etc – *as in Form 60*: **A6.65**].

A6.159

154. Oath for administration (will) to person entitled to estate not disposed of

(*Heading as in Form 1:* **A6.01**)

I, C D, of. . . . . make oath and say that:

1. I believe the paper writing now produced to and marked by me to contain the true and original last will and testament of A B of. . . . . deceased, who was born on the. . . . . . day of. . . . . 19. . . . . . and who died on the. . . . . . day of . . . . 20. . . . . . aged. . . . . . years, domiciled in England and Wales;
2. No executor or residuary legatee or devisee is named in the will which does not dispose of the whole estate of the deceased;
3. The deceased died a bachelor [spinster] [widower] [widow] without issue or parent or any other person entitled in priority to share in the estate by virtue of any enactment [*or as the case may be*];
4. I am the brother of the whole blood and only person entitled to [*or* one of the persons entitled to share in] the estate of the deceased not disposed of by the will;
5. No life or minority interest arises in the estate of the deceased;
6. [*add statement as to settled land*];
7. I will:

   (i) collect, get in and administer [etc – *complete as in Form 149*: **A6.154**].

[Note.–

If a residuary gift in a will fails by reason of s 15 of the Wills Act 1837, the following wording, adapted as necessary, should be used: 'The residuary bequest and devise to E F in the will is void by reason that he was an attesting witness to the will [or that at the date of the will he was the lawful husband of G F, an attesting witness to the will].']

A6.160

155. Oath for administration (will) to person entitled to estate not disposed of following disclaimer (death on or after 1 February 2012)

(*Heading as in Form 1:* **A6.01**)

I, C D, of. . . . . make oath and say that:

1. I believe the paper writing now produced to and marked by me to contain the true and original last will and testament of A B of. . . . . de-ceased, who was born on the. . . . . . day of. . . . . 19. . . . . . and who died on the. . . . . . day of . . . . 20. . . . . . aged. . . . . . years, domiciled in England and Wales;
2. E F the sole executor and residuary legatee or devisee named in the will has renounced probate thereof and administration (with will) of the estate of the deceased; further by a deed dated the . . . . . . day of . . . . 20. . . . . . E F has disclaimed all his right and title to the estate and is treated by virtue of the s 33A of the Wills Act 1837 (amended by the Estate of Deceased Persons (Forfeiture Rule and Law of Succession) Act 2011) as having died immediately before the deceased;
3. The deceased died a bachelor [spinster] [widower] [widow] without issue or parent or any other person entitled in priority to share in the estate by virtue of any enactment [*or as the case may be*];
4. I am the brother of the whole blood and only person now entitled to [*or* one of the persons entitled to share in] the estate of the deceased now not disposed of by the will;
5. No life or minority interest arises in the estate of the deceased;
6. [*add statement as to settled land*];
7. I will:
   (i) collect, get in and administer [etc– *complete as in* Form 149: **A6.154**].

A6.164

159. Oath for administration (will) to testator's widow and a person entitled to share in estate (there being no executor or residuary legatee or devisee)

(*Heading as in Form 1:* **A6.01**)

We, E B of. . . . . and C B of. . . . . make oath and say that:

1. We believe the paper writing now produced to and marked by us to contain the true and original last will and testament of A B of. . . . . de-ceased, who was born on the. . . . . . day of. . . . . 19. . . . . . and who died on the. . . . . . day of . . . . 19. . . . . . /20. . . . . . aged. . . . . . years, domiciled in England and Wales;
2. No executor or residuary legatee or devisee is named in the will;
3. No minority but a life interest arises in the estate of the deceased;
4. [*add statement as to any settled land*];
5. We are respectively the lawful widow, and a son and two of the persons entitled to share in the estate of the deceased not disposed of by the will;
6. We will:
   (i) collect, get in and administer [etc – *complete as in Form 149*: **A6.154**].

A6.173

168. Oath for administration (will) to person authorised by Court of Protection where executor is lacks capacity to manage his affairs within the meaning of the Mental Capacity Act 2005

(*Heading as in Form 1:* A6.01)

I, C D, of. . . . . make oath and say that:

1. A B of. . . . . deceased, was born on the. . . . . . day of . . . . 19. . . . . . and died on the. . . . . . day of. . . . . 20. . . . . . aged. . . . . . years, domiciled in England and Wales, having made and duly executed his last will and testament and thereof appointed E F sole executor;
2. E F is now lacks capacity to manage his affairs within the meaning of the Mental Capacity Act 2005;
3. By an order of the Court of Protection dated the. . . . . . day of . . . . 20. . . . . . I was duly authorised to apply for letters of administration (with will) of the estate of the deceased for the use and benefit of E F;
4. [*add statement as to minority or life interest*];
5. [*add statement as to settled land*];
6. I believe the paper writing now produced to and marked by me to contain the true and original last will and testament of the deceased;
7. I will:
   (i) collect, get in and administer according to law the real and personal estate of the deceased for the use and benefit of E F until further representation be granted;
   (ii) when required to do so by the Court [etc – *complete as in Form 149*: A6.154].

A6.174

169. Oath for administration (will) to attorney acting under a registered enduring power of attorney or registered lasting power of attorney; for the use executor who lacks capacity within the meaning of the Mental Capacity Act 2005

(*Heading as in Form 1:* A6.01)

I, C D, of. . . . . make oath and say that:

1. A B of. . . . . deceased, was born on the. . . . . . day of . . . . 19. . . . . . and died on the. . . . . . day of. . . . . 20. . . . . . aged. . . . . . years, domiciled in England and Wales, having made and duly executed his last will and testament;
2. E F, the sole executor named in the will, is now by reason of mental incapacity incapable of managing his affairs [*or* now lacks capacity to manage his affairs within the meaning of the Mental Capacity Act 2005];

3. No one has been authorised by the Court of Protection to apply for a grant of representation of the estate of the deceased for the use and benefit of E F;

4. I am the lawful attorney of E F acting under a registered enduring power of attorney [*or* I am the lawful attorney of E F acting under a registered lasting power of attorney];

5. [*add statement as to minority or life interest*];

6. [*add statement as to settled land*];

7. I believe the paper writing now produced to and marked by me to contain the true and original last will and testament of the deceased;

8. I will:

    (i) collect, get in and administer according to law the real and personal estate of the deceased for the use and benefit of E F until further representation be granted;

    (ii) when required to do so [etc – *complete as in Form 149*: **A6.154**].

A6.174A

169A. Oath for administration (will) to person appointed by district judge or registrar; for the use of an executor who lacks capacity within the meaning of the Mental Capacity Act 2005

(*Heading as in Form 1:* **A6.01**)

I, C D, of. . . . . make oath and say that:

1. A B of. . . . . deceased, was born on the. . . . . . day of . . . . 19. . . . . . and died on the. . . . . . day of. . . . . 20. . . . . . aged. . . . . . years, domiciled in England and Wales, having made and duly executed his last will and testament;

2. E F, the sole executor and residuary legatee and devisee named in the will, is now by reason of mental incapacity incapable of managing his affairs [*or* now lacks capacity to manage his affairs within the meaning of the Mental Capacity Act 2005];

3. [*add statement as to minority or life interest*];

4. [*add statement as to settled land*];

5. I believe the paper writing now produced to and marked by me to contain the true and original last will and testament of the deceased;

6. By order of District Judge [*or* Registrar] . . . . . dated the . . . . . . day of . . . . 20. . . . . . it was ordered that letters of administration (with will) of the estate of the deceased be granted to me under and by virtue of rule 35(4) of the Non-Contentious Probate Rules 1987, the grant to be for the use and benefit of E F limited until further representation be granted;

8. I will:

    (i) collect, get in and administer according to law the real and personal estate of the deceased for the use and benefit of E F until further representation be granted;

    (ii) when required to do so [etc – *complete as in Form 149*: **A6.154**].

Subpoenas

A6.206

201. Order for examination of person with knowledge of testamentary document

(*Heading as in Form 1:* **A6.01**)

Elizabeth the Second, [etc *as in Form 200:* **A6.205**]:

To. . . . . of

We command you to appear before the [Right] Honourable Sir. . . . . Knight, the President [or Judge] of the Family Division of our High Court of Justice at the Royal Courts of Justice, Strand, London WC2 on the . . . . . . day of. . . . . 20. . . . . . at. . . . . . o'clock, to testify the truth according to your knowledge [*or* to answer any question to be put to you], relating to a certain document, being or purporting to be testamentary, namely [*here describe the document, and give its date as accurately as possible*], of which said document there are reasonable grounds for believing that you have knowledge.

Witness the Right Honourable [Lord Chancellor], the. . . . . . day of. . . . . 20. . . . . . .

(Signed)

District Judge/Registrar.

[*Name and address of solicitor.*]

[Note.–
To be indorsed prominently on the front of the copy to be served:] You the within-named . . . . are warned that disobedience to this order would be a contempt of court punishable by imprisonment.

PART II – FORMS FOR USE IN PROBATE CLAIMS

A6.210

CPOA. Heading for all claims issued in the Business and Property Courts

In the High Court of Justice. . . . . Claim No. [PT[1]] – [*year*] – [*number*]

Business and Property Courts of England and Wales

Property, Trusts and Probate List (Ch)

[Business and Property Courts in [. . . . .][2]

Property, Trusts and Probate List (Ch)

[In the County Court at . . . . hearing centre][3]

In the Estate of A B, deceased (Probate)

Claimant	C D
Defendant	E F

[**Notes.–**

1 PT is the prefix for claims issued in London in the Property, Trusts and Probate List after 2 October 2017.

2 This must be one of the B&PCs District Registries.

3 This must be a hearing centre where there is also a Chancery District Registry, or be the county court at Central London (Chancery List).

A6.210A

CP0B. Heading for claims issued outside London in a Chancery District Registry which is not one of the B&PCs District Registries

In the High Court of Justice. . . . . Claim No. [. . . . .]

Chancery Division

[. . . . . District Registry]

In the Estate of A B, deceased (Probate)

Claimant	C D
Defendant	E F

Affidavits and witness statements

A6.214A

CP4A. Handing out Testamentary Documents for examination1 (Form CH27)[1]

(*Heading:* **A6.210**)

UPON the application of the [*party*] by application notice dated [. . . . .]

AND UPON HEARING [. . . . .] for the Claimant and [. . . . .] for the Defendant

AND . . . . [*name*], the Solicitors for the [*party*] having undertaken (1) that they will on or before [*date*] or earlier if so directed by this Court return the testamentary documents specified in the attached Schedule to Masters' Appointments, Ground Floor, Rolls Building, Fetter Lane, London EC4A 1NL and (2) that until the specified testamentary documents are returned as stated above they will remain in the possession of [*name*] and [*name*] who are handwriting experts

IT IS ORDERED that

1. the testamentary documents be handed out to [*name*] the Solicitors for the Claimant/Defendant for the purpose of handwriting analysis being examined by microscope and immersion tests
2. an officer of the Chancery Division attend [*name*] at [*address*] and produce to him for the purpose of handwriting analysis the testamentary documents specified in the attached Schedule
3. [*name*] return the specified testamentary documents to Masters' Appointments, Ground Floor, Rolls Building, Fetter Lane, London EC4A 1NL on or before [*date*] or earlier if so directed by the Court
4. the costs of the Application shall be costs in the case
5. this order shall be served by the [*Claimant*] on the [*Defendant*]

Service of the order

The court has provided a sealed copy of this order to the serving party:

ABC Solicitors LLP at [*address*] [*reference*]

SCHEDULE

[*Identify the testamentary documents the subject of the order*]

[1] Note CPR 57.5(5) provides that except with the permission of the court, a party is not allowed to inspect the testamentary documents or written evidence lodged or filed by any other party until he himself has lodged his testamentary document and filed his evidence.

Notices

A6.218

CP8. Notice of claim to non-parties (CPR 19.8A) (based on Form CH7)

(*Heading:* **A6.210**)

TAKE NOTICE THAT:

(1) Proceedings have been commenced in the Chancery Division of the High Court of Justice in accordance with the attached claim form.

(2) You are or may be one of the persons who are interested in the estate to which the claim relates.

(3) You may within 14 days after service of this notice acknowledge service of the claim form by completing the attached acknowledgment and handing it in at, or sending it by post to the Issue Section, Ground Floor, The Rolls Building, 7 Rolls Buildings, Fetter Lane, London EC4A 1NL [*or* . . . . District Registry] and thereby become a party to the claim.

(4) If you do not acknowledge service of the claim form you will be bound by any judgment given in the proceedings as if you were a party to them.

Dated

To

Signed

Orders

A6.220

CP10. Order in probate action involving compromise (Form CH26)

(*Heading:* A6.210)

UPON the application of [. . . . .]

by application notice dated [. . . . .]

AND upon hearing [. . . . .] for the [. . . . .] and for the [. . . . .]

AND upon reading the written evidence filed

AND UPON [probate of the alleged last will and testament of the above named deceased bearing date. . . . . having been granted on. . . . . to. . . . .] [*or* letters of administration of the estate of the above named deceased having been granted on. . . . . to . . . .]

AND UPON the parties having agreed the terms set out in the attached schedule

[[And the Court being satisfied

(1) that consents by or on behalf of every relevant beneficiary (as defined by s 49, Administration of Justice Act 1985) have been given to the making of this order hereinafter made and

(2) that the said order is for the benefit of those relevant beneficiaries who are children

The Court pronounces for [against] the force and validity of the last will and testament of the above named deceased a completed copy of which is the script bearing the date [. . . . .] being the exhibit marked [. . . . .] referred to in the [witness statement] [affidavit] of testamentary documents of [. . . . .] dated [. . . . .] and against the force and validity of the last will and testament of the above named deceased a completed copy of which is the script bearing the date [. . . . .] being the exhibit marked [. . . . .] referred to in the [witness statement] [affidavit] of testamentary documents of [. . . . .] dated [. . . . .]]]

AND it is ordered that

(1) this claim [and counterclaim] be discontinued

(2) the said probate [letters of administration] be revoked

(3) the terms set out in the Schedule be carried into effect

(4) [probate of the will] [and. . . . . codicil] [letters of administration of the estate] of the above named deceased late of [. . . . .] be granted to the claimant/the defendant [. . . . .] the executor named therein [*if entitled thereto - see Note*]

(5) on application for such a grant the caveat numbered [. . . . .] and entered on [. . . . .] do if still subsisting cease to have effect

(6) there be assessed if not agreed

(a) the costs of this claim [and counterclaim] of the claimant/defendant [. . . .] the executor named in the said will

(b) the costs of this claim [and counterclaim] of the claimant/defendant [. . . . .] and [. . . . .]

(7) that the costs specified in (a) and (b) above be paid out of the estate of the said deceased in the due course of administration.

Service of the order

The court has provided a sealed copy of this order to the serving party:

ABC Solicitors LLP at [*address*] [*reference*]

Schedule

[*Set out the agreed terms*]

[Note.–

The words 'if entitled thereto' must be included unless it is proved that the named person is solely entitled without the exercise of any discretion under the Non-Contentious Probate Rules or unless all persons to whom a grant could be made are before the Court ([1972] 1 WLR 1217).]

Text in [[ ]] is only applicable in cases where the court is being asked to pronounce for or against the validity of one or more wills under s 49 of the Administration of Justice Act 1985. Section 49 permits a probate claim to be compromised without a trial if every 'relevant beneficiary', as defined in that section, has consented to the proposed order. It is only available in the High Court.

A6.223A

CP13A. Revocation/refusal of revocation of grant of probate (Form CH28)

(*Heading:* **A6.210**)

UPON the application of the [*party*] by application notice dated [*date*]

UPON THE TRIAL of this Claim and Counterclaim

AND UPON HEARING [*names of the advocates and/or those given permission to address the court*] for the Claimant / the Defendant

AND UPON READING [Probate of the alleged last Will and Testament of the deceased dated [*date*] granted on [*date*] to [*name*] *or* Letters of Administration of the estate of the deceased granted on . . . . [*date*] to . . . . [*name*]]

THE COURT PRONOUNCES FOR the force and validity of the Last Will and Testament of the deceased dated [*date*]

AND THE COURT PRONOUNCES AGAINST the force and validity of the alleged Last Will and Testament of the deceased dated [*date*]

AND IT IS ORDERED that

(1) the Probate / Letters of Administration be [revoked] [handed to the [party] or [his] Solicitors]

(2) this Claim and Counterclaim be dismissed

(3) there be a detailed assessment if not agreed of

(a) the costs of this Claim and Counterclaim of the Claimant / Defendant / Executor named in the Will dated [*date*]

(b) the costs of this Claim and Counterclaim of the Claimant / Defendant

that the costs specified in (a) and (b) shall above be paid out of the estate of the deceased in the due course of administration

that the Claimant / Defendant do pay to the Claimant / Defendant [his] costs of this Claim and Counterclaim such costs to be subject to detailed assessment if not agreed [*delete as required*]

(4) this order shall be served by the Claimant on the Defendant

Service of the order

The court has provided a sealed copy of this order to the serving party:

ABC Solicitors LLP at [*address*] [*reference*]

A6.223B

CP13B. Order pronouncing for some words, against others (Form CH29)

(*Heading:* **A6.210**)

UPON the application of the [*party*] by application notice dated [*date*]

AND UPON HEARING [*names of the advocates and/or those given permission to address the court*] for the Claimant / the Defendant

AND it appearing from a Witness Statement / an Affidavit of the Claimants that the testamentary documents of which they had knowledge and which they produce in this Claim included [three] paper writings now remaining in Court each bearing the date [*date*]

One ("Testamentary document A") beginning with the words " ", another ("Testamentary document B") beginning with the words " " and a third ("Testamentary document C") beginning with the words " " [*amend as appropriate*]

THE COURT PRONOUNCES FOR the force and validity of the last Will and Testament of the deceased late of [*address*] dated [*date*] and of the Codicil of the last Will and Testament being so much of Testamentary document A and Testamentary document B as is mentioned below that is to say the whole of Testamentary document A except the following:

the words beginning with " " down to and including the words " " [*as appropriate*]

AND THE COURT PRONOUNCES AGAINST the force and validity of [*as appropriate*]

(1) the words beginning with " " down to and including " "

(2) the whole of Testamentary document B except the words " " and the signature of the deceased and its attestation and

(3) the whole of Testamentary document C

AND IT IS ORDERED that this order shall be served by the Claimant on the Defendant

Service of the order

The court has provided a sealed copy of this order to the serving party:

ABC Solicitors LLP at [*address*] [*reference*]

Statements of case

III.

Defences

A6.254

CP44. Claimant propounds privileged will: Defendant pleads claimant was not in actual military service and propounds earlier will

(*Heading:* **A6.210**)

Defence and Counterclaim

The defendant says that:

1. The alleged will dated the. . . . . . day of. . . . . 20. . . . . . . was not executed in accordance with the provisions of the Wills Act 1837.

Particulars

[*As in Form CP32*: **A6.242**, *or as the case may be*.]

2. The said letter is not a will.

Particulars

The said letter is not in the form of a will and was not intended to take effect as such, as clearly appears from the language thereof.

3. The deceased was not in actual military service at the time the said letter purports to have been written.

Particulars

The said letter was written before the outbreak of war and before any order for mobilisation had been issued.

4. That the deceased was not at the time the said letter purports to have been written domiciled in England and Wales.

Particulars

The deceased was born in Scotland of Scottish parents. His domicile of origin was in Scotland, and he at all times retained such domicile.

And by way of counterclaim:

5. The defendant is the surviving executor named in the true last will and testament dated the. . . . . . day of. . . . . 20. . . . . . of the said deceased.

The defendant counterclaims:

1. That the Court shall pronounce against the force and validity of the said alleged will dated the. . . . . . day of. . . . . 20. . . . . .
2. That the Court shall pronounce for the force and validity of the said true last will and testament dated the. . . . . . day of. . . . . 20. . . . . . in solemn form of law.

Index

D